Only the Stars Are Neutral

Other Books by

QUENTIN REYNOLDS

The Wounded Don't Cry

London Diary

Convoy

QUENTIN
REYNOLDS

Only the Stars
Are Neutral

Random House · New York

Sixth Printing

To Mom

Contents

Desert; if you wish to lie in a three-foot-deep trench shuddering as shells falter over you to drop fifty yards away; if you want to know what it feels like to lie with your nose in the sand and with your toes curled tensely as five airplanes dive-bomb you for nearly an hour; if you wish to drink with us and play with us and argue with us in bars from Fleet Street to Cairo and if, by any incredible chance, you want to know what sort of life a foreign correspondent actually lives in war time—why, come along.

Because that is the tenuous texture out of which this book is made.

Only the Stars Are Neutral

I

No. 10 Downing Street

NEWS IN ENGLAND during the spring of 1941 was as scarce as charity in the heart of a tax collector. Every operational trip that we were allowed to make with the Navy or the RAF had been covered; everyone of importance had been interviewed and profiles of Cabinet officers and generals had long since ceased to interest either our editors or the public. There was only one story we could not get. None of us had interviewed Winston Churchill. Churchill had flatly denied himself to all of us. In vain we begged Brendan Bracken, then his Parliamentary Secretary, to persuade Churchill to hold semi-monthly press conferences.

"The Prime Minister is too busy," Brendan told us.

"The President has press conferences twice a week, and he's pretty busy," we countered.

"But the P.M. reports to the House of Commons a couple of times a week," Bracken said wearily. "Any member can ask him any question at any session. You fellows represent the public and, of course, the President sees you in Washington. But members of Parliament represent the public here in England, and the P.M. submits to what amounts to interviews by them every time he enters the House."

It was hard to answer that one. Some months before I had written a personality article on the King for *Collier's Weekly*.

3

It was not an interview, and I never spoke to the King or met him, but I was allowed to trail around with him when he visited Southampton, following a particularly vicious blitz on the port. I heard him ask intelligent questions of those in charge of clearing the debris from the still-smoking city; I heard him give practical advice to men and women engaged in fire fighting and rescue work. Twelve hours with the King gave me a profound respect for the shy, tall monarch who is perhaps the hardest-working civil servant in Britain. I wondered if I couldn't persuade Bracken to let me trail around with Churchill on one of his tours. By now Churchill was becoming a legend. In his own lifetime the legend was threatening to obscure one of the most fascinating personalities of our time. He should be "humanized." What did he eat and drink? How did he spend his leisure hours? What did he do for mental relaxation? This was the argument I put up to Brendan, and he half-heartedly agreed to see what he could do.

"He's very fair though," Bracken said. "And if I arranged it for you he'd want to know why Bill Stoneman or Ed Beattie or some of the other correspondents were excluded."

"Tell him I thought of it first," I urged Brendan.

"Sure, and then tell him to make it up afterwards with the rest of the boys," Bracken said sarcastically. "You know we try to treat you fellows all the same. We can't give one man a facility which we don't allow the others."

"I just want to follow him around some day. I don't even want to meet him. I just want to find out what makes him go."

Bracken looked at me suspiciously. "You'd cut my throat to get an interview with the P.M., wouldn't you?"

"I'll say I would," I confessed. "But I'll be satisfied to do what I did with the King. I didn't bust up to him and say, 'Hey, King, say a few words for *Collier's Weekly*,' did I?"

4

"You probably didn't think of it," Bracken said, and there it rested. I kept after Bracken because there wasn't another good story in sight. I sounded out Bill Stoneman of the *Chicago Daily News* (president of the Association of American Correspondents and always the one to run to for advice) and Ed Beattie of the United Press, and they told me that they wouldn't be sore at Bracken if he arranged the trip for me. After all, I wasn't in direct competition with any of them. They were interested in news. I was after what we call features. But for a long time nothing happened. Duff Cooper was relieved of the unhappy burden of heading the Ministry of Information. I think he was happy to lose that job. Brendan Bracken did his best to dodge the nastiest job in the world—a job that in two years had defeated about eight men, but in the end he succumbed to Churchill's insistence. We all liked Bracken and were sorry to see him take the job. Correspondents have an instinctive hatred of censors, and from now on he would be our natural enemy. Bracken, of course, was now in charge of all censorship, and he automatically became Public Enemy No. 1.

One night I was having dinner at the Savoy with Arthur Christiansen, editor of the *Daily Express* and Red Mueller of International News Service. It was nearly midnight when a page came up with an awed look on his face.

"Telephone call for you from 10 Downing Street," he said, very impressively.

I looked searchingly at Chris and at Red, but the surprise on their faces was too authentic to be assumed. But someone was pulling a gag on me. Correspondents seldom get telephone calls from 10 Downing Street—and never at midnight. I looked around the dining room. Bill Stoneman was at one table; Helen Kirkpatrick of the *Chicago Daily News* at another, Mary Welsh of *Time* and Frank Owen, editor of the

5

Evening Standard were there with Grace Owen, Frank's American wife. Larry Rue of the *Chicago Tribune* was looking too demure at another table. One of them was responsible for this, but I didn't know which. Well, I wouldn't fall for it.

"I really wish that Winston wouldn't phone me so late," I yawned to Chris and Mueller. Then I turned to the popeyed page boy. "Tell 10 Downing Street I'm busy, to get in touch with me tomorrow."

That settled, we went back to our nightly task of reshuffling the Cabinet and arranging the entire future conduct of the war. But the page boy came back more popeyed than ever.

"They are sending a car for you and will you be ready in five minutes," he said.

"Sure, sure, I'll be ready," I said, looking balefully across the room at Larry Rue who appeared much too innocent not to be guilty. I turned back to Chris. "I suppose the P.M. is having trouble with that production speech he is to make next week. Well, I'll be glad to straighten it out for him."

"Nuts," Chris said, pouring a drink.

In about five minutes the doorman of the Savoy stalked into the dining room. This was most unusual. He came to our table and said with more respect than he had ever shown to me, "There is a car waiting for you, sir. It is from 10 Downing Street."

"Is it really from 10 Downing Street?"

He smiled and nodded. "Oh, yes, I know the car."

Chris and Mueller sat there open-mouthed. I was as amazed as they, and quite as puzzled. It still might be a gag; things had been so dull lately that we spent half our time thinking of practical jokes to play on each other. But still . . .

"If you boys will take care of the bill," I suggested, "I'll bring you back anything in the way of news I get. And, Chris,

6

in case Beaverbrook or Eden should phone while I'm gone, take the call for me and tell them where I am."

Before Chris could make a fitting answer, I made my exit. But I felt more reassured when I saw the car. It certainly had a 10 Downing Street look about it. I was sure when the driver went straight down the Strand, turned left at Trafalgar Square, entered Whitehall, made a sharp right turn and stopped. We were actually going to 10 Downing Street. Downing Street is a dead-end street only one block long. There were two policemen at its entrance where we had stopped.

"You're expected," one of them said laconically, and we went on, while I still wondered what it was all about. I rang the bell and, when it opened, gave my name. "Oh, you're expected; come this way," the major-domo of No. 10 said smilingly. For a moment I had the uneasy thought that No. 10 Downing Street was too easy to get into. Then he ushered me into a large office, the office Lord Beaverbrook used in the building. Brendan Bracken was sitting behind the desk and Averell Harriman was sitting next to him.

"We thought you'd like to drink a toast to the new Minister," Harriman said.

"If he'll supply the drink." I liked Harriman a lot and saw a great deal of him when he was in London.

"A friend of yours just came in from Washington," Harriman went on. "He said he wanted to see you."

"Who is it?"

At this point I was hit on the back of the head and, turning around, I saw Harry Hopkins. There is no one in the world I'd rather see at any time than Harry Hopkins. Harry is deeply loved by all who know him. When he is in London, he usually works all day and all night. In London he was given the name, "Hurry Upkins." Months later in Russia I heard Molotov

7

and Vyshinsky talk about Hopkins with awe. They'd never seen such a bundle of dynamite in Moscow as Harry. But tonight Harry was through working. He had landed that evening by plane, and he, Harriman and Bracken had been with the Prime Minister for the past three hours. It was no use my asking them what they had discussed. Harriman, Hopkins and Bracken can be nicer to reporters without telling them anything than any three men I ever met—except, perhaps, Beaverbrook. But tonight, having a drink with them, toasting the new Minister of Information and welcoming Hopkins to London, I wasn't being a reporter. I was an old friend.

We talked of many things, sitting there with our feet perched comfortably on Beaverbrook's desk and then, finally, I remembered that I was a reporter and that I was wasting time.

"I regret to say our friend Bracken is a rat," I told Averell and Harry.

"We know that, but why?" Harriman asked.

"I asked him for a very simple favor," I explained. "I just want to trail around some day with the P.M. and do a story on him. But will he fix it? No!"

"I don't see any harm in it, Brendan," Harriman said. "If he does a story and it's no good, you can always kill it. How about that trip we're taking on Friday to see those tanks? Of course, I don't want to interfere. . . ."

"No, I can see that," Bracken said coldly. "Anyhow, I'll see what I can do."

"I'm spending the week end with the P.M.," Hopkins said, thoughtfully. "Maybe . . ."

"Same old run-around," I said, in disgust. "You'll see what you can do. Listen, I only get paid when I write stories. I haven't found a story in two months, and if I don't find some soon I'll be putting the bite on all three of you."

8

"For God's sake, Brendan, dig up some stories for Quent," Hopkins said in alarm, and then we talked of other things. Eventually, we started to talk of the grandest man any of us had ever known—Heywood Broun. Harry Hopkins and Broun and I frequently met at race tracks. I recalled a story Broun used to tell about Hopkins. He said he'd been standing with Harry at Pimlico as the horses started, and Hopkins was in a state.

"Come on, Somethin'!" Hopkins yelled, as the nags passed the grandstand. "Come on, Somethin'!"

Broun said that he looked at his card and couldn't find any horse named "Somethin' " on it. He called Hopkins' attention to that and asked him why he was rooting for a horse that wasn't even in the race.

"There are four horses in the race," Broun reported Hopkins as saying. "I've got two dollars on each of them. That's why I'm just rooting for something. I can't lose if something wins."

Like most of Heywood's stories, that one is undoubtedly untrue. Hopkins swore that it was a libel and that he had never bet on more than three horses in a single race. Broun's stories never had to be true. After he told them a few times he firmly believed them himself and then you had to believe them too.

Harriman used to bowl a lot with Broun. Broun could bowl pretty well with his shoes off. He couldn't hit a hundred wearing them. After a night's bowling, Broun's socks were usually spats. Bracken had met Broun a few times and had liked him as much as we did. It was fun sitting there in 10 Downing Street with the President's personal representative, with the Administrator of Lend-Lease and with a Cabinet Minister talking until dawn about a friend of ours who had been dead nearly two years. But people like Heywood Broun

9

don't die. The little men who used to criticize him are all dead, even though they're still sitting at their puerile typewriters going through the motions of writing and living their smug little lives. But Broun wasn't dead that night in 10 Downing Street, and I doubt if he'll ever be dead to those of us who loved him.

2

The Unfamiliar Churchill

THE NEXT MORNING the phone rang before I was awake, and I made believe I didn't hear it. I've been trying that trick for years but it never seems to work. Then I swore at my secretary for not answering it on the office extension, looked at my watch, saw it was nine o'clock and remembered I had told her that she was fired if she ever appeared before 10:30. So I picked up the phone and woke up quickly when a voice said, "10 Downing Street calling. Commander Thompson wishes to speak to you."

Commander Thompson was the Prime Minister's aide, a dapper, pleasant Naval Commander who wore a look of perpetual worry on his face. He was "Tommy" to all of us in London.

"The Prime Minister is going to inspect some tank maneuvers out of town tomorrow," Tommy said. "He has invited you to go along and spend the day with him. We'll let you know later what time and from where the train leaves. All right?"

"All right? Hell, it's perfect, Tommy!" I told him. I knew then that Averell had been working behind the scenes. You can always depend on Harriman. My bright, good-looking, young secretary came in while I was having breakfast. I told her to break any dates I had for the next day. I was spending it with the Prime Minister.

The phone rang again and she reached for it. A look of awe spread over her pretty face.

"It's Mrs. Churchill," she gasped. And so it was. The greatly loved "Clemmy" was asking me to lunch on Sunday. Hopkins had not forgotten his promise. I knew Mrs. Churchill. I told her I'd love to come, and then I added, "This time I'll tell you the truth about Hess."

When I hung up, my secretary glared at me. "You tell Mrs. Churchill the truth about Hess?" she said scornfully. "The nerve of you! As if she didn't know more about it than you do."

As a matter of fact, she didn't. Some weeks before, just after Hess had made his one-way trip to Scotland, Harriman had asked Helen Kirkpatrick and me to lunch. To our surprise and delight, Mrs. Churchill was present. She is one of the world's loveliest-looking women. Her hair is softly white; her cheeks are ivory-tinted and she looks as though she had just stepped graciously out of a cameo.

"I'm so glad to meet you two," she said eagerly. "Now at last I'll hear the truth about Hess."

Helen and I choked on our soup. "I really think," I assured Mrs. Churchill solemnly, "that the Prime Minister knows more about the Hess case than we do."

"Oh, he never tells me anything," she pouted.

Now, after a year, none of us who work in London knows any more than we did the night Hess landed. We do know that Churchill, instead of treating him as a prisoner of war, gave him the doubtful distinction of a prisoner of state. The difference is more than a nominal one. A prisoner of war ceases to be a prisoner when the war ends. The prisoner of state can be tried afterward. There is no doubt that even in

12

those dark days of early 1941, Churchill was visualizing the world after the war, thinking of the punishment that would be given to the Nazi leaders who had plunged the world into war. Hess, as guilty as any, will undoubtedly go on trial for his life when the war is over.

To get back to my day with Churchill. A message came late that afternoon that we would leave Paddington Station at nine o'clock the next morning in a special train bound for Salisbury Plains.

I reached Paddington Station at 8:45. The railroad official looked at my note and waved me on. The train was waiting patiently enough, but, except for three policemen and a Scotland Yard man, there was no one else on the platform.

The man from Scotland Yard had his watch out. In three minutes it would be nine o'clock. The stationmaster stood there nervously. Paddington Station was almost deserted. The brilliant morning sunlight filtered through the open spaces of a roof that had once been glass. We stood there beside the train, and then silently, almost casually, two large black cars drove up. Averell Harriman climbed out of one. Winston Churchill climbed out of the other. He was smiling, and when Churchill smiles he smiles with his eyes as well as with his lips. When he saw the Scotland Yard man standing there with his watch in his hand, the smile broke into a laugh. He glanced up at the big station clock. It read 8:59. Churchill shook hands all around. He has the same phenomenal memory for names that Jim Farley has.

"Get in," he said. "We'll get going right away. In with you."

He ushered us all into the train. He stepped in last of all. As he boarded the train, the clock struck nine. There were only nine of us: Harriman; Commander Thompson, the Prime Minister's aide-de-camp; General Sir Hastings Ismey; Major

13

John Churchill, the Prime Minister's brother; two American generals in London as observers; Churchill's two secretaries, Mr. Martin and Mrs. Hill; and myself. The special train that was taking us to the tank maneuvers some two hundred miles from London was very comfortable. The Prime Minister is the perfect host. If he is in his office, in his home, or on a train he must play the host. He enjoys seeing that everyone has a cigar or a cool drink.

"It's awfully hot today. Let's take off our coats," he said, and then he retired to the farther end of the car with his two secretaries, who had the morning mail with them.

Winston Churchill has kept a nation of 44,000,000 in fighting mood now for nearly two years. Churchill, who is called "Winston" by three quarters of Britain, is worshipped in every army encampment, in every RAF mess, in every ward-room of His Majesty's Navy, and in every pub in Britain.

Churchill the statesman is well known to the world. Churchill the writer, Churchill the war leader of Britain, Churchill the orator—these Churchills are familiar wherever newsprint is made, wherever men read and write. In the two days I spent with him on this trip, I had the opportunity to observe another Churchill—one who is not so well known. I speak of Churchill the man.

It was a pleasant trip, and the luncheon on the train was good. It wasn't as good as one would get on any decent train in America, but even the Prime Minister and his guests are rationed in England. And, of course, the cigars were excellent. Averell Harriman and I sat and talked of our friends in New York. The train slipped through the lovely countryside, which was wearing its brilliant summer dress, and then finally it stopped. The Prime Minister had been talking about tanks to the two American Army officers. It was hot when the train stopped.

14

Five thousand uniformed men were drawn up at the station when we stepped off the train. The General and his staff were at attention and they saluted sharply as Churchill left the train. Each one of us had to be introduced to the officers. For the moment we were his family. Churchill radiates friendliness. It is awfully difficult not to start calling him "Winston" after knowing him for two hours. This implies no disrespect. It is merely the remarkable power he has of making you feel that here is a friend you have known a long time.

"I suppose they've been standing here a long time," he said, pointing to the lines of soldiers standing rigidly at attention. "Let's walk along and say hello to them."

The General could hardly restrain his delight. The rest of us groaned. We had to trail after the Prime Minister, who, apparently unaware of the heat, smiled and chatted with the men as he walked along. You knew that each one of them would treasure this moment; each felt that Winston had come down from London just to see him. Finally, it was over. We climbed into cars and drove to the tank maneuvers five miles away.

Now, I can take a tank or leave it alone. Not Churchill or Harriman. Harriman has become a great authority on tanks. Churchill discussed the technical details of the tanks on even terms with the experts. I just wanted to get back to the train, where I hoped I might find a glass of cold beer. Finally, we headed for it. We drove past five miles of cheering troops.

A block from the station our cars halted. A long table had been set up by the side of the road and soldiers stood behind it ready to serve drinks and sandwiches. The General in charge said, "Would you stop for some refreshment, Mr. Churchill?"

Churchill was about to refuse. He'd be more comfortable in the comparative coolness of the train with his coat off and with iced drinks, if he wished them. Then he looked at the soldiers standing behind the long table. He smiled and nodded.

Like a mother hen clucking her chickens to her side, he called to us, "Come on, come on, we'll have a cool drink," and we followed him to the table. He spoke to every one of the men who stood there serving; he said something different to each, and each undoubtedly felt that the Prime Minister had come only to say hello to him. Churchill has that amazing knack. Jim Walker has it and Jim Farley has it and so has Jack Dempsey. I never met anyone else who could convey that impression with nothing but a smile and a half dozen words.

"It was a good show today, oh, a fine show," Churchill said to the General in command. "Wasn't it, Averell? Wasn't it a fine show?"

"It was indeed," Harriman said earnestly. "I hope you'll find those tanks of ours up to standard."

"I know we will," the General said, smiling.

"Aye and there's more of them coming," Churchill chuckled. "Isn't that right, Averell?"

"Plenty more," Harriman said gravely.

"Time to go. We're leaving at five." Churchill looked at his watch. "Get along with you all now. Cars enough for everyone? Tommy, Tommy, are there cars enough?"

Churchill shook hands all around. He spread his charm upon General and private, and the charm was contagious. Looking down the street, you could see the villagers infected with the delightful aroma of it, laughing and waving to the Prime Minister. Once more troops were lined up in front of the station and a military band played "For He's a Jolly Good Fellow." A few of the troops began to sing it, and then the chorus swelled to a roar and they were all singing it, and he stood there with his hat off, smiling not only with his mouth

16

but with his whole face, and then he waved his hat and we all stepped into the train.

We were hot and tired. He had his coat off in a moment and was calling for cool drinks for everyone and a fresh box of cigars. When he saw that we were all settled he said reluctantly, "Ah, well, I must get to work." He sat with his two secretaries, dictating, and his voice rose and fell and never stopped until we were pulling into Waterloo Station in London.

"You'll come to lunch tomorrow?" He shook my hand before he stepped into his car. "You can make it?"

"I can make it," I said gravely. Reporters can usually make it when a Prime Minister asks them to lunch.

I was twenty minutes late for luncheon at Chequers, the estate all Prime Ministers of Great Britain are loaned during the term of their office. That is hardly the way to win the friendship of a Prime Minister. But he didn't seem to mind. Neither did Mrs. Churchill. Pretty eighteen-year-old daughter Mary, vivacious and eager-eyed, didn't mind either. Only Sukie seemed annoyed. He barked and leaped and in general behaved as any young puppy would at the intrusion of a stranger into the family circle.

"He's a Free French poodle," Mary explained proudly. "Have you a dog?"

I told her that the Savoy Hotel where I lived took a very dim view of guests who kept dogs.

"Have you a cat?" she asked. I told her that my secretary took a very dim view of cats, and I had to choose between her and a cat. And, after all, I explained, a cat can't take dictation.

"I have a goldfish, though," I told Mary.

"I shouldn't think they'd be much fun," Mary said thoughtfully.

Winston and Harry Hopkins were talking production. When Harry made a statement, Winston would lean back and say thoughtfully, "You know, friend Hopkins, you could make a good case against that. Now, for instance . . ." Then, having made a good case against Harry's statement, he would add mischievously, "Of course, I don't believe a word of what I've been saying. I agree with you entirely. I just wanted to see if I could make a case against it."

After lunch, Mary had to rush to the hospital where she works. The Churchills all work. Sister Sarah, an actress, gives concerts for the troops. Brother Randolph is in Egypt with his regiment. Mrs. Churchill heads a dozen committees doing war work; she works in a canteen and she is on duty as a fire-watcher near Downing Street two nights a week.

Churchill, Hopkins, Thompson and I walked out of the house. It was difficult to believe that this wasn't Long Island, or Connecticut or even Beverly Hills. There was a badminton court and a lawn studded with croquet wickets.

"Harriman would go crazy about this court," I said. "He loves croquet. He and Bob Sherwood play it by the hour."

"Mary gave him a beating here the other day," Winston chuckled.

Light rain began to fall. Churchill doesn't notice minor things like the weather. He was dressed for it. He was wearing what his staff calls his "rompers" and what we usually call a "shelter suit." It is a one-piece all-over garment with a zipper. He always wears it in the country. He also wears it because he is a great one for prowling around at night, especially on blitz nights.

In the afternoon the Prime Minister worked with his secretaries, who go everywhere with him. Mrs. Hill, Martin and

"Tommy" are indispensable to him. Always one of them is within shouting distance.

I wandered about the house with Tommy and Harry Hopkins. We went into one enormous room where Winston keeps his toys. Here is the largest globe of the world I've ever seen. Churchill loves to twirl it around, finding places where his armies are fighting, and when he does this, you can tell by the look in his eyes that he wishes he were there. Then there is a refined, mechanical version of the old-fashioned stereopticon. Here pictures of bombed German cities are shown. On his desk was a book, one book. It was the history of the Washington family in England; Churchill reads everything, including the comic strips in the papers, but most of all he prefers biographies.

"The P.M. wants you to stay for dinner," Thompson said.

"I have no dinner clothes with me," I protested.

Tommy laughed. "Do you think that will worry the P.M.? And you know Mrs. Churchill. She doesn't worry about what people wear."

We assembled in the big, high-ceilinged hall before dinner. This room was probably 500 years old. Portraits of great figures of the past crowded the walls. You seldom have cocktails in England now. There are no lemons, no limes, and practically no vermouth is left. We had our choice of sherry or whisky. Hopkins had double-crossed me and had put on a dinner coat. So had Thompson and Martin, who were dining with us. The Prime Minister wore a new set of "rompers." Mrs. Churchill had a slight cold and was resting. Mary was the hostess tonight, and she played her part beautifully.

"I feel like a French refugee in these clothes," I said to Mary.

"How about Pa?" she laughed. "Look at his clothes!"

"It's easy to see," Winston chuckled, looking at our dinner-

19

jacketed companions, "which two men in the room worked all afternoon. Mary, where's Nelson?"

Mary didn't have to answer. From out of the dark recesses of a corner there strode a cat—Nelson. Nelson is a huge, baleful-eyed, black cat, who ignores everyone else but tolerates the Prime Minister. He takes a rather patronizing view of him, but occasionally allows Churchill to stroke him, and when there are no dogs around to chase, Nelson even listens to the P.M.'s attempt to draw him into conversation.

"Bravest cat you ever saw," Churchill laughed. "Once chased a big dog right out of the Admiralty."

Nelson yawned, and stalked majestically into the dining room.

"Nelson knows we're having salmon for dinner," Mary said. "He's hoping that Pa will feed him."

It was fun at dinner. We talked about Mary's enlistment in the ATS (Auxiliary Territorial Service). She is to go on active service with an anti-aircraft battery.

It was a cozy family dinner. The Churchills all have the knack of making you feel at home. We talked of many things —of food, which is topic number one all over England, and of the cigarette shortage. Churchill chuckled, "Thank goodness," he said, "I smoke only cigars." We talked of motion pictures (both Churchill and Beaverbrook are fans) and, inevitably, of the war.

After dinner Mary left us to the port and the cigars. She kissed her father good-bye. "Don't be long," she pleaded. "I so want to see the picture. It's that wonderful *Target for Tonight*—the bombing picture. If you love me, you'll hurry."

"I am very fond of you," he said gravely, and Mary, satisfied that he would be there, left.

A report came about the sinking of an Italian destroyer.

Churchill chuckled happily. He has made no secret of his contempt for the Italians.

"Tommy," he said, "have you got that letter about the Italians? Good, good. Let me read it. It is a letter to Charles Colebaugh, managing editor of *Collier's Weekly*. It is from W. B. Courtney, his correspondent who was then with the Italians in Ethiopia. Best letter I ever read."

He read the letter, and Hopkins laughed. Thompson roared; Churchill himself had to stop several times to repeat lines he liked especially. The letter is really one of the all-time classics of invective.

Everyone laughed but me. Reading that letter merely plunged me into a state of heavy gloom. Churchill noticed my change of mood.

"Great letter, isn't it?" he boomed.

"Sure," I said bitterly, "but I have to live with that Bill Courtney who wrote it. His office is next to mine at *Collier's*. When I tell him that the Prime Minister read his letter to his dinner guests, there'll be no living with him."

"Don't tell him," Churchill said. Then he turned to Tommy. "Have some copies of that letter made. We'll send them around."

"If you read it at a Cabinet meeting, don't let me know about it," I said.

Over our cigars and port, which nobody drank because there was also brandy, and brandy gets scarcer every day in England, we talked of the war, and of after the war, and Churchill talked of governmental problems of the present and the future. He talked freely, as one who knows and trusts his guests. Nor did he ever preface what he said with the usual, "This is off the record, of course," which we reporters hear so often. But a guest at the Prime Minister's has the same,

21

self-imposed responsibility which a guest at the White House has. However, one can quote a word or two.

"Things have been looking up a bit lately," the Prime Minister said. His voice is the same in conversation as it is in speeches. It has the same slight lisp—if that word can be applied to anyone as virile as Winston Churchill; the same long, beautifully rounded sentences; the occasional armchair phrase; the by now perhaps unconscious use of alliteration as an aid to description. He talked of the dark days after Dunkirk and his face clouded at the remembrance.

"Oh, we have a long way to go," he said thoughtfully. "But with the help of our great friends across the sea, we'll get there. I expect that we'll get it badly in London again and again, but, mind you, every time they come over, our night fighters will be taking huge bites out of them. I am not over-optimistic, I hope. But then, I am at heart an optimistic person." Then his face clouded again as his thoughts turned back to Dunkirk.

"Oh, that was bad. We needed Spitfires most of all. I said to Beaverbrook, 'Get those Spitfires into the sky,' and Max said, 'If God will give me three months I'll have Spitfires for you.' Well, God gave him three months but there still weren't enough. I said, 'Max, we need more Spitfires,' and he said, 'If God will give me two months more I'll have them for you.' Well," Churchill smiled, "God gave him two more months and when the Luftwaffe came over by day, we were ready.

"Now, we're getting stronger," he went on. "Yes, and that horrid man knows it. He knows he's beaten, even at this moment when his submarines are sinking our vessels in the North Atlantic; even now when his planes are bombing this island, he knows he's beaten."

Churchill lit a fresh cigar. Everyone was quiet. He was thinking aloud now, gazing reflectively through the clouds of

22

blue-gray smoke from the cigar. He pointed to an empty chair across from his place at the table.

"Hitler would like to be sitting right there now," he said gravely. "He'd like to be talking to me and asking me if there wasn't some way out for him. Aye, he'd like to meet me alone somewhere—alone."

"If you ever have a date to meet him alone, be sure that Beaverbrook is around some place with a club in his hand," I suggested.

"Good, good," he laughed. "Max would come in handy then. Ah, that man Hitler! When I think of the crimes he has committed. When this war has come to a successful conclusion"—even in private dinner conversation, Churchill never abandons the rounded, sonorous, rhetorical phrase—"then something must be done about that man. His philosophy, his tyranny must be stamped out. If my allies agree, I would be in favor of trying him and exterminating him. I am sure that he feels the same about me. If, which for the moment I do not believe, he should be victorious, I am sure that he would have me shot. Mind you," he chuckled, looking archly over his glasses, "I would not like that. But I cannot say that my sense of righteousness would be outraged."

He switched suddenly. "Do you know why I hate the Nazis? I hate them because they frown when they fight. They are grim and dull-faced. They don't go into battle with a song in their hearts. Now take our magnificent RAF lads. They grin when they fight. Ah, yes, they grin when they fight. I like a man who grins when he fights."

His conversation was like a chameleon on a rock. It darted back into antiquity; it touched on Greece and that reminded him of a canto in *Don Juan* and he talked of Byron; it somehow streaked halfway across the world to India, and that reminded him of Kipling.

"I've gotten a lot from Kipling," he said enthusiastically. "Ah, there was a singer of songs! But, of course, there was only one. I mean Shakespeare. Do you remember in *Hamlet* when . . ."

It was exciting to hear Winston Churchill recite Shakespeare. On and on his sonorous voice rolled. He was acting the part now. He was Hamlet, and not a word in a long passage did he miss.

"Not one real poet has emerged from the war as yet, do you think?" Harry Hopkins asked.

Churchill shook his head. "No, and very few from the last war. But there was one who died too soon. Rupert Brooke. Do you remember that lovely thing he wrote called 'The Fish'?

"In a cool curving world he lies
And ripples with dark ecstasies.

"And further on"—Churchill's eyes were blazing with enthusiasm now; he loved this poem—"those lines:

"The dark fire leaps along his blood;
Dateless and deathless, blind and still,
The intricate impulse works its will;
His woven world drops back; and he,
Sans providence, sans memory,
Unconscious and directly driven,
Fades to some dank sufficient heaven.

"And how about these lines to apply today?" Churchill chuckled. "Can you fit them to anyone?

"But there the night is close, and there
Darkness is cold and strange and bare;
And the secret depths are whisperless . . .

"That was a poet," Churchill said softly. "Ah, yes. And he, you'll remember," he said sharply, "was killed by the Hun."

He went on, and something Hopkins said awakened a memory of Thomas Moore, and from the store of that incredible memory there came forth stanza after stanza of Moore. And then, amazingly, Bret Harte, and he laughed because neither Hopkins nor I could recall the passages he quoted. Outside of this quiet dining room, dominated by the resonant, insinuating voice, outside of this personality that dominated the room the way a sunrise dominates a dawn—there was bloody, murderous war going on. But for the moment we had declared a moratorium on terror and bloodshed and governmental problems. I'd even forgotten that I was a reporter.

And then, "But Mary will be waiting," Churchill said ruefully. In the long run, fathers, even Prime Ministers, are always bossed by their eighteen-year-old daughters. We went upstairs to the room where a projection booth had been installed. The picture, we all agreed, was the best film to come out of the war. *Target for Tonight* is the honest, sincere story of the bomber pilots. Churchill smoked and was as tense as any movie fan when things looked bad for the bomber that was over Germany. He chuckled when the bombs hit the Nazi target; he breathed with relief when the pilots returned safely.

Downstairs again, Thompson said that my car was ready. The Prime Minister walked to the door with me. It was a dark night. The rain still slanted down dismally.

"Sure now you won't have a drink before you go?" he asked solicitously. "It's a chilly night. No? It's been nice having you. You must come again. Let me know when you go to Moscow. Good night."

The car pulled away. I looked back. Just for the moment the Prime Minister had forgotten the black-out. He stood

25

there in the huge Gothic doorway, and the dim light from the hall silhouetted him—sturdy, rocklike, immovable. He stuck his cigar in the corner of his mouth at a jaunty angle. His hands were dug deep into the pockets of his blue "rompers." He waved once and grinned. I, too, admire a man who grins when he fights.

3

When Britain Won
the War

DURING THE SPRING OF 1941, the city of Plymouth was virtually destroyed by German bombing, and London received two raids which will prevent her from ever outwardly being the city she was before. The story of Plymouth should be recorded lest one day time may dull the shock we all felt when it happened. The story of the most brutal raid London had to endure should be recorded too for the same reason and for yet another reason. It was on that night, May 10, 1941, that I believe Britain won the war.

I had seen Coventry and Southampton and Liverpool and had, of course, lived in London during all of the 1940 and 1941 blitzes; but nothing I had seen prepared me for the sight of Plymouth after it had been bombed five nights in one week. Any time an enemy airplane comes over dropping bombs, that is a raid. It is not a "blitz" unless at least a hundred airplanes come over. At least one hundred bombers each loaded with dynamite came over Plymouth town on five out of seven nights.

Plymouth was never a very large city. At the time it received what was intended to have been its death blow, it had a population of about 204,000. This included the suburb of Devonport. In Britain Plymouth has always been known as

27

the city of Sir Francis Drake, not because he was born there, but because he sailed from Plymouth so often when he went to fight the Spaniards. A huge statue of Drake stands overlooking the sea, on the Hoe, a large limestone plateau 120 feet above the water. There were no factories, virtually no industry, in Plymouth, outside of the docks, and the city was more than 90 per cent residential. That is what gave the city its clean, tidy look; that and the fact that most of the houses were built of native limestone. Plymouth was a city of shrines. Down in the town proper, there were twenty-five ancient churches, each steeped in tradition. There was the famous fourteenth-century church of St. Andrews, teeming with memories; Catharine of Aragon knelt here giving thanks for her safe return from Spain; here the congregation rose to welcome Drake back from Nombre de Dios.

Within an hour many tangible evidences of the past glories of Plymouth were wiped out by the invader. Two hundred bombers, each carrying at least 1,000 pounds of explosives, flew over the city dropping death and destruction from the skies. Plymouth was ablaze.

Drake, in addition to being perhaps the greatest of English admirals, was also a great engineer. To give Plymouth drinking water, he built a leat bracket, a stone-lined trench bracket from Lake Burrator on Dartmoor just twelve miles away from Plymouth. Gravity brought the clear, sparkling waters of the lake to the town. For fifty years the reservoir has been a curiosity, nothing else. But the firemen piped the water from the reservoir, hurled it at the flames, and soon the fires were under control. So Drake, dead 350 years, had come out of the past to help his own home town.

But they came back again the next night, and the next, with redoubled fury and with thousands of incendiaries to start more fires. Shops were destroyed. Twenty-three churches

28

were in ruins. Many hospitals were merely smoking funeral pyres. Unidentified bodies lay on slabs in the morgue. Lovely St. Andrews was a charred mass.

Then Plymouth began to fight back. Civilians can't use the ordinary weapons of war. Their weapons are courage, ingenuity, physical and spiritual strength. These weapons Plymouth had in abundance.

First there was the question of feeding the people. Every city in England has emergency rations well cached away from the devil's fingers of bombs and flames. They consist of canned goods: milk, corned beef, tongue, soup. Thirty centers were established in the city; schools, public halls, any untouched building large enough was commandeered by Lord Astor, Mayor of Plymouth. All of the schoolteachers were impressed as cooks.

Meanwhile, Britain was rallying to the aid of her stricken city. From London came the Queen's messengers—mobile canteens sent by America. From elsewhere came huge steam ranges—stoves that generated their own steam. Thirty of these were set up at various points outside the city. Lord Woolton, Minister of Food, rushed great quantities of beef, vegetables, soup and bread to Plymouth. The emergency rationing ceased after three days. Now the huge stoves were ready for action, ready to help Plymouth fight back. The cooked food was put into huge containers capable of keeping it hot for two hours and rushed by truck to centers in the city, to wherever men and women were hungry. When people could pay, they paid twelve cents a meal. A typical meal would be vegetable soup, beef stew, rice pudding, bread, tea or coffee. Even during those horrible days when the invader returned five nights out of seven, no one went hungry.

Those nights were bad. Nancy Astor, the Mayor's wife, turned her terrific energy to the task of evacuating and finding homes for the children. She phoned a thousand people she knew, told them what their quota of children would be and then delivered them. They say now in Plymouth that neither the Mayor nor his wife slept a wink during those first three days of horror.

Today Plymouth is virtually a city without children. Every large, untouched building not used as a hospital or feeding center is a rest center. Mayor Astor believes, and experience has taught all of us here, that people are not frightened when they are with others. These rest centers are open all night. If your house is hit and you have been shaken up or wounded slightly, you rush to the nearest rest center. There is hot tea and a chocolate bar and a hundred of your friends and someone to play the piano.

Lord Astor managed to get a military band to play on the Hoe. Everyone left in Plymouth came to listen to the band and to dance. A group of Welshmen came to help out. Astor got them to sing. Their voices carried over the water and they might well have reached German territory to tell the Nazis of the defiance and of the endurance of this city which fought back so magnificently. One of the Welshmen wrote a song for the occasion. This verse is typical:

We'll be coming back to Plymouth by and by.
When old Adolf's in the sweet by and by;
When we've made a mess of Goering and Goebbels is in
*   mourning,*
We'll be coming back to Plymouth by and by.
We'll cheer our Winston Churchill by and by.
When he makes our skies more clear by and by.
We will welcome Franklin Roosevelt and thank him for his
*   help;*
To smash the blinkin' Nazis from the sky.

30

Three thousand people danced and sang, until it grew dark. They knew that the raider would be over later, but this was their way of telling him to do his worst.

I talked to a tall, helmeted policeman. He was smiling at the dancers and he said, unexpectedly, "How can old Jerry beat us? They're all going to get it again, and here they are dancing and singing. No, old Jerry can't beat us. Not as long as we've got Drake's drum."

He told me the legend—to him a living legend—of the drum which Drake carried on the *Golden Hind* around the world. The drum is now at near-by Buckland Abbey. Back in 1918, when the German fleet surrendered and the British ships closed in around the enemy vessels, men on board the admiral's vessel heard the long beat of a drum. When, after careful search, neither drum nor drummer were found, even the admiral accepted the fact that this was Drake's drum. They remembered the poem:

Take my drum to England, hang it by the shore, strike it when your powder's running low.
If the Dons sight Devon, I'll quit the Port of Heaven and drum them up the channel as we drummed them long ago.

"Now and then that drum sounds again," the helmeted policeman assured me. "Our forefathers heard it when the *Mayflower* beat its way out of the sound. It was heard when Nelson came to Plymouth to be made a freeman of the city, and it rolled again when Wellington sailed from here to fight Napoleon. Aye, on the first night of the bad blitz we heard it roll again, and you'll not find a man, woman or child who'll deny it. It told us to fight on and we will."

Plymouth is still very much alive, although her shrines and her buildings are dead. Her shops are ruined, her churches and homes are hopeless masses of debris. One thing remains

31

untouched—the tablet commemorating the departure of the Pilgrims to Plymouth, Massachusetts.

If I were a citizen of Plymouth, Massachusetts, I would ask my fellow citizens to make a great sacrifice. I would ask them to give up their shrine, the Plymouth Rock, and ask them to smash it into a million pieces. I would give the rest of the country the privilege of sharing that shrine. I would sell the bits of rock to the citizens of America. Each of us would be proud to have a bit of the original rock in our homes and we would be glad to pay for that privilege. And with the money raised, Plymouth, Massachusetts, could rebuild her mother city—Plymouth, England.

Saturday in London on May 10th started off like any other Saturday night. The night was soft and the moon was full and London is very pleasant on a Saturday night like that. So many people are in the country that you get the illusion that you have London all to yourself. The Savoy dining room was only half full, a rare occasion at that popular hotel. I was having dinner with Ed Beattie.

This is the cable I sent *Collier's* on what happened that night:

QUOTE EYE DON'T LIKE WALKING UNQUOTE EYE TOLD ED BEATTIE STOP BEATTIE IS A MEMBER OF THE LONDON BUREAU OF THE UNITED PRESS STOP HE IS ALL RIGHT IN EVERY OTHER WAY BUT HE LIKES TO TAKE LONG WALKS IN THE COUNTRY STOP WE WERE DISCUSSING PLANS FOR SUNDAY STOP PARAGRAPH QUOTE ALL RIGHT COMMA ALL RIGHT UNQUOTE HE SAID STOP QUOTE EYE KNOW A PLACE IN KENT WHERE WE CAN HIRE BICYCLES STOP WE'LL TAKE A BICYCLE

RIDE THROUGH THE COUNTRY STOP INCIDENTALLY THE PLACE EYE HAVE IN MIND HAS A FINE PUB STOP UNQUOTE PARAGRAPH THE IDEA SEEMED MORE REASONABLE STOP SPRING IN ENGLAND IS ALL RIGHT STOP YOU DO GET A BIT TIRED OF LONDON AND A DAY IN THE COUNTRY SOUNDED FINE STOP THE DINING ROOM WAS ONLY HALF-CROWDED AND CARROLL GIBBONS THE ORCHESTRA LEADER WAS PLAY-ING AMERICAN TUNES STOP THEN CUTTING SHARPLY THROUGH THE MUSIC CAME THE SOUND OF THE SIREN STOP PARAGRAPH QUOTE THERE'S THAT NASTY MAN UNQUOTE BEATTIE SAID STOP PARAGRAPH QUOTE IT'S FULL MOON TO-NIGHT STOP EYE THOUGHT HE'D BE OVER UNQUOTE PARA-GRAPH BUT NO ONE PAID ANY ATTENTION TO IT STOP THE MINUTES PASSED AND WE HAD FORGOTTEN THE SIREN STOP GIBBONS WAS PLAYING QUOTE WHEN THAT MAN IS DEAD AND GONE UNQUOTE STOP THE GUNS WEREN'T FIRING STOP IN THE RESTAURANT WHICH IS BRICK-WALLED WE COULDN'T HEAR THE PLANES IF THERE WERE ANY UP THERE STOP THEN CAME THE DEEP-THROATED ROAR OF A BOMB EXPLODING AND THE GLASSES ON THE TABLE RATTLED COMMA THE FLOOR UNDER OUR FEET SHUDDERED STOP THE ECHO OF THE EXPLOSION HUNG IN THE ROOM STOP THIS HAD BEEN A VERY BIG ONE VERY CLOSE STOP WE HADN'T HEARD IT SCREAM ON ITS WAY DOWN STOP THE VERY BIG ONES FOR SOME REASON OR OTHER DON'T SCREAM THE WAY THE SMALLER ONES DO STOP A MOMENT LATER THREE MORE EXPLOSIONS CAME STOP THEY USUALLY DROP A STICK OF THREE STOP PEOPLE BEGAN TO LEAVE THE RESTAURANT STOP THE SAVOY RESTAURANT IS ON THE GROUND FLOOR WHICH ISN'T GOOD ENOUGH STOP PARAGRAPH AND THEN SUDDENLY BEATTIE AND I REALIZED THAT THIS WAS NO ORDINARY BLITZ STOP THE SAVOY IS VIRTUALLY ON THE BANKS OF THE THAMES STOP WE WALKED TO THE BACK

33

OF THE HOTEL AND INTO THE STREET STOP THE ANGRY BUZZING OF THE PLANES INCREASED AND THE BOMBS RAINED DOWN SEMICOLON LITERALLY RAINED DOWN STOP WE HUGGED THE SIDE OF THE BUILDING STOP NOW THE FIRES APPEARED STOP A LARGE BOMB DROPPED ACROSS THE RIVER BURST IN A BRILLIANT ORANGE FLAME SEEMED TO DIE AND THEN SPURTED HIGH INTO THE AIR STOP THERE WERE WAREHOUSES OVER THERE STOP ONE BY ONE THEY CAUGHT FIRE STOP THE FIRE ENGINES CLANGED SHARPLY AND THEN THE AIR WAS FILLED WITH A GREAT HISSING AS THE WATER MET THE FLAMES PARAGRAPH WE WENT BACK INTO THE HO- TEL STOP WE HAVE TWO ROOMS ON THE FIRST FLOOR WHICH ARE KEPT OPEN ALL NIGHT FOR THE CONVENIENCE OF COR- RESPONDENTS WHO LIVE AT THE SAVOY STOP ONE BY ONE THEY APPEARED PARAGRAPH TELEPHONE REPORTS BEGAN TO COME IN STOP THE UNITED PRESS BUILDING WAS ON FIRE PARAGRAPH QUOTE EYE'LL HAVE TO GET TO FLEET STREET UNQUOTE BEATTIE SAID PARAGRAPH QUOTE YOU'RE CRAZY UNQUOTE EYE TOLD HIM STOP QUOTE IT'S A MILE WALK AND STUFF IS DROPPING ALL OVER UNQUOTE PARAGRAPH QUOTE EYE'M IN CHARGE OF THE OFFICE TONIGHT UNQUOTE BEATTIE SAID SIMPLY STOP QUOTE WE HAVE RECORDS THERE AND EYE WANT TO GET THEM UNQUOTE PARAGRAPH QUOTE YOU'RE A FOOL UNQUOTE EYE SAID PARAGRAPH QUOTE ANYBODY GOT A TIN HAT QUERY UNQUOTE BEATTIE ASKED STOP NO ONE HAD STOP WE NEVER HAVE OUR TIN HATS HANDY WHEN WE NEED THEM STOP THEY'RE NO GOOD ANY- HOW STOP EYE DROPPED MINE ONCE AND IT CRACKED IN THREE PLACES PARAGRAPH CLAIRE LUCE THE AMERICAN ACTRESS HAD COME INTO OUR SHELTER STOP WE CALL IT A SHELTER BUT IT'S ONE FLIGHT UP STOP SHE WAS PLAYING CHESS WITH LARRY RUE OF THE CHICAGO TRIBUNE STOP SHE LOOKED UP WHEN BEATTIE ASKED FOR A TIN HAT PARAGRAPH

34

QUOTE CAN EYE GO ALONG WITH YOU QUERY UNQUOTE
SHE ASKED STOP BEATTIE SAID SHE COULD IF SHE WANTED
TO BE A FOOL AND THEY BOTH WENT OUT TO FACE A MILE
WALK IN THE MIDST OF THE WORST BLITZ LONDON OR ANY
OTHER CITY EVER HAD STOP THE NOISE HAD INCREASED AND
WE COULD HEAR THE RATHER TERRIFYING ROAR OF THE
FLAMES ACROSS THE RIVER STOP EYE WENT UP TO THE ROOF
TO CATCH A QUICK LOOK OF THE GENERAL SCENE STOP WE
ARE NO LONGER ALLOWED ON THE ROOFS DURING HEAVY
RAIDS PARAGRAPH QUOTE EYE'M FROM THE AIR MINISTRY
INTELLIGENCE DEPARTMENT UNQUOTE EYE TOLD THE ROOF
SPOTTER PARAGRAPH QUOTE YOU'RE FROM ROOM 554 UN-
QUOTE HE SAID AND EYE RECOGNIZED HIM AS THE MAN IN
CHARGE OF THE SAVOY BAR STOP HE LET ME STAY A FEW
MINUTES STOP OFTEN THE GERMAN RADIO HAS TOLD US
QUOTE LAST NIGHT LONDON WAS IN FLAMES UNQUOTE
STOP IT HAS NEVER BEEN TRUE STOP IT WAS TRUE TONIGHT
STOP LONDON WAS IN FLAMES STOP ACROSS THE RIVER A
SOLID SHEET OF LEAPING MADDENED FIRE BANKED THE
RIVER FOR NEARLY A MILE STOP A GERMAN PLANE DROPPED
A FLARE AND IT HIT THE RIVER STOP IT BURST IN A BRILLIANT
CASCADE OF BLUE AND GOLD SPARKS DASH A NEW KIND OF
FLARE TO ME STOP THEN THE INEVITABLE STICK OF BOMBS
FOLLOWED AND THE SAVOY TREMBLED STOP THERE WERE
FLAMES ON EVERY SIDE STOP EYE LOOKED TOWARD FLEET
STREET AND WINCED STOP TWO LARGE FIRES WERE REACHING
UP INTO THE NIGHT STOP EYE HAD A LOT OF FRIENDS WORK-
ING DOWN THERE PARAGRAPH THIS DWARFED ANY BLITZ EYE
HAVE EVER SEEN STOP STILL BOTH INCENDIARIES AND HIGH
EXPLOSIVES SCREAMED DOWN STOP THE NIGHT WAS FILLED
WITH NOISE DASH ALL OF IT FRIGHTENING NOISE STOP AND
ABOVE THE PLANES STILL ROARED STOP IT WAS SO LIGHT THAT
THE BALLOONS FIVE THOUSAND FEET UP COULD BE SEEN

35

CLEARLY STOP NOW AND THEN THERE WOULD COME THE RATTLE OF MACHINE GUN FIRE HARDLY HEARD OVER THE CRACKLING OF FIRES AND THE NOISE OF THE BOMBS STOP BUT IT TOLD US THAT THE NIGHT FIGHTERS WERE UP THERE PARAGRAPH EYE WENT DOWN TO OUR QUOTE SHELTER UN-QUOTE STOP A BOMB WHICH HAD HIT OUTSIDE WHILE I WAS AWAY HAD KNOCKED TWO DOZEN GLASSES OFF THE BAR STOP TITCH OUR ALL-NIGHT BARTENDER WAS SWEEPING UP THE BROKEN GLASS STOP EARL REEVES IN CHARGE OF THE INTERNATIONAL NEWS SERVICE CAME IN PARAGRAPH QUOTE OUR PHONES ARE GONE UNQUOTE HE SAID STOP QUOTE WE HAVE NO WIRES LEFT DASH CAN'T CABLE A THING UNQUOTE PARAGRAPH YOU CAN SHARE MY OFFICE UNQUOTE BOB POST ACTING CHIEF OF THE NEW YORK TIMES SAID STOP QUOTE IT'S ONLY UPSTAIRS AND WE HAVE PLENTY OF ROOM STOP EYE'VE TOLD THE UP AND AP TO MOVE IN STOP USE MY WIRES UNQUOTE PARAGRAPH IT'S LIKE THAT DURING A BAD BLITZ STOP TOMORROW THE BOYS WOULD BE QUOTE OPPO-SITION UNQUOTE AGAIN DOING EVERYTHING TO BEAT EACH OTHER STOP BUT THIS WAS AN EMERGENCY STOP THE NIGHT HAD LEADEN FEET STOP IT SEEMED AS THOUGH IT WOULD NEVER END STOP THERE WAS NOTHING WE COULD DO STOP WE'D GOT THE STORY OF THE NIGHT MERELY BY BEING WHERE WE WERE STOP DETAILS SUCH AS TARGETS HIT COMMA CAS-UALTIES ETC. WOULDN'T BE AVAILABLE UNTIL THE MORN-ING STOP WE SAT THERE STOP BEN ROBERTSON OF PM WAS PLAYING CHESS WITH AN ENGLISH REPORTER STOP JOE EVANS OF THE HERALD TRIBUNE CAME IN AND DROPPED WEARILY INTO A CHAIR STOP QUOTE ABOUT ALL THE TELE-PHONE LINES ARE OUT UNQUOTE HE SAID STOP QUOTE CEN-TRAL IS GONE STOP PADDINGTON AND GERRARD WENT STOP AND NOW MUSEUM IS GONE STOP CAN'T GET THE MINISTRY OF INFORMATION UNQUOTE PARAGRAPH QUOTE THE NIGHT

36

FIGHTERS GOT FOURTEEN UP TO ONE O'CLOCK UNQUOTE
WHITE-HAIRED JIM MACDONALD REPORTED GLEEFULLY
PARAGRAPH QUOTE HOW MANY JERRIES ARE UP THERE UN-
QUOTE EYE ASKED HIM PARAGRAPH QUOTE AROUND FOUR
HUNDRED I HEAR UNQUOTE JIM SAID STOP QUOTE THAT'S
A LOT OF AIRPLANES UNQUOTE PARAGRAPH TITCH THE
WAITER BROKE IN QUOTE WHY DOESN'T SOMEONE INVENT
A DEATH RAY QUERY UNQUOTE PARAGRAPH QUOTE HOLD
MY DRINK TITCH UNQUOTE EYE TOLD HIM QUOTE EYE'LL
INVENT A DEATH RAY UNQUOTE PARAGRAPH THEN WE
ARGUED AS TO WHICH BLITZ WAS WORSE COMMA THIS ONE
OR THE FAMOUS WEDNESDAY ONE IN APRIL STOP BOTH HAD
THEIR POINTS BUT WE AGREED THAT THIS WAS MORE
SEVERE STOP IN ANY CASE IT WAS CONCENTRATED HERE AT
OUR END OF LONDON STOP THE OLD GAL WAS TAKING A
REAL PASTING TONIGHT AND NONE OF US FELT GOOD STOP
EYE'M SURE THAT MOST OF US WERE AFRAID STOP BOMBS
WERE DROPPING THAT CLOSE PARAGRAPH GEORGE LAIT AND
RED MUELLER OF INS WALKED IN STOP THEIR CLOTHES WERE
FILTHY AND THEIR FACES HEAVY WITH SOOT STOP THEY HAD
HAD A BAD TIME STOP THEY LIVE IN A WOODEN HOUSE
COMMA ONE OF A BLOCK OF THEM STOP THREE BOMBS HAD
DROPPED AND DEMOLISHED EVERY HOUSE IN THE ROW BUT
THEIRS STOP THEY HAD PULLED WOUNDED FROM THE BURN-
ING BUILDINGS AND BROUGHT THEM INTO THEIR HOUSE
STOP THEY HAD SOME IODINE AND THEY TORE THEIR SHEETS
INTO BANDAGES AND DID WHAT THEY COULD FOR THE TOR-
TURED MEN AND WOMEN WHO LAY BLEEDING THERE STOP
FINALLY DOCTORS AND AMBULANCES HAD COME TO RE-
LIEVE THEM STOP NOW THEY WERE REPORTING FOR WORK
STOP THE BLITZ WAS AT ITS VERY HEIGHT AND MORE THAN
ONCE THE BIG SAVOY SHOOK UNDER THE FURY OF THE
BLAST FROM THE BOMBS PARAGRAPH QUOTE EYE WONDER

37

HOW MANY OF US WILL BE ALIVE IN THE MORNING UN-
QUOTE A WOMAN SAID CALMLY STOP WE LOOKED AT HER
INCURIOUSLY STOP NONE OF US KNEW HER STOP SHE WAS
A STATELY MIDDLE AGED WOMAN IN EVENING CLOTHES AND
SHE WAS SIPPING A TALL DRINK PARAGRAPH QUOTE WELL
ANYWAY SO FAR SO GOOD UNQUOTE EYE SAID TO HER AND
THEN INCREDIBLY MERCIFULLY CAME THE LONG JOYOUS
SOUND OF THE SIREN STOP IT WAS JUST SIX THIRTY ON SUN-
DAY MORNING PARAGRAPH LAST FALL AFTER A BAD RAID
PEOPLE IN LONDON WOULD SHRUG THEIR SHOULDERS AND
SAY COMPLACENTLY QUOTE WE CAN TAKE IT UNQUOTE STOP
ALL THAT FEELING IS GONE NOW STOP EYE WALKED AROUND
THE STILL BURNING STREETS OF LONDON ON SUNDAY MORN-
ING STOP THE STREETS WERE FILLED WITH GRIM FACED
SULLEN LOOKING MEN AND WOMEN STOP THEY WERE
THROUGH TAKING IT STOP THEY WANTED TO GIVE IT STOP
EVERY BOMB THAT THE NAZIS DROPPED DURING THE NIGHT
CARRIED GERMS WITH IT DASH GERMS OF HATRED STOP EYE
COULD FEEL THE HATRED RISING FROM THE RUINS INFECT-
ING EVERYONE STOP TIGHT LIPPED MEN AND WOMEN STARED
AT THE DEBRIS OF TREASURED LANDMARKS AND YOU COULD
FEEL THE HATRED OF NAZI BARBARISM EMANATING FROM
THEM STOP THIS WAR IS TOO IMPORTANT TO BE FOUGHT BY
GENERALS DASH IT IS BEING FOUGHT BY THE PEOPLE STOP
THE PEOPLE HAVE BORNE THE BRUNT OF THE ATTACK STOP
THE PEOPLE WILL INSIST UPON MAKING THE PEACE STOP
THE PEOPLE WILL NOT BE GENEROUS VICTORS PARAGRAPH
PEOPLE STOOD STARING AT THE SMOKING WRECKAGE OF
ST CLEMENT DANES WHICH WAS DOCTOR JOHNSON'S CHURCH
SEMICOLON EVERY CHILD IN LONDON HAS SUNG THE NUR-
SERY RHYME WHICH BEGINS QUOTE ORANGES AND LEMONS
SAY THE BELLS OF ST CLEMENTS DASHES UNQUOTE THE
CHURCH WAS STILL BURNING AND THE LIGHT FROM THE

FLAMES WITHIN SHOWED SOFTLY THROUGH THE STRAINED GLASS WINDOWS STOP SOMEONE WILL HAVE TO PAY FOR THAT ONE DAY THE FACES OF THE PEOPLE SAID STOP THE VENERABLE TEMPLE CHURCH WHERE THE CRUSADERS WERE BLESSED BEFORE GOING ON THEIR PILGRIMAGES COMMA WHERE THEY WERE BURIED WHEN THEY DIED WAS NOTH-ING BUT SMOLDERING RUINS STOP HISTORIC BIG BEN WAS HIT BUT ALTHOUGH HIS VOICE WAS STILLED THE HANDS OF THE HUGE CLOCK STILL TRAVELED SLOWLY AROUND THE FACE OF BIG BEN STOP WESTMINSTER HALL ADJOINING THE HOUSE HAD THE LARGEST WOODEN ROOF IN THE WORLD COMMA BUILT BY WILLIAM RUFUS IN THE YEAR 1200 STOP INCEN-DIARIES HAD DESTROYED THE ROOF STOP BOMBS HAD FOUND THE TWO SYMBOLS REPRESENTING WHAT ENGLAND IS FIGHT-ING FOR DASH THE HOUSE OF COMMONS THE SYMBOL OF FREE SPEECH AND WESTMINSTER ABBEY SYMBOL OF A CHRISTIAN WAY OF LIFE STOP PEOPLE WALKED ABOUT THE CITY GRIM FACED PARAGRAPH IT WAS A BEAUTIFUL DAY STOP A SPRING SUN BATHED THE CITY WITH ITS WARMTH BUT THERE WAS A PALL OF SMOKE OVER THE CITY AND THROUGH IT THE SUN SHONE BLOOD RED STOP A BREEZE CARRIED SOOT FROM STILL SMOKING BUILDINGS AND YOUR HANDS AND FACE GREW GRIMY STOP THE FIREMEN UNEXHAUSTED AFTER A BITTER NIGHT'S WORK KEPT AT THEIR JOB METHODICALLY STOP MOBILE CANTEENS DASHED UP AND UNIFORMED GIRLS SERVED THEM TEA AND SANDWICHES STOP AIR WARDENS AND POLICE WERE SEARCHING AMONG RUINS HOPING AGAINST HOPE THAT THEY MIGHT FIND SOMETHING LIVING UNDER THEM PARAGRAPH TWO MEN GOT OUT OF A CAR IN FRONT OF THE SMOKING HOUSE OF COMMONS STOP THEY PASSED THROUGH THE POLICE LINES STOP ONE MAN WAS BULKY AND HE SMOKED A LARGE CIGAR STOP THE OTHER WAS SMALL ALMOST GNOMELIKE STOP THEY WALKED THROUGH THE

39

RUINS OF THE HOUSE SCENE OF SO MANY OF THEIR BATTLES
STOP THEY WASTED NO TIME IN BEING SORRY FOR THE OLD
HOUSE STOP THEN THEY CAME OUT STOP THE VERY ANGLE
OF WINSTON CHURCHILL'S CIGAR SHOWED ANGER AND DE-
TERMINATION DASH NOT COMPLACENT ACCEPTANCE AND
LORD BEAVERBROOK'S FACE WAS GRIM STOP THESE TWO MEN
WERE TIRED OF TAKING IT STOP LIKE THE PEOPLE THEY GOV-
ERN THEY TOO NOW WANTED TO GIVE IT.

All that day I sensed a new and intensified hatred of Germany in the people of London. That hatred has lasted. It is
as true today as it was on that Sunday morning. The steel had
entered the soul of Britain. No matter how long this war
drags on Britain will be inspired and encouraged by her
hatred. Hatred is an honest emotion—as honest as love. You
can't beat fascism with halfway measures. Czechoslovakia,
Poland, Belgium, Holland, Norway, France—none of them
hated fascism enough. To beat fascism, you have to hate it
as a preacher hates sin. Ever since that Sunday the people of
Britain have nursed that hatred. I heard them in pubs, in
theatres, in homes, in RAF messes, in wardrooms of destroyers, in the offices of Cabinet Ministers. That hatred would destroy anyone in Britain misguided enough to associate himself with the servants of that horrible word, "appeasement."
No one in Britain will ever forget that Saturday night or the
Sunday that followed it.

There are two things I will never forget seeing as I walked
about the city in the half gloom. The statue of George Washington looked down from his pedestal in front of the Royal
Gallery in Trafalgar Square. He looked puzzled. In his day,
churches and civilians were not military objectives. Then there
was the huge statue of Abraham Lincoln with the House of

40

Commons to his left and Westminster Abbey to his right. Lincoln didn't look puzzled. He looked grim but understanding. From the Nazi point of view, both were military objectives, and Lincoln, brooding there solemnly, looked as though he understood.

The House of Commons in Britain is the symbol of free speech, and Westminster Abbey has always been the symbol of a Christian way of life, a symbol of tolerance and decency and faith. These, too, have been objects of Hitler's scorn and wrath. Yes, Westminster Abbey was indeed a military objective.

4

Bombers' Moon

DURING THE BLITZ of May 10th, the RAF fighters brought down forty-four Nazi airplanes. The Air Ministry had always said that if 10 per cent of the invading planes were destroyed, night bombing as a serious menace would cease to exist. No air force, the Air Ministry argued, could afford to expend its capital in aircraft and personnel at such a rate and survive. It must be remembered that the larger Nazi bombers have trained crews of from four to six men, and a loss of forty-four aircraft might mean a loss of close to 200 pilots, wireless operators, navigators and air gunners. Difficult as it would be to replace forty-four airplanes, it would be even more difficult to replace 200 trained airmen. In the long run, men not machines still win wars.

There will probably never be any complete answer to night bombing, but the radio locator gave eyes to the night fighter, and it has become far more effective against invading planes than the comparatively innocuous anti-aircraft barrage which does little except keep them way up there. Britain became night-fighter conscious after that May 10th raid. The night-fighters, the lads with the cat's eyes, became the new glamour boys. One heard that they ate nothing but carrots, which gave them phenomenal eyesight. We heard that they slept all day in darkened rooms, to become accustomed to the night. I knew a few of the night fighters who were stationed in Kent, and I spent quite a lot of time with them. In general, they were more mature than the youngsters who flew the Spitfires and the Hurricanes by day.

There was a grand pub only three miles from their airport, and the boys made it their headquarters. It was a fine, decent pub, the type found only in rural England, run by a nice middle-aged woman and her two daughters. Closing time was ten o'clock in the pub, but one of the pilots more affluent than the rest kept a room upstairs. This made him a resident of the pub, and of course license laws in England do not apply to residents. So at ten o'clock each night the ordinary village customers would be shooed out of the bar and we would take over. We were guests of the resident pilot and (by stretching the point) we, too, were entitled to drink after hours.

At this particular airdrome there were four squadrons. A Squadron and B Squadron would alternate with C and D Squadrons on night duty. Of course the two squadrons not on duty had to stay reasonably near the airport in case of an emergency call. Staying a week end at the pub (the George and the Dragon) was really an ordeal. You had to spend a night drinking with two of the squadrons, and then the next night you'd be faced with two fresh squadrons, ready to take you on.

I found out quite a bit about the RAF night fighters. To begin with, very few of them ate carrots at all. They didn't eat carrots because they didn't like carrots, no matter what helpful vitamins lurked in their ugly yellow insides. They wore dark glasses during the daytime, but, as one of them said, "What the hell, dark glasses are good to hide a hangover." This was one of the few airdromes in Britain devoted entirely to night fighters. There was friendly rivalry and much argument, mostly ribald, as to which was the superior plane. At the airport, there

43

were Defiants, Beaufighters, Douglas Havocs and Spitfires. The Spitfires were used only on very bright nights. The Spitters land at a hundred miles an hour, and they don't have the sturdy legs which the two-motored airplanes have. It takes a lot of landing to set a Spit down when you can't see exactly where you're going. There is one cardinal rule in the RAF: Any pilot who "shoots a line" is a marked man. He can rave all he wants about his aircraft or his guns, but if he starts telling how good he himself is, God help him. I have been in fifty RAF messes and know perhaps 300 RAF pilots well, and I never heard one of them "shoot a line." But they can rave about their airplanes. One of the pilots who flew a Spitfire was taking a ride from his mates one night in the George and the Dragon. He hadn't been up for nearly a week, the weather had been so bad. Meanwhile, the Defiants and Beaufighters and Havocs had been doing the patroling.

"Well, I'll tell you fellows something," he said, reaching for another glass of beer. "You may be right about the old Spit being no good, but this is all I know about it. The other day I was down to Tunbridge Wells to visit a chum of mine who's in the hospital there. A squadron leader, nice fellow, too. Wasn't shot down. He was flying a Defiant, and it just came apart in the air."

He was interrupted by loud and very rude cries of derision, but he calmly pushed his glass toward the barmaid and said, "Give me the other half, sweetheart."

"At this hospital, now, they had some wounded Hun airmen," he went on. "In fact, they had twelve of them. I thought it would be fun to take a look at them."

"You might have had a chance to finish the job," someone growled.

"No bloody fear," he said. "They watched me like a hawk, thinking I was up to something. Anyhow, I went into the room and there they were—twelve of them. The doctor looked at them and was furious at the nurses. 'Look at the black and blue marks on these men,' he yelled. He went from bed to bed and sure enough, eleven out of the twelve were covered with black and blue marks. The twelfth one was unmarked. 'Are you nurses allowing these prisoners to be beaten?' he yelled at them. When they swore they hadn't touched the Hun patients, he said, 'Well, where in hell did they get those black and blue marks?' The head nurse said, 'Well, Doctor, it's like this, that twelfth man was delirious all night and he kept yelling "Spitfire, Spitfire," and every time he yelled "Spitfire" why, those other eleven just naturally bailed out of bed.' "

He turned back to his beer complacently. They made him buy the next round after that story. These kids averaged about twenty dollars a week salary, out of which they had to pay an income tax, but after hours I was never allowed to pay a round of drinks. They considered the pub to be part of their mess. Sure, I was their pal and all that, but I couldn't buy a drink.

The Defiant Squadron at this airport is one of the most famous in England. This bunch made its name around the time of Dunkirk. Over Holland they got thirty-seven German planes in one day. Between May 14th and May 30th last year, the squadron got sixty-five Jerries—the best record made by any squadron. During that time they lost five airplanes and five crews. The Defiant, of course, is a two-place airplane. The pilot flies and the gunner shoots. When the Defiant first came out, the Germans were baffled by its turret. The gun turret with its armor and guns weighs a ton and a half. That slows the aircraft down a bit but gives it great firing power.

One pilot and his gunner held the D.F.M. with bar, which merely means that they have been decorated twice. Legends grew up about this great team. One day their Defiant got a bullet through its radiator. The same thing happened that happens to your car when your radiator leaks. Their glycol (the same stuff you use in winter to keep your radiator from freezing) leaked out, the motor heated up and then stopped. They were at 20,000 feet directly over the Channel. They did the only thing possible to do; they glided toward the English coast. They made it, all right. That is a routine operation, but what made the experience remarkable was the fact that while gliding toward England, they managed to dive on a Junkers and the gunner calmly blew the Junkers to bits. He was a butcher's boy before the war.

I learned the squadron secret: A scion of a great English family was anxious to enter the air force. He was thirty-eight, however, and for that reason was turned down. He changed his name, secured a fake birth certificate saying that he was twenty-five and was accepted. He is doing great work, too. His colleagues in the House of Lords sometimes wonder why he never appears any more at sessions. They don't know that he and his cat's eyes are knocking down Germans.

We had some wonderful talks in that pub and we settled many a problem. There was one lad named Terry who was like a character out of a book. He was twenty-four and he had just become a proud father. Every time I saw him he found a new anniversary to celebrate. First, it was when his wife returned from the hospital. Then, there was the baby's christening. Another time, the baby was a month old. Terry and I did more damn celebrating because of that kid. (Although I am writing this far from the British censors, I must respect the Air Ministry rule which does not allow us to use the full names of pilots, except in special cases.)

Terry was D.F.C. with bar and a D.S.O. with bar. He had already shot down sixteen Nazi planes, seven of them at night. He flew a Defiant. Often the boys would talk about the inva-

46

sion. Would there be an invasion? They all hoped that there would.

"Suppose there was an invasion; the Home Guard would take care of it," I told Terry. "You fellows would be in here shooting a line to each other, telling how you were up there at 20,000 feet, your wings full of ice, hanging by your knees to the rudder-bar . . ."

"Sure, and the sky full of Messerschmidts and the clouds full of sky weed. There I was and my gun jammed. But was I afraid? No, sir." Terry began to grow eloquent. "I just grabbed a bunch of that sky weed, strung it together, made a ladder out of it, and then hung it over the side of my aircraft and climbed right down. Yes, sir, and I got home in time for tea."

"But suppose there was an invasion," I persisted. "What part would you all play?"

"I'd love to see an invasion," Terry said softly. "Oh, I would love it. I would like to see those nice fat troop-carrying aircraft come over the Channel, each of them carrying forty dirty Huns."

The others stood at the bar quietly and suddenly no one was fooling. Everyone was listening to Terry.

"I would pick out the biggest and the fattest troop-carrying aircraft," Terry went on, "and I would fly alongside it. He wouldn't worry at first, because he'd forget that my Defiant has a turret. Then I would call to my gunner, 'Tallyhoo, Andy,' and I would look at the troop-carrying aircraft. I would hear our bullets hitting the Hun. It would sound like the quick beating of a drum, like this." Terry struck his beer glass sharply on the bar a dozen times, rat - rat - rat, rat - rat - rat. He took another sip of his beer.

"And then I would watch where the bullets had hit," Terry went on. "I would see our bullets cross-stitch the fat troop-carrying aircraft up and down, back and forth, as Andy swung

47

his gun. Then I would wait for the blood to come out of the holes made by our bullets. I'd wait for the blood from the Huns inside to drip out of those bullet holes until the whole fuselage was covered with blood. That's what I'd do, by God, that's what I'd do."

He was breathing hard and his hands were clenched.

"Then when I knew that they were all dead except the pilot, you know what I'd do then? You know what I'd do? I'd give the motor everything it had, and I'd ram the God-damn troop-carrying aircraft, that's what I'd do."

Terry was trembling now, and I looked at the other pilots. Their faces were tense and their eyes were hard. They weren't just pleasant boys sitting around a country pub having a glass of beer. They were men fighting for their country; they were men whose pals had been killed fighting; men whose relatives and friends had been killed in air raids.

"I hate Germans," Terry said finally. "Let's drink up. Fill 'em up, Sadie. Fill 'em up. This is my drink. And now let's drink a toast. Fill 'em up, Sadie, all of them. Ready. Here we go, boys. . . . Death to the bastards."

We drank it and meant it.

"Let's get some air," Terry said. "Let's go over to the field."

Seven of us piled into Terry's car, a horrible-looking contraption that had once been a respectable Rolls-Bentley. It had nothing much left but one of the best engines ever tossed into an automobile. We bumped over dirt roads while the boys sang, "All day long we haven't flown below six hundred . . ."

We walked into the large dugout where a dozen pilots were waiting their turn to go up. On a night like this, quiet so far, two airplanes were always circling the field just in case of the unlikely contingency that a Nazi plane had managed to penetrate the radio defenses without having been picked up. As we went in, a small and very nondescript-looking dog of dubious

48

ancestry made a bounding leap for Terry. Terry grabbed the dog and started tossing him around, and the dog made small growling noises in his throat. He leaped at Terry's gloved hand and worried the glove, and then when Terry picked him up in his arms, he looked reproachfully at him, as if blaming him for the unpalatable taste of the gloves, and then decided to lick Terry's face instead.

"Easy to tell he's your dog," I laughed to Terry.

"He's not my dog," Terry said quietly. "He belonged to Al ———. You remember Al? I brought him up to your place about three weeks ago. Remember him, a tall, blond chap, D.F.C. with bar? Flew Beaufighters. Well, Al didn't get back last Sunday night. Damn fool dog, can't tell me from Al." Terry turned and looked at me. "Do you blame me for hating Germans?"

"I don't blame anyone for hating Germans," I told him.

I talked awhile with them, and then the Commanding Officer walked in. He waved them down as they half rose to salute. The RAF dispenses with strict and unnecessary regulations when the pilots are standing by, preparing for active duty. This, incidentally, is no sign at all of slack discipline. The discipline is perhaps better in the RAF than in any other service because so often, especially when orders are given to pilots who are in the air, a man's life and the safety of an aircraft may depend upon exact and immediate obedience. We chatted with the Commanding Officer and then, surprisingly, he invited me to go up to the control room with him.

We walked across the airdrome. It was a bright night with a real bomber's moon. The Germans hadn't been over in force for several weeks, but you felt that this was too good a night for them to waste. The airdrome was about a mile square and, scattered over the field, you could see airplanes crouching, as though eager to take off. The control room was brilliantly

49

lighted. There were a dozen men at telephones, at maps, bending over charts. Most of the mechanics of a control room come under the "hush hush" category, but the Commanding Officer explained everything to me.

"You've been to enough control rooms to know what you can write about and what you can't write about," he laughed. "Here's an interesting thing perhaps you haven't seen. Lights out," he called.

Under a heavy plate glass there was a map of France, Belgium, Holland and Germany. The map was dotted with small red lights. There must have been eighty of the tiny electric bulbs aglow, and there were a third that many green lights.

"They are Jerry airports which we know about," the Commanding Officer said, indicating the red lights. "The green lights indicate probable Jerry airports. We'll learn about those soon."

The lights went on, and one of the men, without turning from his position at his telephone, said, "Forty plus coming this way. Forty plus coming this way. Last located at . . ."

The Commanding Officer smiled and went off to give orders. Now these men with whom I'd been talking and laughing and drinking beer would have to start earning their twenty dollars a week. "Forty plus" might mean anything. Actually, it meant "over forty German planes."

Out on the field the motors started to roar. The pilots and their gunners sauntered out of the hut where they had been waiting. They walked to their planes.

"I'd just ordered a beer," a pilot named Cecil said to me. "When Frank brings it, grab it."

"I'll buy you one when you get back," I told him.

"I'll be back," he said. They all think that; they all believe in their own luck. If you don't believe in the absolute infallibility of your own luck you won't be much good as a night

50

fighter. In fact, if you don't believe in your own luck you'd better stay out of the war zone.

One plane after another soared away. They all show lights when they take off. They circle the field once to get the sleep out of their motors, and then they switch their lights off and go to work. They show lights on returning. The Germans do the same thing and often the RAF night fighters try to guess what color lights the Germans will show on a particular night. They will circle high over German airports, mingling with German bombers, showing the German landing lights, and then let them have it. It is a difficult operation, but the night fighters have become very proficient at it. They call the operation "intruding."

I stood with two pilots who hadn't been sent up yet and we watched the planes circling. Twenty-four of them were up there. They would fly at different levels, forming a protecting wall 35,000 feet high between our airport and London. It was bright enough for the Spitfires to go up, and now they took off. Even the night couldn't conceal the slim beauty of this greatest of fighting planes. The blunt Beaufighters and Defiants are decidedly masculine-looking. The Spitfire looks like a debutante, eager-eyed, youthful, dressed for her first big party. In the distance the guns were roaring, and occasionally the sky was studded with quick, golden flashes from the exploding shells.

"Why don't you fellows ever get hit by our own ack-ack?" I asked one of the pilots.

"That's what they call co-operation between the air force and the ground force," he said. "They know where we are most of the time."

The nearest guns stopped, and now we could hear the German planes. The two pilots could tell the difference between the German motors and the motors of the night fighters.

Now and then we'd hear the unmistakable loud singing of a Spitfire. It has a sound all its own. The sky above and on all sides was almost filled with planes but, bright as the moon was, we couldn't see any of them. Then we heard the rattle of machine-gun fire. It is a quick, sharp bark, quite unlike the sound of other guns. A great drama was being played up there above us. German planes loaded with thousands of tons of high explosives were trying to get through to London. London slept all unaware.

Then, ten thousand feet above and two miles to the east, a tremendous golden and purple ball of fire appeared. It lit the whole countryside. It seemed to hang in the air for seconds.

"That's a new kind of flare they're dropping," I said.

The two pilots looked at me with pitying eyes. "That's not a flare," one of them said quietly. "That's an aircraft on fire—I hope one of theirs."

The light changed to sullen yellow and then suddenly dropped. It was hard to believe that it was a burning plane. It dropped and suddenly died. Two seconds later there was a tremendous explosion. Its bombs had found the ground. The world seemed very quiet now; the planes were very high and their motors sang a soft litany.

The men were quiet. The Commanding Officer smiled.

"I hope we're putting on a good show for you."

"It's a good show," I told him. "Was that plane one of theirs?"

"It was a Jerry, all right."

It was good to know that one of these men I'd been with all evening hadn't got it. The hours went on. Dawn was breaking now and the pigeons were coming home to roost. One by one they approached, circled, showing their identification lights, and then settled down. It was 5 A.M. The night's work was about over. A Spitfire landed. The pilot who climbed down

52

was Cecil, the one who had told me about his glass of beer.

"I nailed one," he said. "Made quite a blaze. Could you see it from here?"

"You could see that one from London," I told him.

"They can't call that one a probable," he growled. He told me about getting it. He was as casual as though he were telling of a movie he'd seen.

"I came up from below," he said, "and just had time to get in one cannon shot. It was the luckiest shot I ever made. Mind you, if you hit a Jerry kite at all that's good shooting. If you hit his petrol tank that's a miracle. Anyhow, I hit his tank and the whole thing went up in flames. I was climbing as I shot and I zoomed over him. My aircraft got the full force of that blast, and damned if it didn't turn us right over on our back! It was pretty hot for about five seconds."

"What did you do?"

"I got the hell out of there quick," he laughed. "I didn't know when those bombs were going off."

"How about some lunch now?" he suggested. It seemed a good idea, though it was the first time I had ever had lunch at 5 A.M. We went into the mess. Things were very informal here. It was warm and we took off our coats and sat in our shirt sleeves. We had thick, juicy chops, fried potatoes and peas and beans, and there was plenty of butter on the table. Then the mess attendant brought in a plate of something that made me exclaim, "What is that?"

"Cheese, just cheese," Cecil said.

Just cheese. I hadn't seen so much cheese since I had left New York.

We had cheese and I ate as much as I could with decency, and we had rolls and coffee and the boys talked of the squadrons.

"Lunch" over, we got a full report of the night's operations.

In all, the boys had got seven German planes. More important was the fact that they had prevented the German planes from reaching London. I drove back to London and went to my hotel. It was just 7 A.M. A sleepy-eyed charwoman scrubbing the lobby floor had just turned on the radio to hear the morning news.

"This is the BBC Home and Forces program," the voice droned out of the loudspeaker, "giving you the news. There was some enemy air activity over the country last night. Seven enemy aircraft were destroyed by our night fighters. London had a warning which lasted four hours, but not one enemy aircraft was heard over the city . . ."

"I wonder," the charwoman said sleepily, "if you can always believe those reports."

"You can believe that one, sweetheart," I told her.

5

Two Boys and a Girl

I HAVE A SECRETARY in London named Betty Marais who is worth her weight in gold and, if she doesn't stop eating pastry, she will soon be worth all of the gold in Fort Knox. Betty worked for a friend of mine named MacAlpine, one of the smarter BBC executives. I had done some work for MacAlpine, who was in charge of broadcasts to America. I'd always be late with my script, which Mac had to censor, and more than once I finished it in longhand while hurrying to the studio in a cab. As I have never been able to decipher my own longhand, it was perhaps not unreasonable of Mac to complain that he couldn't read it either. So I got into the habit of tossing my script to Mac's secretary as I entered the studio and asking her to type a clean copy. She, by some uncanny second sight, was able to decipher the penciled corrections and additions which were merely esoteric hieroglyphics to Mac and myself. And she was the fastest typist I ever saw.

One day MacAlpine said to me, "Do you know anyone of any importance in the Wrens?"

Wrens are the Women's Royal Naval Service, perhaps the most popular women's service in Britain. Girls like to be in the Wrens because of the uniforms. Officers in the Wrens wear very chic tricolor hats. Last spring, there were no vacancies in the service, but I told Mac I did know a few of the head

55

women in the service if he had someone he wanted to get into the Wrens.

"It's Betty Marais, that young secretary of mine," he said in a worried tone. "This place is no good for her. I want to get her into either the Waafs or the Wrens."

This rather amazed me. I could think of no more pleasant or circumspect place for a girl to work in than Broadcasting House.

"What's it all about, Mac?" I asked.

"You don't know her story?"

"I don't go around asking the secretaries of my friends to tell me the story of their lives," I said coldly.

"Well," he said thoughtfully, "her nerves are bad. This place is getting her down. About six months ago, she married a boy who had worked here. They had a lot of fun here working together. Anyhow, he joined the RAF. Then, as I say, six months ago they were married. A couple of weeks later he was killed."

"That isn't good," I said.

Mac shook his head. "No. She came back here to work, thinking she would get over it better if she were working. But the trouble is that every time she turns a corner here, she meets Derek; every time she goes into the commissary she remembers the meals they had together. The youngster is only twenty, and I think a change of scenery would do her good. I've talked it over with her, and she agrees that she'd like to enter either the Wrens or the Waafs."

"Not the ATS?" The ATS are the women's part of the army.

"She doesn't like the ATS' uniform," Mac said.

"Too bad she has her heart set on that," I told him. "My secretary left two weeks ago to join her husband in South Africa. He's a district commissioner down there and now I'm looking for a secretary."

56

Mac shrugged his shoulders. "She might be better off working for you," he said. And so, a week later, Betty Marais came to work for me. If I seem to spend too much time in discussing my secretary, it is because a secretary to a foreign correspondent holds a much more important place than does the ordinary business man's secretary. Betty was my whole office force. My office, since the May 10th Blitz when so many Fleet Street offices went west, was a room in my suite at the Savoy. In addition to typing, a correspondent's secretary has to be a model of tact; she has to take stories to the censor and sometimes argue with him if he makes cuts that are too drastic; she has to arrange parties that you give and see that you attend parties that you should attend, but with a little mental encouragement on your own part might miss; she has to pay your bills and chase away unwelcome visitors and entertain those visitors who might be useful. In my case, Betty had an additional duty. I had, in a manner of speaking, adopted several American lads serving in the RAF. When they got leave, it was Betty's job to see that they had accommodations, drinks, girls to go out with and theatre tickets, if they wanted them. She was especially good at entertaining Red Tobin, Bill Malkemus and other young pilots.

Once I found her in the Savoy bar, happily doling out champagne to Red and Bill. I really felt as though these three healthy, fine youngsters were my family. But I had to bawl Betty out a bit, just for fun.

"What's the idea of giving them champagne?" I yelled at her. "They'd be just as happy drinking beer. And what are these loafers doing here? Why aren't they up there protecting us?"

"Red was over France on a sweep today," Betty said as proud as though Red (who was 21) was her son. "He thinks he got an M.E. 109, too. And he came home with twenty bullet holes

57

in his Spitfire. And, oh, Quent"—Betty could never get into the habit of calling anyone mister—"where do you think Bill was last night?"

"At that pub near Huntington where his squadron goes," I suggested.

"No," Betty said breathlessly. "He was over Berlin. Think of it! He bombed Berlin only last night! And his birthday is next Friday, and you're giving him a big party, and Red is coming and a lot of Squadron 71. And you," she said scornfully, "won't even buy them a bottle of champagne! I'll pay for the champagne and you can take it out of the wages you owe me."

I was so proud of Red Tobin of Eagle Squadron 71 that to keep from showing it I had to bawl him out because he hadn't written home to his father in Hollywood for six weeks. Red was a wonderful boy. So was gentle-voiced Bill Malkemus of Louisville, Kentucky, a bomber pilot. We sat and talked of whom we would ask to his birthday party. When these RAF kids come to London on leave, they don't go haywire, as one might expect. For the most part they go to a show, have a few beers and let it go at that. Red and Bill were like that. We made great plans for Bill's birthday party.

"My folks sent me some candy," Bill said. "I'll bring that along and I can get some sugar and butter from our mess."

"I thought maybe we'd get Pat Burke from *Up and Doing* and Judy Campbell and Frances Day. They'd come, I'm sure." Betty was a born Elsa Maxwell. "And suppose I get tickets for *Black Vanities* and after the show you can take them all around to Bud Flanagan's dressing room and he'll have drinks and sandwiches. You know he loves the Eagle boys. And we'll have Chris and Harry Watt."

"Must have Harry Watt," Red Tobin said firmly. "I won't come otherwise."

Harry Watt is the man who made the phenomenally suc-
58

cessful picture *Target for Tonight*. Harry and Red were great pals. "The bank phoned to say you'd overdrawn your account," Betty said casually. "And this party will cost at least fifty quid. But the Sunday *Graphic* phoned. They want a story from you for next Sunday. They'll pay fifty pounds. That will pay for the party."

"I'll do it; remind me," I told Betty.

"I'd like to bring a couple of the boys from my squadron," Bill said, in that voice that had the richness of the blue grass in it.

"Bill, do you know it's the first week in May?" I reminded him.

"That's right," he said. "Derby time. The juleps will be flowing at home right now."

"We'll have mint juleps at Bill's birthday party," I told Betty.

"Where am I going to get mint juleps in London?" she demanded.

"Everyone tells me you're the best secretary in town," I told her. "Find someone who can make them and have him here at the Savoy that night. Tell Santarelli to have the right things."

"Got to have Uncle Ed and Dr. Stoneman and Red Mueller," Tobin said. Uncle Ed is Ed Beattie of the United Press.

Carrol Gibbons, the American orchestra leader who had the band at the Savoy, knew Red and Bill. He came up and asked them what they wanted.

"Just hit me with a hot note," Bill drawled, "and watch Betty and me bounce."

Both the kids were great swing fans, although Red loved cowboy dirges too. When they were on leave in London, Betty called a moratorium on work. All three were great movie fans. They lived at movies. Tobin used to bounce into my place and

59

I'd hear him yell from the hall, "Here's Leon the Great Lover." He'd usually bring a carnation for Betty; then he graduated to gardenias and, finally, to orchids. I was a bit worried about Red spending so much money on flowers and told him that Betty would be just as happy with a carnation as with an orchid.

"Expense doesn't matter to Leon the Great Lover," he said airily. "Besides, since Betty told me that you had a charge account at the florist's in the lobby I have been using it. You want us to be happy, don't you?"

Tobin had worked as a messenger boy for MGM in Hollywood. He had learned to fly week ends and had then gone to France to join the French air force. He got there just in time to get away from the Germans. He made his way to England and applied to the RAF. He said that he had lost his log book and all of his credentials. They took his word for it that he'd been flying fighter aircraft for the French Army and promptly gave him a Spitfire to fly. Red, who had never flown anything with more horse power than a Waco, almost dropped dead. But he took it up and didn't kill himself.

Red had become a fine pilot. So had Bill Malkemus who was on bombers. Bill was an idealist. When he went to Canada to enlist he wrote a long letter to his father whom he worshipped saying that he was doing this because he believed in Britain's cause and he hoped that his family would feel the same way and be proud of him. Often he read me extracts from letters his father who now lived in Tennessee had written him. Evidently his father and sister were proud of him.

I was out of London that next week and now and then I thought of the great time bright-eyed Betty was having arranging her party. Every party I ever had in London became Betty's party in the end. I arrived in London the day before Bill's birthday. I sent my things upstairs and went in to see Santarelli, the maître d'hôtel of the Savoy.

"How's Miss Betty's party going for tomorrow night?" I asked him. She was Miss Betty to everyone in the Savoy.

Santarelli said, "It's been postponed."

"Why?" I asked, but Santarelli evaded my eye and shrugged his shoulders. I walked into the bar. Ed Beattie and Bill Stoneman were there not looking very happy.

"Have you heard about Red Tobin?" Beattie said, and something in his voice made me look up sharply.

"What about him?"

"He got it today," Ed said. "A daylight sweep over France. Squadron 71 went over and seventy-five M.E.'s dropped on them. They got Red. The last they saw of Red he was going down pretty fast with smoke coming from his engine. It looks bad."

The boy in the bar said there was a phone call for me. Almost automatically I answered it. It was Bob Montgomery, the film actor, now a naval attaché in London.

"Have you heard about Red?" he said. I told him I had and hung up. Then I went upstairs. There was a light in my office. Betty was sitting at her desk.

"The birthday party is off," she said, and her face was white and miserable.

"I know. I heard about Red."

"Bill didn't come back last night, either," she said dully. "He went over Berlin again. His plane is missing. Bill and Red both."

I sat down and never hated the war so much as at that moment; never hated the Germans more; never hated complacent isolationist fools who even then were making speeches and building political fences. None of this hatred was logical, but when people you know and like are killed in a war, you can't think—you feel. I sat there at my desk and Betty brought me something she had typed.

"What's this?" I said indifferently.

"That's the story you wrote for the Sunday *Graphic*," she said in a small voice. "I typed it up. Shall I send it along?"

I looked at the story. I couldn't read it very well. This was the story that was going to pay for Bill's birthday party. I tore it up and dropped it on the floor.

6

He Never Worked
in Brooklyn

"For long centuries Germany and Russia lived side by
side in peace. Why not in future too? Each attempt to
make it impossible will be frustrated because the motives
of such attempts will be clearly understood by all."
Adolf Hitler, New Year's Day, 1940

ON JUNE 22, 1941, Hitler attacked Russia, and by that one
act completely justified Stalin's 1939 demand on Finland
(with compensation) for the removal of Finland's frontier
from its eighteen-mile proximity to Leningrad. We (Britain
and America) severely criticized Stalin for his action, and
we waved flags for "brave little Finland" but, had Russian
arms not removed that frontier in 1940, Germany would
dominate Leningrad and Moscow (and thus Russia) today.
Stalin, the great realist, had been right once more. The admiration we must feel for the fine fight Finland put up must
be tempered by the realization that Stalin at that time was
not fighting Finland—he was preparing to fight Germany;
he was preparing to fight for Russia's life.

When we heard the news of Germany's march into Russia
in London, our first reaction was to get there as quickly as
possible. I went running to Ivan Maisky, Soviet Ambassador

to Great Britain, and applied for a Russian visa. It would take time, Maisky assured me, but he would do his best; he could only forward my request to Moscow with a recommendation that it be granted. Days went by; weeks went by. The news of Germany's rapid advance into south Russia overshadowed anything happening in Britain. I went to see Maisky every eight or nine days. He was doing all he could, but such things were handled directly from Moscow. Could Oumansky help? Maisky thought a word from the Soviet Ambassador in Washington might facilitate matters. I cabled my office in New York to appeal to Oumansky.

September came and I was no nearer to Moscow than I had been on June 22nd, the day Germany walked into Russia. I had tried every legitimate and illegitimate means I knew to get a Russian visa. My office had prevailed upon Ambassador Oumansky in Washington, and he had been cabling Moscow. There was nothing against *Collier's Weekly* or against me. They just didn't want any more foreign reporters in Moscow. I had cabled Harry Hopkins and Averell Harriman and they, too, used their influence with Oumansky. Brendan Bracken had talked to Ambassador Maisky in London, and poor Maisky was horribly embarrassed because he could not do anything.

Bright Arthur Christiansen, editor of the *Daily Express,* caught what he thought to be a good idea. It might be, he decided, that they didn't want American reporters or representatives of American newspapers and magazines in Russia. After all, American periodicals had been pretty unkind to Russia during the twenty-three years of her communistic experiment. Perhaps, if I represented an English newspaper . . .

"Sure, you louse," I told Chris coldly, "you get me the visa and I have to work for you in Russia. That's fine. Nuts to you, sweetheart."

"Now, chum," Chris' voice dripped honey. "You know I wouldn't interfere with your work for *Collier's*. But if we told Maisky that we were sending you to Russia for the *Express* perhaps Moscow would take a better view of your application for a visa. After all," Chris' voice was so sympathetic, "you must remember that you are still a neutral. . . ."

"I've never been a neutral," I stormed.

"Well, your country is neutral. Maybe the Russians don't like neutrals. Maybe they're just allergic to neutrals. If I made an application, you might get the visa. I wouldn't want much. Just a small news story every day and one or two feature stories each week. My God, Quent, you could do those in your sleep."

"I only work for *Collier's*," I said stubbornly.

"All right," Chris sighed. "Seems to me you're throwing *Collier's* down. They want you to get to Russia. They don't care how you get there. All ordinary methods have failed. *Collier's* would be tickled to death if I could fix it up for you to go. Any stories you did for me wouldn't interfere with your *Collier's* articles. I'd put a world copyright on your pieces so they couldn't be reprinted in America. Of course, maybe you're right at that. After all, you haven't done daily stuff for years and Moscow is a pretty fast league. Philip Jordan of the *News Chronicle* is there and Chollerton of the *Telegraph* and Alexander Werth and Maurice Lovell of Reuters and, if you did news stories for us, you'd be in competition with them and after being away from the newspaper game so long, I don't blame you for not wanting to compete . . ."

"Don't give me that baloney, Chris." I saw through that one. "If I can't get my visa any other way and you get it for me, I'll work for you, all right."

"Well, now," Chris said, very happy, "and how much would you want?"

65

"All the traffic will bear," I snapped. "I want your highest rates, but we'll talk about that when I come back. First get me that visa."

Chris then applied to Maisky. Poor Maisky was so unhappy. About this time a Russian picture called *A Day in the Life of Soviet Russia* came to London. It ran an hour and a half. It was too long and too slow but there was some magnificent stuff in it. It was frankly a Russian propaganda film but a good one. They asked me to do the English commentary for it. Would I? I would have joined the Communist Party, learned to speak Russian and sold my two brothers into slavery to get that visa, and by doing the film I thought I'd put the Russian Embassy under such obligations that Moscow would have to let me in. I did the commentary for the picture and we cut it down to fifty-five minutes. It made a good picture. At least it showed that all Russians weren't born with two heads, as a few puka Britishers apologizing for their new ally seemed to believe. Thank God, they were few in number.

We had a grand opening for the picture with Maisky and his whole Embassy present. I made a speech and did everything but sing the "Internationale." I wound up by talking of Maisky as though he were a combination of John the Baptist, Clark Gable and Albert Einstein. When I finished, the spotlight flashed to where Maisky was sitting and the place went wild. London was very, very grateful to Russia last September. Maisky wasn't Minsky any more.

The next day I waited patiently for a phone call from the Russian Embassy, but nothing happened. Another week went by and then came the announcement that Averell Harriman and Lord Beaverbrook were to head a joint Anglo-American mission which was to go to Moscow within a few days. Harriman arrived in London. One morning the long-awaited phone call did come. It was Maisky, and he was very happy.

66

"At last," he said, "your application for a visa has been granted. Come over to the Embassy any time with your passport and we'll stamp it. I'm sorry it took so long to arrange, but I finally managed to persuade my colleagues in Moscow to give it to you."

A few moments later Chris called. "Well," he said heartily, "I fixed it for you, pal. Let me be the first to tell you. I finally got you your Russian visa."

"Maisky just told me about it," I said suspiciously. "What do you mean you fixed it?"

"Of course I fixed it. You're going as a representative of the *Daily Express*. Really, Quent," there was a hurt note in his voice, "we did make a deal, didn't we? Naturally Maisky phoned to tell you he had received word from Moscow. As Ambassador it is his job to inform you of these things. But I knew it last night."

"Well, all right," I said, ungraciously. "Now, how the hell do you get to Moscow?"

"You take a No. 22 bus from Marble Arch," he advised. "After all, I got your visa. Do I have to arrange transportation for you?"

"Well, I'm going for you, Chris," I reminded him. "After all, if you don't want me to go, don't bother. But . . ."

"All right, all right." Chris hung up and went to work. Getting to Moscow from London is not quite like going from Philadelphia to New York. Chris found out that there were no airplanes going; the cold weather had set in up north and planes couldn't risk flying over Norway even at night. However, Brendan Bracken had assured Chris that there would be a boat within two weeks and I could take that. It was a three-week trip to Archangel and then at least a three-day train ride to Moscow. It was hardly an inviting prospect but, after all, I did have my visa and I was on my way to Moscow.

67

The next morning Harriman phoned me and asked if I could drop into his office. He was very busy and secretaries flounced in and out making vague gestures with papers he had to sign.

"I hear you're all set for Moscow," Averell said. I told him I was, but that I couldn't get off for two weeks and that it would be a month after that before I'd reach Moscow.

"How would you like to leave tomorrow—fly?" Harriman asked casually.

I looked at him suspiciously, but he wasn't joking.

"Beaverbrook and I are going by ship tomorrow," he said. "A cruiser or a destroyer. We're going to be very busy over there. We'll be having committee meetings all day long, and at night I think we'll be having conferences with Stalin. Now, this is going to be an important conference. The public has a right to know what goes on at these meetings; that is, in so far as no secrets are given away to the Germans. I mean the conference is going to be real news for a week or so, yet Max and I will be too busy to see the reporters very often. This is where you come in. I've talked it over with Max and he agrees. You could come along with us, attend some of the meetings, trail along with the Beaver and me and get news out of us on the run. Then you can pass it on to the newspapermen each night. In short, if you wish, you can be a full-fledged member of our mission; but mind you, Quent, you can't write anything about what takes place while you're a member of the mission. That wouldn't be fair to the rest of the correspondents."

"Now that I'm a diplomat . . ."

"All right, you'll go. Here's your ticket. You leave Euston Station at 9:30 tomorrow night for a place in Scotland. You fly to Moscow and bring plenty of warm clothes because that

68

plane trip will be cold. I'll see you in Moscow in a few days. Have things lined up there for us when we arrive. Okay?"

"Okay," I said. "Have a nice trip."

"I bet Marie is going out of her mind today," Harriman said thoughtfully. Marie is Mrs. Averell Harriman. "I got a cable from her saying that the Dodgers won the pennant. You know what a Dodger fan she is."

"I know." I did know. "If only we can beat those Yankees. Do you suppose we can?"

"Well, Wyatt ought to win the first game for the Dodgers and . . . Look, we're leaving tomorrow. I haven't packed yet. Neither have you. I've got a million things to do. . . ."

"I'll see you in Moscow," I said, and ran like a mad thing to the Russian Embassy. It is a big, dreary building in Kensington Gardens that looks as though the brothers Karamazov had designed it, and all the unhappy, suicidally inclined heroines of Russian literature had lived in it and left their sad history in the gloomy rooms. Maisky was in and he would see me. It was the first time in weeks I had seen him smile and Maisky was born to smile. He is one of the nicest little men I have ever met: small, with twinkling eyes, a caricature of a black goatee, and very small hands and feet. When I went in Maisky wasn't alone. A chunky dark man who showed white even teeth was with him—Ambassador Constantine Oumansky. I looked at him in surprise.

"I thought you were in Washington?" I said, when Maisky introduced us.

"I'm not," he said, in his slow deliberate but perfect English. I can't imagine Oumansky doing anything on the spur of the moment, impulsively. "In fact, I am traveling with you tomorrow. Have you your passport? Good, good. Mr. Maisky will have it stamped for you. It took a long while to get your visa. I suppose you were impatient."

69

"I was impatient," I admitted.

"Ah, well, I finally managed to arrange it," he said carelessly. That gave me a start. First, Maisky said that he had obtained it. Then Christiansen said that he had arranged it. Now it was Oumansky. I supposed if I went into the gents' room at the Savoy Hotel, the attendant there would have told me that he'd fixed everything for me.

Parenthetically, I found out months later in Russia that actually it had been Harriman whose influence and insistence had persuaded the Moscow Foreign Office to give me my visa. Typical of Harriman is the fact that to this day he hasn't mentioned to me that he had any hand in it. And, of course, Chris won. I sent stories to the *Express* all the time I was in Russia. You can't beat editors—there's no use trying.

"Shall we have a little drink to celebrate our departure? Maisky has something very special." Oumansky rubbed his hands and smiled at little Maisky. Maisky pressed a bell and a uniformed lackey came in with a tray. I wondered what exotic Russian drink the "something special" was, but it turned out to be Haig and Haig Scotch whisky. Maisky poured us drinks. Ever since I met Maisky I had been haunted with the thought that I had met him before. I have one of those annoying memories that retains the most useless bits of information for years and years. It had troubled me because I couldn't place Maisky. I was sure that I had known him before but I didn't know where. Now, sitting there in his office, it came to me.

"Did you have a job in Brooklyn in 1911, Mr. Ambassador?" I asked him.

He shook his head. "I've never been to Brooklyn."

In 1911 I had two swell jobs. I sold the *Saturday Evening Post* and had a weekly route of thirty, which meant a clear profit of sixty cents. We also got premium coupons which

70

eventually might result in a pair of skates or even a bicycle. In addition to that I had a job lighting the candles and electric lights in a synagogue on Jefferson Avenue, Brooklyn, every Friday afternoon. I got fifteen cents for that job, so it can readily be seen that I was one of the wealthiest nine-year-old men-about-town in Brooklyn. For fifteen cents, I would have not only lit the candles and electric lights, I would have set fire to the whole building.

The sexton of the synagogue was so orthodox that he wouldn't even light a candle or turn on an electric light on Friday, so he always hired one of the Irish boys from the neighborhood. He was a nice little man and he always paid me in cash and promptly. Put a skull cap on Maisky and he'd be a dead ringer for my 1911 sexton of the synagogue on Jefferson Avenue in Brooklyn.

"You're sure," I persisted, "you never had a job in Brooklyn? Back in 1911. Now think back."

"But, my dear Reynolds," Maisky's eyes were full of sympathy. He would like to oblige, but after all. . . .

"All right," I admitted defeat a bit ungraciously. What good is a trick memory like mine if it goes wrong on you?

Oumansky and Maisky and I talked, and it was mighty pleasant being knee-deep in Ambassadors and good Scotch. We discussed the press censorship in Moscow, about which I had heard dire things, and Oumansky waved a casual arm and said confidently, "Things will be better. Please remember that neither Britain nor your country trusted us very much during the past twenty-three years. It is perhaps a little hard for my colleagues in Moscow to trust correspondents 100 per cent now. You will recall that many correspondents went to Russia during the past few years, stayed only a few weeks and then went out to make violent attacks upon my country and our form of government."

71

Oumansky had me there. The boys who spent a few short weeks in the country and then went out to write "The Truth About Russia" are numerous enough to start the nucleus of a new political party. Russia does something to good reporters. They go there looking for facts and come away believing that they have a mission. The mission is either to convert the world to Communism or to destroy Communism. In either case they cease to be reporters.

"What's the news from Russia today?" I asked Maisky, to get away from the subject of my erring colleagues.

"The Germans continue their advance," Maisky said, without change of expression.

"Well, your fellows have done all right so far," I said weakly. "They've done better than anyone here expected them to do."

Maisky nodded. "I know that no one here expected much of us. It is strange to me, too. Several years ago, they sent me a film from Moscow about our parachute troops. I had a party here at the Embassy for the Diplomatic Corps and I asked several British generals and several War Office men to see the picture. I thought they might be interested. It was the first time that parachute troops had been heard of or had been filmed. But they all looked at the motion picture and they laughed. All except one man. He didn't laugh. He asked me if he could see it again. He was General Sir John Dill who is now, you know, I am sure, Chief of the British Imperial General Staff."

"Yes," Oumansky smiled, "everyone thought that we slept while Germany armed, while Germany built her huge mechanized forces. Stalin did not sleep. Believe me. We are having reverses now, that is true, but wait."

"How do you feel?" I asked Maisky. "Optimistic?"

Maisky put his small soft hands in front of him on the

desk, then placed them together. "Not optimistic," he said thoughtfully, "but confident."

It was dark now and I remembered I had a cab waiting for me for the past hour. That would be a good ten shillings, but still I had had three drinks of beautiful Scotch and I had met Oumansky, who might be, in fact certainly would be, useful in Moscow. They walked to the door with me and the doorman handed me the visaed passport I had forgotten about.

"I'll see you on the train tomorrow night." Oumansky smiled, showing those even white teeth again.

I shook hands with them both. "You're sure?" I pleaded with Maisky.

"No," he said gently, "I never worked in Brooklyn."

7

I Don't Like to Travel

AIRPLANES ARE COMFORTABLE ENOUGH and they are safe. My only objection to airplane travel is its slowness. Airplanes never seem to start on time; they always have head winds to keep them back and they always arrive late. I never remember a pilot saying at the end of a trip, "We had a tail wind helping us all the way." I don't think such a thing as a tail wind exists.

We had to wait two days in Scotland for the right weather. We stayed at an RAF mess which was only a few miles from the birthplace of Bobbie Burns. Mr. Burns would be horrified to know that you can't buy a bottle of whisky in the village of his nativity. In fact you can't buy a bottle of Scotch whisky in Scotland, but then I understand you could never buy a Spanish omelet in Spain. In Scotland, you can buy a drink at a pub or a hotel, but whisky is so scarce that no one will sell you a bottle. Before Lend-Lease, whisky was pretty much Britain's only important export to America. Britain needed dollars desperately in America, so most of Scotland's whisky supply had to travel across the ocean to provide dollars for airplanes and guns.

We were to travel on a nice new Consolidated Liberator (B-24), one of the world's best airplanes. It is an enormous four-motored affair, and ours was stripped to go into action as a bomber. A Liberator was never made to be a passenger plane. There were eight of us, and we sat in the bomb bay on benches arranged parallel to the fuselage. The crew handed out fur-lined flying suits and boots to us, but they must have been designed for the seven dwarfs. Happily, I had my own flying suit with me, a fine RAF issue outfit given to bomber pilots. A bomber pilot pal of mine got into a little difficulty over his mess bill and I helped him out. He was very grateful, and two weeks later he showed up in London with this rather valuable token of his gratitude. The inner part was fur-lined and over it went a heavy blue overall of wool. It was a fine flying suit; it fitted me perfectly. I knew those suits were worth about two hundred dollars, and I began to wonder where my pilot pal had obtained it. I tried to find out, but he was very evasive. Finally, he broke down.

"There was a chap in our squadron about your size," he said sheepishly, "and he had two flying suits. What the hell does any pilot want with two outfits anyhow? So I kept watch for a week or so and one night I managed to grab it out of his locker. So there you are."

I was horrified. "Take it back," I told him. "I can't be wearing stolen clothes. You'll get into trouble over this and it'll be one jam I can't get you out of."

"No, it's all right," he said carelessly. "The chap was killed two nights after I grabbed his suit. He'll never need it now."

"I'm not going to wear a dead pilot's clothes," I said firmly.

"Why not?" He was surprised. "Why not?"

I thought awhile and I said, "You're right. Why not?"

So I kept the flying suit and it has come in mighty handy on more than one occasion. In fact, I've often been annoyed with my bomber pal for not having stolen a pair of boots too. Those RAF flying boots are beautifully warm. Anyhow, I wore the suit on the flight from Scotland to Moscow.

We roared down the long concrete runway at five o'clock. It was dusk and the sun was just beginning to drop below the horizon. Loaded down with 3,600 gallons of gasoline we weighed 56,000 pounds, yet the enormous aircraft was airborne twelve seconds after we had started down the runway. Sitting in the bomb bay we were completely blacked out There was a compartment in the rear where we could go, one at a time, to smoke. Because of our big load of gasoline, we would be a bit tailheavy if more than one of us occupied the compartment. So we just sat in the semi-darkness until they switched on tiny electric lights. We were to travel about 3,000 miles and I had brought three detective novels with me; one for each thousand miles. I couldn't bring any more. We were only allowed forty pounds. It seems to me that I've been living for years under the rule "Forty pounds and a typewriter." I always carry my typewriter and class it as "hand baggage"; and so far I've gotten away with it, though my portable itself weighs twelve pounds.

We were one hour out when we had our first taste of excitement. Montgomery, the co-pilot, rushed back from the pilots' compartment, stumbled over our feet in the confined belly of the airplane, and cried to Greene, the mechanic, who stayed in the rear compartment, "Get to the guns." We sat there wondering what it was all about—none too comfortable.

"The three pursuit ships below us," Monty called over his shoulder, as he stumbled back to his compartment. That puzzled me for a moment, then, of course, I remembered that in the United States Army, airplanes are often called "ships" and that "pursuit" meant "fighter." In the RAF a Spitfire or a Hurricane is merely a "fighter" and, if you called either of them a "pursuit ship," the kids wouldn't know what you were talking about. Sometimes they call their airplanes "kites" or "machines" but nearly always, even in casual conversation, they refer to them as aircraft. Anyhow, "three pursuit ships" could do dire things to our big Liberator, poorly armed as we were; poorly armed only because we weren't supposed to be fitted for combat.

I had seen our "guns." We had one miserable little rear gun that might have stopped a bird in flight but not much else. There were two huge American flags painted under and atop the fuselage of our Liberator. The day before, one of the British ground crew was lying on his back under the airplane painting the flag. It was a long, tedious job.

"I wish to hell you didn't have so many states over there," he grumbled. "I've been painting these stars for seven hours."

However, American flags, no matter how plainly painted, wouldn't do us any good if German planes found us. To begin with, being naturally suspicious people, they wouldn't have believed the flags. Then too, we were in the No Man's Land of the air where anyone who was a German could be safe in assuming that an airplane which wasn't German was British. Suddenly our big Liberator swung from side to side, but it was only our pilot tipping his wings in salute.

"They were three Spitfires," Montgomery told us, shouting from the pilots' compartment. "Came up like bats out of hell and then saw what we were."

I went back to reading Peter Cheney's *It Couldn't Matter Less,* a very tough detective story. Then our lights went out and we were told that we'd have no more light until morning. That was just lovely. I walked back to the "smoking compartment." Greene, the combination mechanic-gunner, gave me an American cigarette, the first I'd smoked in some months and I choked on it. Once you are accustomed to Players, American cigarettes seem awfully strong. But then, when I arrive in England after a spell at home and have to switch from Chesterfields to Players, I find that I choke on them too. Apparently the cigarette that doesn't make you cough is the cigarette you are accustomed to smoking. By kneeling on a sort of table hinged to the side of the fuselage, I could see out of the one small window that had not been covered. Night had come, but it wasn't dark. The coastline had disappeared and we were over very cold water.

"Nice weather," I ventured to Greene.

"Too nice," he grunted. "The Old Man said it was too nice before we left. Them Germans might intercept us on a night like this."

The "Old Man" was Major Al Harvey, our pilot. I had learned something else about United States Army bomber crews. Evidently they use nautical language, calling their aircraft a "ship" and calling the pilot the "Old Man." Perched above us, at the front end of the "smoking compartment," was the wireless operator. He shrugged his shoulders when I asked him if he was getting any news.

"Get some music," I asked him. "Try a German station. They always have musical programs at night to keep their pilots awake."

Finally, he got a Nazi station and I listened to some German folk songs, but even the lilt of them couldn't disguise the fact that it had become bitter cold. I went back into our bomb bay and tried to sleep. I slept for two hours and awoke to find that I was numb from tip to toe. There was no heat in the Liberator at all and we were up about 16,000 feet off the Norwegian coast.

I went back to have a smoke and found Greene asleep. It was 2 A.M. now and quite light outside. I stamped my feet and banged my gloved hands together, but the cold had too firm a grip on them. I went into the tail of the airplane for want of something better to do. I thought I'd try our gun. There was an ingenious arrangement to keep you steady while you handled the gun. There was a heavy strap and you rested your buttocks against it and put your feet into stirrups. This gave you a firm stance no matter how the airplane rolled. I grabbed the gun, swung it around and knocked off two M.E. 109's. I imagined I saw two more leaping out of a cloud. Then I gave the cloud itself a burst and aimed at the North Star. I guess it was the North Star. Anyhow, it was a very bright star. Then (I was playing soldiers) I saw a big Junkers 88 waddling along, and what I did to that crate! It just went down in flames and I saw it hit the water with a mighty splash. Before I was through I had finished off half a dozen other Nazi planes, six clouds, eight stars and I had shot a good-sized bit out of the moon. Of course, had a Jerry airplane actually appeared, I would have given one despairing yell for Greene and then fallen in a dead faint. I find I am allergic to enemy airplanes.

We must have been very high because the walk to the smoking compartment (about fifteen feet) seemed very long. The thin air made you feel dopey. A cigarette tasted funny. We were high enough for oxygen, but it was so bitterly cold that nothing else mattered much.

"I've never been colder," I told the half-awake Greene.

"It's thirty below," he muttered.

"What's it doing so cold?" I asked him.

"Why the hell shouldn't it be cold?" he grumbled. "We're only about 600 miles from the North Pole."

The hours crept on numbly. Once a buzzer sounded. It was an insistent buzz. I was sitting across from Colonel Philip Faymonville.

"What's that, Colonel?" I asked him.

"That's the alert," he said.

"What are we supposed to do, go to a shelter?"

He looked at me reproachfully. Colonel Faymonville was

afterward to gain fame (in the correspondents' eyes) by being the only man in Moscow during its siege who insisted that the Germans would never take the city. But meanwhile there was this alert. Montgomery came back after awhile to tell us about it.

"An aircraft zoomed right by us awhile back," he explained. "We couldn't see what it was, so the Major banked us into a cloud and we've been hopping from one cloud to another. Anyhow, we've shaken it."

I went back again, suddenly remembering that we'd put some thermos bottles of tea in the aircraft before leaving. Greene dug them out. The tea was still steaming. At the moment I thought that the thermos bottle was a far greater invention than was the 56,000 pounds of steel that was carrying us at 300 miles an hour. There were several boxes of sandwiches too. I opened one. It was roast beef, something you don't see very often in London. I bit into it and almost broke a tooth. The meat was frozen stiff. There were also lettuce sandwiches, but they were merely thin green wafers of ice. It was morning now and the sunshine was brilliant. There were clouds below us billowing softly and then we came out of them and there was land. It was dreary-looking land, dotted with lakes and rivers and sparsely forested. We had no idea what land it was. We only knew that we were headed for Moscow.

"Do you know where we are, Greene?" I asked.

"Don't know, don't care," the laconic Greene yawned. "The skipper knows and that's good enough for me."

Our crew all had a terrific respect for Major Al Harvey. Before our flight was over we passengers made eight additional hero-worshippers.

"Yeah, you got nothin' to worry about," Greene went on. "You're ridin' in the best airplane in the world with the best damn pilot in the world aflyin' you. You got hot tea, and it ain't costin' you a dime. What more do you want?"

"A cigarette," I said, still too cold to feel anything but sorrow for myself. The big airplane went steadily on, hardly vibrating. I'd never been in an easier-riding aircraft than that lovely Liberator.

"Ever been to Florida?" Greene asked.

"I'd like to be there now," I said. "I'd like a job driving a bus or something there. This is a hell of a way to earn a living."

"There's an airplane," Greene said, looking out of the window. Sure enough—there were two of them. On their sides was the Red Star and they looked mighty comforting. The planes were fighters, looking a great deal like our P-40 (Tomahawk). Then we circled twice over something which on closer inspection proved to be a landing field. We were over Archangel. Harvey came down quite close but didn't like the look of the wet field. He had intended to land, but Mr. Harvey was taking no chances on having his lovely airplane mired in Archangel mud. We lit out straight for Moscow, flying low. An airplane flying very low is almost invisible to enemy planes above. The camouflage of the upper wings and fuselage seems to blend into the countryside. Then, flying low, no over-zealous Russian anti-aircraft gunner could take a pot shot at us.

Gradually the bleak countryside changed and we passed over thousands of farms, neat and tidy and clean under the brilliant morning sun. The country looked lush and fruitful— something like Iowa or Kansas. There were huge patches of cultivated land with rivers and streams feeding it. And then we were over Moscow. The streets in the center of Moscow are wide and, from the air, the city looked not unlike Cleveland. Harvey made a beautiful landing, setting the big aircraft down as though she were a Piper Cub. We climbed out, stiff-legged, trying to shake the chill out of our limbs.

I said to Harvey, "It wasn't a bad trip."

Harvey looked at me pityingly. "It wasn't a good trip. We flew 3,200 miles, most of it over water. That's the longest non-stop flight ever made over water by a United States Army airplane. I think it's the longest flight carrying passengers any airplane ever made. We iced up badly twice up there. We didn't get one radio signal from the time we left Scotland, and we couldn't break our radio silence. A nice trip you call it. Me, I didn't like it. No, sir, I've been flying twenty years and that was the nastiest one I ever made."

We climbed into cars and headed for the National Hotel in Moscow. It felt awfully good to be on land again. Fifteen hours is long enough to stay in any man's air. The hotel was reasonably warm. My colleagues were there. Alice-Leon Moats of *Collier's Weekly;* Philip Jordan of the *News Chronicle* (London); Arch Steele of the *Chicago Daily News;* Henry Cassidy of the AP; Henry Shapiro of the UP; Cy Sulzberger of the *New York Times;* Maurice Lovell of Reuters and the others. There was caviar and vodka.

"The vodka is lousy," Jordan said. "There's no good vodka left. It's all at the front. The good vodka was all imported from Riga and Poland and Esthonia."

I winced at that. I never knew that Russia imported her vodka. "I suppose you'll tell me now," I said to Jordan, "that the caviar in Russia all comes from the Fulton Fish Market."

"The caviar is nice, plenty of it, too," Jordan said, and then added, "at New York prices."

"What are the censors like here?" I asked casually. That started it. They all talked at once, giving their grievances. I felt that things couldn't be as bad as they made out. I was to find out that they were worse.

I looked out of my hotel window across the square to the Kremlin. That was pretty exciting. Moscow was a strange city to me. A correspondent's job is to make friends with strange cities. It is exciting and it is fun to walk into a strange city, knowing that within a week you'll know plenty of government officials, embassy people, censors, fellow correspondents, and then the city will no longer be strange. Looking out across the Kremlin, I decided that mine wasn't such a bad way to earn a living after all. Except for the traveling . . .

8

Dinner with Stalin

No MISSION EVER worked as fast or as thoroughly as did the Harriman-Beaverbrook group during its seven days in Moscow. Harriman and Beaverbrook proceeded on this theory: "Germany is an enemy of Britain and of America. Germany as a conquering power must be destroyed for the sake of the future security of both Britain and America. Circumstances have made Russia the immediate instrument of destruction. To do a good job, Russia must have the proper tools. It being to our mutual advantage that the Russian Army and Air Force be as well equipped as possible, the only logical thing for Britain and America to do is to see that Russia has the tools needed if we can possibly provide them, without weakening our national defenses."

The work of the mission resolved itself into Harriman and Beaverbrook asking, "What do you actually need?" The Russian representatives stated their needs and then Beaverbrook and Harriman consulted the military and naval experts and economic advisers they had brought with them to find out if Britain and America could, in safety, spare this material. In no case did the Russians make demands which any members of the mission thought to be unreasonable. In many cases, notably in the case of certain raw materials, the Russians surprised the Anglo-American members with the modesty of their requests. The various committees met early in the morning and kept at it all day. Late each afternoon they reported to Beaverbrook and Harriman, and the two mission heads examined the work done. Then, nearly every night, Beaverbrook and Harriman went to the Kremlin to confer with Stalin. They were terrifically impressed with the technical knowledge shown by the Soviet leader. He knew American tanks and airplanes as well as Harriman did; he knew British aircraft production and the capabilities of British guns and aircraft as well as Beaverbrook did.

"He checked me up on something tonight," Beaverbrook chuckled, when he and Harriman came back from one of their long sessions at the Kremlin. "I was talking about the Hurricane motor. I was telling Stalin how good it was. 'Ah, it's a fine motor, Mr. Stalin,' I said. 'It has 1,350 horse power.' Stalin smiled and said, 'Oh, no, it has 1,250 horse power.' "

Beaverbrook, always relishing a joke, even one on himself, laughed at the recollection of how he, a former Minister of Aircraft Production, had made such a slip.

"That would make a nice little bit of news for the boys," I told him. "Let me give it to them. News is scarce enough."

"Sure, sure," he said. "Give it to them."

I did, but the censors wouldn't pass it. When I heard that, I ran to the Foreign Office to register a protest. If I gave out news from Beaverbrook and Harriman, it came officially from them, I said. I was their personal representative. Beaverbrook had okayed the little item.

"It would be discourteous to allow that item to go," Solomon Lozovsky, who was in charge of the censors, said to me gravely. "It would be discourteous to Lord Beaverbrook."

"Beaverbrook told me the story," I said, exasperated. "He suggested I pass it on to the correspondents. It is a great tribute to Stalin that he can correct Beaverbrook on anything

85

to do with British airplanes. It is a good joke on Beaverbrook and he himself is laughing at it."

"Oh, no, we can't pass it," Lozovsky smiled. "The story would serve no purpose."

The story never passed. Only stories which served a purpose could pass the censor. My criticism of Soviet censorship is in no sense a criticism of Communism or of Russia. I've criticized censorship in lots of countries, including England, where it is comparatively innocuous. Any correspondent hates all censorship, but the Soviet brand was particularly obnoxious. It was just as bad as German censorship, except that so far as I know we were never given false information.

There was an air raid on Moscow every night during the conference, but to those of us who had been as it were brought up on London raids, the Russian variety lacked spontaneity, variety and frightfulness. But the Moscow authorities took them very seriously, and their air-raid precautionary measures were, I think, more thorough and intelligent than those of London. As soon as the sirens sounded, all citizens had to get off the streets. There were no exceptions. Hotels and restaurants stopped serving food and shooed their customers into shelters. One night Beaverbrook and Harriman came back to the hotel and were about to order dinner when the sirens began to sing. The hotel authorities polite, suave, but firm, suggested that they go to the subway shelter across the square; dinner would be served to them there.

This was perhaps the best and most comfortable shelter in the world. To begin with, the escalators took us down 150 feet below street level. There was a large room just off the subway platform. It was a magnificent room, perhaps ninety feet long and thirty feet wide, and it had tables, chairs, divans and eight very small rooms opening off it for sleeping purposes. There were attendants present all night, and we had a fine dinner quite undisturbed by even the echo of the anti-aircraft barrage. This room was reserved especially for members of the mission. It was brilliantly lighted. There was a piano in the room and soon the inevitable trio of musicians appeared. Beaverbrook and Harriman, after little sleep for a week, were in no mood to listen to the solemn dirge of Russian chamber music. Of course the NKVD boys were with us—eight of them; four for Beaverbrook and four for Harriman. These are the secret police and they had been assigned to protect the heads of the mission. The correspondents always called them the "Y.M.C.A." boys. I went to them and told them that both Beaverbrook and Harriman had very early appointments at the Kremlin the next morning and that they were anxious to get to bed. Very reluctantly they agreed to allow us to leave. They were not being officious; they had been told to protect Harriman and Beaverbrook and they'd do that if they had to keep them both up all night. So we went home. They didn't realize, of course, that the raid in progress that night was one which neither Beaverbrook nor Harriman would have noticed in London.

The Anglo-American missions met together on the last day of the conference at the British Embassy. In this instance I am going to disregard Harriman's orders about writing anything that happened at the closed meetings because it is the only way I can show the spirit which actuated the whole Moscow conference. Like all of the meetings, this, too, was informal. Harriman asked for the written reports from the heads of each of his committees. Brilliant Bill Batt in charge of raw materials handed his across the table. So did General Cheney and Admiral Standley. The others followed. Beaverbrook called for his final reports.

"We're scheduled to leave tomorrow," Harriman said. "This afternoon you'll hold your last meetings with the Soviet representatives. When we leave we don't want any loose ends left over. We want to have everything absolutely completed. To do this, you may have to work all night. Well, work all night. Don't forget, these Russians trust us—we must trust them. They have been reasonable in their requests. Remember that everything we give them is going to be used to destroy the German Army. Don't quibble over small differences in your meetings. The issues at stake are too big for that. But, above all, don't let these people down." Harriman pounded on the table. "We've given them our words, Beaverbrook and I have, that everything we have promised them will be delivered. Let me repeat, don't let them down."

This wasn't the smiling, quiet Harriman who is so well-liked in New York and Washington and London. This, for the moment, was a very tough executive intent upon doing his job well, and insisting that all of his associates do their jobs well.

"Got anything to add to that, Max?" Harriman turned to Beaverbrook.

"No, Averell." Beaverbrook didn't even stand up. "Except let's get on with the work."

On that note the conference came to an end. It is too early to judge the effect of the Moscow conference. I do know that within a week Beaverbrook and Harriman removed much of the suspicion which Soviet Russia quite rightly felt about Britain and America. For twenty years, Russia had seen its form of government ridiculed and vilified in the British and American press. She had seen Communism, which in Russia amounts to a religion, dragged in the mud by every member of Parliament who couldn't find an honest issue to debate, and by publicity-seeking band-wagon hoppers in our own Congress who sought to find favor with voters by talking of a Red Menace which existed only in their own distorted imaginations. Russia had no reason to like or trust either Britain or America. In one week, Beaverbrook and Harriman swept away much of this feeling. They loved the Beaver's showmanship, his loud laughter, his jokes and his absolute disregard of protocol and red tape. They admired Harriman's sincerity, his obvious knowledge of the problems involved and his eagerness to work all night every night if need be to help solve those problems. "Garriman" became a very popular figure among members of the official Soviet family. There is no "h" in the Russian language and for some reason it is always pronounced as a hard "g." Harriman was Garriman and Hitler was Gitler.

As a final wind-up to the affairs of the conference, Stalin asked both missions to dinner at the Kremlin. The Moscow correspondents were amazed. It was the first formal state dinner Stalin had held in many years. Most of us, of course, were tremendously excited.

"Remember," Harriman warned me, "you're not to write anything about tonight."

"I won't," I said regretfully. As far as I knew, no reporter had been inside the Kremlin for many, many years. Two publishers, Roy Howard and Ralph Ingersoll, had made it, but no reporters. And I was to have dinner with Stalin and not be allowed to write about it. At least, until long afterward. It was a very annoying spot for a reporter to be in but, of course, as I had to admit to myself, if I'd been in Moscow merely as a reporter I wouldn't be going along that night.

The Kremlin is an amazing combination of buildings. There are churches, barracks, office buildings and palaces within the high brick wall that surrounds it. There are only three entrances. We left from the National Hotel in cars provided by our respective Embassies. Where they got them I don't know, because cars for hire in Moscow were few and far between. A

"Y.M.C.A." boy sat in front of each car beside the chauffeur. Nearly always the "Y.M.C.A." boys in Moscow wear black caps and black leather coats. They couldn't look more sinister. Most of them were young and when they smiled they just looked like pleasant, healthy young men. But they didn't smile very often.

We swept through the big Gothic archways (all archways are Gothic to me) and found ourselves inside the wall. We were on the river side and I was surprised to find green grass and trees growing within the wall. The whole atmosphere was that of a college campus on an autumn night.

The former palace of the Czars is, of course, the main building inside the Kremlin wall. It is a huge building, ugly now with its camouflage; rather futile camouflage in view of the fact that the Moscow River flows right by it and on a night with any moon at all, the river would point out the way to the Kremlin as unerringly as the Thames points the way to central London. You can't black-out a river, although the Russians have done a rather ingenious job in hiding that part of the river which is near the Kremlin. How successful it is, Nazi pilots would be able to tell better than I and, as to the method employed, it seems hardly the duty of a correspondent to divulge such information to the Nazi air force.

The building was brilliantly light inside. A large staircase of white marble led to the rooms above. There were 137 steps to climb, if my arithmetic was correct. Then we turned left, went through a door and came out into an enormous room, perhaps 150 feet long. At each doorway there were two officers on guard and significant was the fact that they were regular army captains. Guarding the Kremlin, apparently, was not the work for ordinary soldiers. We walked the length of this room feeling dwarfed by the immensity of its high ceilings and huge crystal chandeliers. Then we entered the Chamber of Deputies with its 1,000 seats. Empty of course, it looked larger than it was. We turned left and walked through what had once been the throne room; now it was the state banquet room. The walls were relieved by red tapestry framed with gilt and three large crystal chandeliers hung from the ceiling. It was a beautiful room, now set for a hundred people. We walked through it into the next room where we were to await Stalin.

Waiters passed around trays of vodka and thin sweet pastry sticks. There was a seating list and when we found where we were to be, we took stock. By now I knew many of the government figures. Oumansky, who was there acting as interpreter for Beaverbrook, introduced me to the others. Vyacheslav Molotov was there. He is a small man with a Groucho Marx mustache. As Commissar for Foreign Affairs, the equivalent of our Secretary of State, Molotov is perhaps the second most important man in the régime, if a one-man régime can be said to have a Number Two man. Molotov is not very well liked by the diplomatic and journalistic corps in Moscow. They think him cold, ruthless, and no doubt he is. The correspondents, to a man, mistrust him. They think that he engineered the Russian-German pact. They all think that he was too friendly with Von Ribbentrop when the latter visited Moscow. Molotov always looks as though he is watching someone else sucking a lemon. It may be because he is near-sighted and wears very thick spectacles. When he smiles, the set crust of his face seems to crack reluctantly, and you feel that it costs him a physical effort. Molotov is not the kind of man you'd want to sit up with late at night over a bottle.

Smiling Maxim Litvinov was there, a little to our surprise. For some years Litvinov had been in the doghouse. He always hated fascism, so he couldn't even pretend a half-hearted acquiescence when the Russian-German economic pact was signed in August, 1939. Because he was always better known and more highly regarded in Britain and America than perhaps any other Russian, we thought that he had been dusted off and presented just for the duration of the conference. We were afterward to find out that we had been quite wrong. That evening he was assigned to be Harriman's interpreter.

Marshal Voroshilov was there. Voroshilov is rather small and dapper, but he looks every inch the general. But then anyone wearing that magnificent Red Army uniform, greenish-gray with red and green tabs on the collar, and with the large decorations (which correspondents call "sardine tins" in Moscow) on his chest and with the red sash showing his marshal's rank, would have looked impressive. The Russian officers wear uniforms which are much better-looking than any uniforms I have ever seen, with the possible exception of those worn by the regal doormen who stand outside of New York motion-picture houses. Voroshilov is a likeable person, good-looking, with a neatly trimmed mustache and with very small feet. Voroshilov never had the military training which either Budenny or Timoshenko had, but he seems to have become Stalin's favorite. A marshal in Russia wears nice uniforms and people cheer him when he reviews troops and the press of the world acclaims him as a military genius when his army wins an important victory, but there is no doubt that there is only one military genius in Russia—Joseph Stalin. Uncle Joe shifts his generals and his armies around as a chess player shifts his pawns and bishops, and his generals talk back just about as much as do the wooden chessmen. Brilliant Andrei Andreiev, sometimes whispered as the Crown Prince of the régime, was there chatting with scholarly-looking, soft-spoken Lavrenti Beria, who looks like a physician but whose innocent-sounding title, Commissar for Internal Affairs, means that he is head of what was once called the Cheka, later the OGPU and now the NKVD. Plump, benign, rosy-cheeked Vyshinsky, animated, easy to smile, stood chatting with Harriman in French, and it was hard to believe that this was the man who prosecuted and sent either to death or imprisonment at least 100,000 Russian citizens in the 1938 purge, unless you noticed that when he smiled his eyes didn't smile. There was a hint of early frost in those pale blue eyes.

We were all horrified by that purge. We forgot the very meaning of the term. The dictionary defines "purge" as "to make physically and spiritually clean." That purge eliminated Russia's Fifth Column. I found no British or American correspondent in Russia who thought that the famous confessions made by Radek, Tukhatchevsky, Bukharin, Rykov, Krestinsky, Pletnov, Rosengoltz and the others had been extorted by torture. Under Soviet law these and the other thousands who had been affiliated with them had been guilty of treason and deserved the death penalty. Had only the Low Countries and Poland and Norway and the other slave states eliminated their own traitors how much happier their fate would have been.

Perhaps some day we will dig up the Congressional Record and see there the voluntary evidence given by our own Fifth Columnists and find a prosecutor as ruthless and relentless as Vyshinsky. But we are pretty soft. If a man in our country rapes a woman he gets life; if he rapes our country he gets a lecture or radio contract. I sometimes wonder if we deserve the wonderful country we've got.

Lozovsky, the Kremlin spokesman, his neatly trimmed black beard streaked with gray, chatted with everyone in Russian, French, German, Spanish or any other language you happened to know. Everyone was there except that little, forgotten man who is President of the Union of Soviet Socialist Republics. Whatever is his name? Oh, yes—Mikhail Kalinin.

Then through the next room we saw Stalin approaching.

93

The hum of talk died down. In his pictures, Stalin looks huge, forbidding, surly. This little man, rather bow-legged, who was walking toward us, was smiling affably, and when he saw Harriman and the Beaver, his face broke into animated welcome. He shook hands with the two mission heads, and those of us who were seeing him for the first time were stricken dumb. His appearance was a contradiction of everything we had ever been led to believe about Stalin. A British correspondent once wrote of Stalin, "He looks like the kindly Italian gardener you have in twice a week." You couldn't find a better description of the Soviet leader than that.

It was not the forbidding, frowning figure of a million posters who circled the room being introduced to everyone by Oumansky. He shook hands warmly and murmured a Russian phrase. He wore the gray semi-military tunic in which he is always pictured, but the simple suit fitted so beautifully that Beaverbrook was right when he said afterward, "Stalin is the best-dressed man in Russia." His left arm is slightly withered and he carries it close to his body, which almost hides the defect. After he had greeted everyone, we went in to dinner. I sat between a Russian admiral and a Soviet Foreign Office man. Happily, Eddie Page of our State Department, a Russian-speaking member of our mission, sat two seats away to help me out. And Lozovsky, with whom I knew I would be fighting in a few days, sat opposite. I turned all of my charm on Lozovsky, but charming a censor is like charming a snake. The best you can get is an even break.

We had a twenty-three-course dinner. A plate was set in front of you and waiters wearing white ties served egg and onion for caviar. The caviar was in huge bowls on the table. There was both natural caviar and pressed caviar. For anyone whose taste was that plebeian, there was red caviar. I am not one of those who can take his caviar or leave it alone. I just keep on taking it. I know when I've had enough, but I don't care. After I had had two huge portions, Eddie Page, alarmed, called, "Lay off the aviarcay. This meal goes on for hours. And you can't refuse anything."

There were several carafes of vodka on the table and as soon as one emptied itself, a waiter refilled it. Every time my glass was half-emptied, the Soviet admiral to my right in great consternation at the lack of hospitality shown me, would fill it, hold up his glass, murmur the conventional "Vashe Zdorovie" and I'd have to drink with him. He talked German happily, so as long as he didn't get too complicated, we got along fine.

Meanwhile one course succeeded another on the same plate. You were supposed to finish what was put on your plate and then, before you could lean back and relax, the waiter was there with another course. And the food was so fantastically good that you couldn't say "No" to it. The three high spots were perhaps the mushrooms fried in sour cream, the sturgeon in champagne and the pilaf of quail. The complete menu, translated as best my Russian secretary could do, was:

COLD HORS-D'OEUVRES

Fresh caviar. Pressed caviar

Smoked sturgeon. Salmon

Kertch herrings

Cold ham. Sausage assorti

Cold pork with horse-radish

Tomato salad. Tomatoes

Game with mayonnaise

Fresh cucumbers

Caucasian cucumbers

Cheese of various kinds. Butter

95

HOT HORS-D'OEUVRES

Tartelettes de volaille
Mushrooms fried with sour cream
Sturgeon in champagne

DINNER

Chicken Crème
Pies
Borstchok (Cabbage soup with beets)
White fish bouilli, sauce muslin
Turkey. Romaine salad
Chicken. Hazel hen-grouse
Pilaf with quails
Cauliflower and asparagus

Parfait of nuts. Petits-fours
Coffee
Liqueur and wines
Fruits
Almonds

Wine kept coming and going; red wine, white wine, champagne and always vodka. White vodka, yellow vodka, red vodka with peppers in it. And inevitably there were toasts. The toasts are the great feature of formal Russian dinners. Stalin started it around the cold pork and horse-radish with a toast to Beaverbrook and one to Harriman, and by the time we reached the *borstchok* there had been twenty of them. Anyone in the room could give a toast any time he felt like it by getting to his feet and tapping his plate for silence. Getting to one's feet became increasingly difficult as the evening wore on. The toasts were all greeted with loud applause; everyone gave one. I expected that any moment one of the waiters would either give a toast or say a few words about the climate of

96

Southern California. There were thirty-six toasts in all, but there were no speeches. Stalin drank every toast. However, he drank a light red Georgian wine. No one could call Stalin a tippler.

Finally we reached the coffee stage, and a welcome stage it was. Then Stalin rose and there was something in his manner which made us all very quiet. All evening he had been chatting volubly with Beaverbrook and Harriman who sat on either side of him and he had been laughing at Beaverbrook's quips, and when Stalin laughs he laughs with his eyes too. Stalin looks like the kind of man you would like to know better. But at that moment he looked very serious. He tapped his glass with a knife and then raised his glass. He spoke for perhaps fifteen seconds and then Oumansky picked it up.

"Comrade Stalin says," Oumansky began, "that he would like to propose a toast to the President of the United States. Comrade Stalin says President Roosevelt has the very difficult task of leading a country which is non-belligerent and yet which wants to do all it can to help the two great democracies of Europe in their fight against fascism. Comrade Stalin says may God help him in his most difficult task."

There was a stunned silence from us and then great applause from everyone. Harriman leaned over and gripped Stalin's hand, thanking him. Stalin wasn't smiling now. He had meant that toast. It was an amazing moment. Stalin the anti-Christ; Stalin who had divorced the Church entirely from the State; Stalin who had acted on the communistic doctrine, "Religion is the opium of the people"—he was publicly, before the world, humbly asking Divine help for Roosevelt. And yet the Russians in the room were not surprised. I spoke to Lozovsky, Litvinov and Oumansky about it afterward and they in fact were puzzled at our surprise. The longer I stayed in Russia, the more I realized the terrific misconceptions we in America and Britain hold in regard to the Soviet Union. The trouble is that for years we have received our information about Russia from salesmen—not reporters. The writing salesmen were either trying to sell Communism to us or to make us hate it. The truth which lay somewhere in between, never was able to grope its way out of either camp.

I remembered that Stalin's wife had been buried in consecrated ground—in a monastery. A little Jesuit priest, Father Braun, said Mass every day in his Moscow church. There was no anti-religion in Russia that I ever saw. In the Czarist days the priests had a wonderful racket in Russia. They were paid by the State and collections taken up in churches went to the State. All Stalin did was to separate the church from the State. The church should be an independent organization divorced from the State. In short, he did the same thing we did in our country back in 1776. People go to church in Russia; I've seen them. But they don't, through the church, pay tribute to the government. Their priests are no longer government officials who have almost the power of life and death over them. Their priests can be elected to Parliament (under the constitution there is no ban on their running for office) but they can neither buy nor graft their way nor be appointed to Parliament. Had any of us ever troubled to read the Soviet Constitution (as vigorously upheld as our own) we might have got the true picture of religion in the Soviet Union. I looked it up the day after the Kremlin dinner. I talked with Father Braun. I mentally apologized as a Catholic for the things I've thought about Russia's attitude toward religion.

I began to wonder while I was in Moscow about the many Senate investigations into Soviet propaganda we have had in Washington these past few years and the thought struck me that perhaps the time and money expended upon those investigations might perhaps have been better spent in the investigation of anti-Soviet propaganda in our country.

Stalin's final electric toast meant that the dinner was over. But we were not yet through. Soviet state officials haven't much use for the morning hours. Stalin, for instance, never makes an appointment before six in the evening. But then he'll work all night. It was midnight when we finished dinner, but midnight to Russians is the hour when they become fully awake. Stalin led the way to another room. We were to see some motion pictures. The Kremlin theatre is a lovely room, beautifully panelled with indirect lighting and large enough to seat about two hundred. Beaverbrook looked around it enviously as we entered. His private motion-picture theatre at Cherkley, his estate at Leatherhead, is nice enough, but this dwarfed it. There was a table in front of each comfortable seat and, even before we were seated, waiters were putting plates of pastry and glasses of champagne on the tables. First we saw a badly done documentary picture called *War of the Future*. It had been made in 1938 and showed a war between Germany and Russia. Prophetically enough, it showed Germany invading the Soviet Union. Unfortunately, the miniature shots of bombed villages were so crude and so obvious that the whole effect of the picture was lost. Then we saw a full-length (and a Soviet picture is really full-length) picture called *Volga, Volga* which was all about a boy meeting a girl. The music in it was beautiful and the picture itself might have been enjoyable, but that huge dinner had so sapped our strength that we could only look up feebly at the screen and wish that we were home in bed. It didn't end until 3 A.M. Stalin pressed everyone to have "just one more" and then we all shook hands with him and said, "Good night."

"What'll he do now?" I asked Oumansky.

"Oh, he has several appointments tonight," Oumansky

said. "He'll go right to the office. Did you like that documentary picture?"

"Frankly, I thought it was lousy, didn't you?"

"Yes," he admitted, "I've been wanting to ask you something. Would you do a picture for us while you are here? Something along the lines of *London Can Take It*? You would work with Eisenstein. You would have our best film unit. We would appreciate it."

"There is one thing I want above all others," I said, ignoring what Oumansky had said. "I want to interview Stalin. I want half an hour with him—that's all. And as for the picture, let's talk about it later."

Oumansky nodded thoughtfully. I like to do business with a man like Oumansky. Oumansky, like all Russians, is an uncompromising realist. He knew what I meant. Hell, I'd make a dozen pictures for him if I could have half an hour with Stalin.

"You will hear from me," Oumansky smiled.

We filed out of the Kremlin. There was a hint of frost in the air and the moon was high and the chauffeur said that there was an air raid on. The news from the front had been bad that day but somehow after seeing Stalin you didn't worry so much. Despite his smallness, despite his bow-legs, despite his withered arm, he gave an impression of enormous strength and made you realize that the Germans had only won the first round in the fight—there were other rounds coming up.

9

Vodka and Caviar

ONCE THE MISSION had left I could really get down to work. There wasn't much else to do in Moscow but work. But there wasn't much work to do. Alice-Leon Moats, who had spent the past six months in Moscow, had done such a fine job that there wasn't a great deal left for me. Meanwhile, we played poker and I spent half my time pulling strings to get that Stalin interview. Henry Cassidy, Llewelyn Thompson of the American Embassy staff, Philip Jordan of the *News Chronicle,* Dennis McAvoy (son of J. P. McAvoy), Cy Sulzberger, Robert Magidoff of the AP, and I played poker at least four nights a week.

They all lived at the Metropole Hotel. I still lived at the National across from the Kremlin. We usually played in my suite. It was a lovely suite with a large balcony overlooking the square. Trotsky had once lived here. It was from this balcony that he had made his last speech in Moscow and had been shouted down by the crowd, angered because of his break with Stalin, inflamed by the fact that he hadn't attended Lenin's funeral, probably the gravest mistake in political history. I had a large double bed and often I'd lie there unable to sleep because of the terrific noise of the barrage, wondering what thoughts filled Trotsky's mind in the days when he too lay there undoubtedly finding sleep difficult.

The food at the National was excellent. We could always get caviar and vodka and eggs and fresh vegetables. Because of the ruinous exchange, living at the National was far more expensive than living at the Savoy Hotel in London or at any New York hotel. Occasionally, one could hire a car from the Intourist garage, but that cost twenty dollars a day. Mostly we walked. Automobiles and gasoline were very scarce in Moscow.

One night we were playing in my room when the phone rang. It was eleven o'clock. Lozovsky was calling. Could I hurry to the Foreign Office immediately to see him? I had no car, I protested. He'd send his. I had a full house and Cassidy was raising, so I went back to the game. Of course he had four eights. As he raked in the pot, we all guessed the reason for the late phone call. I couldn't imagine what he wanted to see me about. Like all government officials, he usually worked until midnight or long after.

"You wouldn't be trying to get an interview with Uncle Joe, would you?" Cassidy suddenly asked, and a chill silence fell.

"I guess there's no chance of that," I said casually. "You've all been here for months and haven't been able to get it."

"You wouldn't use your influence as a member of the Harriman mission to bring some pressure to bear, would you?" Cassidy asked. "You wouldn't be such a rat as that?"

"Would you, if you were in my place?" I said softly.

"You're damn right, I would," Cassidy admitted.

"I'll admit I asked both Beaverbrook and Harriman to put in a word for me, but neither would. They're both too conscientious. They could have done it easily, too. And now they've gone back."

"Good for them," Jordan said. "It would be very unfair if you got that interview. It was bad enough about Ralph

102

Ingersoll getting to see him, although Ralph had to promise that anything Stalin said would be "off the record."

"Unfair, my eye," I told Philip. "What the hell is there fair about our business? Suppose you or Cassidy or Cy got in to see Stalin? I'd be mad as hell, but I'd have to give you credit for pulling it off. Don't tell me you haven't tried."

They all admitted that they had tried and were still trying. All ordinary channels having failed, Jordan only that morning had tried something new. He had merely written a letter to Stalin himself and had dropped it into a mail box. He had small hope that he would get an answer but, like the fine, thorough reporter he is, he'd try anything. The car came and I went off to see Lozovsky. The story of any Soviet government official is an interesting one because each one had earned his job the hard way. Let's take time out to consider the case of Lozovsky.

There are 190 million people in Russia and they speak at least sixty languages and dialects. Today they all speak through a single voice; it belongs to the dapper bearded man who once sold matches and lemons on the streets of a small village far from Moscow. Then, a ragged eight-year-old urchin, he was Solomon Abramovich Dridzo. Today, a polished, suave sixty-three, he is Vice-Commissar for Foreign Affairs, the spokesman for the Soviet Information Bureau and the Kremlin, and is known as Solomon Abramovich Lozovsky. Many years ago, he picked his new name from the city of Lozovaya.

The name Lozovsky was hardly known outside of labor circles until the Germans marched into Russia. Then, as spokesman for the Kremlin, as the only official with whom correspondents had any dealings, he catapulted into fame. Today, next to Stalin, Molotov, Voroshilov and Timoshenko, he is probably the best-known Russian in the world. He occupies much the same position in Moscow as Doctor Paul Josef Goebbels occupies in Berlin. There is one difference between them. Goebbels deals in lies. Lozovsky tells the truth. He doesn't tell nearly as much of the truth as correspondents would wish, but none of us ever caught the Vice-Commissar in a lie. He is far too clever and too evasive in answering questions which policy dictates should be left unanswered to resort to the clumsy fabrication of lies. But, unfortunately, correspondents are not interested in the truth. We are interested in news.

Twice a week Lozovsky held press conferences. We attended religiously, asked dozens of questions, and then left with the uncomfortable feeling that once more the man who sat at the head of the table had completely outwitted us and told us only what he had made up his mind to tell us before the press conference opened. He did it with such charm and humor that it was difficult to become annoyed. In addition to being the spokesman for the Soviet, he was also in charge of censorship. The censor in any country is the natural enemy of reporters. Had he been in any other job, we might have liked the pleasant, affable, well-dressed man with the twinkling eyes. But, after all, he was the head censor.

At twelve, Lozovsky graduated from the matches-and-lemons trade to become a butcher's boy. Later, as a youth he became a blacksmith's helper. No trace of this hard adolescent life can be seen in the slender hands, the well-groomed nails of Lozovsky, nor is there a trace of peasant accent in his cultured speech. In addition to Russian, he speaks perfect French and German; he speaks English reluctantly but much better than he realizes, and his Spanish is good. Obviously, the young blacksmith's helper saw far beyond his forge and learned languages other than that sung by the clash of hammer against anvil. When he was twenty-one, Lozovsky was sent to Kazan for military service. It was in the barracks that he learned the elements of that form of Social Democracy which Lenin later stamped with his own personality and transformed into a high revolutionary doctrine under which nearly 200,000,000 people live today. It wasn't long before Lozovsky, with revolutionary zeal burning brightly in his young heart, joined the Social Democratic Party, the party whose members were known as Bolsheviks.

He moved to Lozovaya where he gave lessons on the new social philosophy to workers. It was here that he found his metier. Unions were being formed surreptitiously in Lozovaya by workers. Our young zealot plunged into this enterprise with joy; it was a chance to transform his theories and his beliefs into practice. But in 1903, the Czarist police were a bit intolerant of those who had the impudence to demand decent conditions and reasonable hours for workers. For the first time, but far from the last, Lozovsky was tossed into durance vile. During the next decade, he was in and out of jail with commendable regularity. By now, Dridzo existed only in police records. He was Lozovsky to the workers of Russia. Once, after a jail-break, he was recaptured and exiled to Irkutsk, but even the wastes of that desolate region could not confine our slippery comrade. He bobbed up in France where he combined revolutionary journalism with union activities.

It was in Paris that he met Lenin and, like nearly everyone else who met the then young, vigorous revolutionist, Lozovsky fell completely under his spell. Lenin had the gift of making men worship him. He backed up all of his eloquence in expounding the Marxist doctrine with an intense practicability and a knack of putting those theories to work. Lozovsky and Lenin were friends until the death of the great revolutionary leader. Lozovsky endured his Paris exile until 1917 when he returned to Russia. Since then, he has given a quarter of a century's devoted service to his country. Lozovsky was no "yes man." When he was not backward about saying what he thought of the Party line during the October Revolution, and when he insisted that the Party was not doing right by the labor unions, he was unceremoniously tossed out of the Communist Party. This should have written "finis" to his political career. But it did not. A few years later, he bobbed up as secretary of the powerful Railway Workers' Union. He was readmitted to the Party, and since then his relations with the Party have been the happiest, even though Lozovsky still does not hesitate to speak his mind. Before the war, his pet scheme was the Profintern, an International Trade Union. But he turned in his dreams of a world-wide labor union in exchange for a heavy red dispatch case out of which at press conferences he sometimes pulls secret German documents with the studied casualness of a conjurer pulling a rabbit out of a hat.

Press conferences with Lozovsky lacked the spontaneous humor and gayety of a White House conference. There was little of the usually good-natured, sometimes acrimonious, discussions of a Brendan Bracken press conference in London. Bracken usually terminates his conferences with a sigh of relief and a cheerful "Thank God, that's over. Now let's all have a drink."

Usually there were twelve of us seated around a long table at Lozovsky's press conferences. There were three Russian reporters, five Americans, three British and one South American. It was a large, pleasant room with pictures of Lenin and Stalin looking down upon us. A door at the end of the room would open and Lozovsky, accompanied by a secretary and by Pulgonov, his chief deputy, would enter smilingly. He would wave an arm and smile a greeting. The press conference was open. We could ask any questions we wished. Lozovsky nearly always stuck to Russian and some of our more linguistically-talented colleagues translated for us.

106

A typical exchange of questions and answers would be these:

Philip Jordan, *News Chronicle* of London, speaking in French: "Mr. Vice-Commissar, yesterday I handed in my daily story at noon. It did not clear the censor until seven hours later. As it takes several hours sometimes for our stories to reach London, I think it not unreasonable to ask you either to add more censors or to ask the present ones to hurry with their jobs."

Lozovsky, looking sympathetic and taking off his rimless glasses, answers in Russian: "That's unfortunate. We will try to do something about it."

Jordan, turning to Robert Magidoff of the AP who knows Russian: "What the hell did he say?" Magidoff tells him.

Henry Shapiro (United Press): "The Russian papers say today that city B near Leningrad has been recaptured by the Red Army. Will you identify city B?"

Lozovsky: "Please, speak Russian."

Shapiro repeats in Russian.

Lozovsky, gently reproving, as one talks to a child: "Mr. Shapiro, if the papers wanted you to know what town it was, they would have named it."

Cy Sulzberger (*New York Times*), speaking Serbian: "The BBC reports that some Japanese fighting boats were blown up by Russian mines. What about that?"

Lozovsky: "What do the Japanese papers say about it?"

Sulzberger: "I don't know."

Lozovsky: "I don't know either."

Jean Champenois, of the Free French News Agency: "When are you going to arrange a trip to the front for us?"

Lozovsky: "In good time, I hope."

Jordan, under his breath to Reynolds: "If he sticks around here long enough, the front will come to him."

Arch Steele (*Chicago Daily News*): "The German radio says that the Nazi troops are pouring through the southern front almost to Moscow. Any truth in that?"

Lozovsky, smiling: "Mr. Steele, you know the German radio? Can you ever believe it? As for Goebbels, remember that if loud braying counted for anything, the ass would be king of the animal world."

And so it went. Lozovsky never refused to answer a question point-blank, but he very cleverly followed the paradoxical admonition of Talleyrand, who said, "Words were invented to conceal thought." When none of us had more questions we wished unanswered, Lozovsky would arise with a cheery good-bye, and the conference would be over. Out of that, plus the two brief daily communiqués, correspondents have to write news stories.

The paucity of news coming out of Russia these difficult days is in no way due to any lack of zeal on the part of correspondents here. Men like Cy Sulzberger, Wally Carroll, Henry Shapiro, Arch Steele, Philip Jordan, Henry Cassidy, Robert Magidoff and Dennis McAvoy are as good and as industrious as any group of reporters in the world. The lack of news is caused entirely by the Soviet attitude toward news. The fact that Soviet censorship is stricter than that of any censorship in the world is well known. The reason for its harshness is not so well known. The Soviet belief is that because there is a censorship, it follows that everything which goes out of Russia is in effect official news having the stamp of approval of the Kremlin. Therefore, individual opinions or speculations are completely out of order. They would not be thought to be opinions of the correspondent under whose name the story appears, but would be official opinion.

Sometimes his love for Russia and his confidence in the ability of the Red Army would shake Lozovsky out of his calm. The day before we were forced to evacuate Moscow, he held his last press conference in the capital. We knew that things were not going well. There was hard fighting in the region of Mozhaisk sixty miles west of the city. If the Germans broke through there they would have a clear path to the city. We asked Lozovsky several questions as to this possibility and the possibility of the government evacuating.

"The government will not move!" He banged the table forcefully. "The Germans will never take Moscow. Understand that. They will never take Moscow." He was a Russian speaking of his soul. He was a Muscovite, talking of his city.

This then was the man I was on my way to see. The Narkomindel housed the Foreign Office under whose jurisdiction the censors operated. It is a large building just opposite the gloomy-looking Lubianka, scene of a thousand stories of fiction and fact, technically, the Central Prison of Moscow. It didn't look like a prison. It looked like a huge office building. It was here that the confessions were extracted from those who were tried in the purge of 1938. I spoke to Poles who had spent considerable time there. They liked it better than most prisons.

"Has a fine library," one of them told me. "Full of Soviet literature, of course, but none the less excellent. And they leave you alone in the Lubianka. My God, how they leave you alone! That is the worst that can happen to you, just to be left alone, week after week, month after month."

Pulgonov was with Lozovsky when I went in. Pulgonov was our *bête noir*. He was so short-sighted that when he read our stories, he had to hold them within a few inches of his eyes. Then he didn't know a hundred English words. We often remonstrated with Lozovsky and Oumansky about the personnel of the censors. Couldn't they get men who understood English? After all, we all wrote in English. This is a criticism of censorship in general and Russian censorship in particular. One could not, for example, inquire too closely, in English or Russian, about the so-called enemies of the State. Stalin has his own way of defining them. Once more let me emphasize that this is no criticism of Communism. In Russia, anyone who criticizes the government is an enemy of the State. Harsh as Stalin's methods are, he has a complete answer, a complete justification for the ruthless quelling of opposition. Today, there is not one Fifth Columnist, not one Quisling at liberty in Soviet Russia. The Germans tried desperately to set up local tribunals with local citizens as nominal heads of the tribunals, when they captured cities like Odessa, Kiev and the others which fell to them during their successful march through the South, last autumn. But in no case were they successful. Potential Quislings were all in the work camps of the far North. Stalin knew what he was doing back in 1938. Russia's magnificent unity today and her completely unbroken spirit after the dreadful tragedy of that German advance, is proof of the fact that Russia accepted the purge and approved of Stalin's "You can't make an omelet without breaking eggs," policy.

Lozovsky got to the point quickly. "I have been talking to Oumansky," he said. "We would like you to make a film for us. A film about how Moscow is fighting back today. We have such a film made and you can see it and use what you want, throw away the rest and send camera men anywhere you wish to get new material. We have all seen *London Can Take It,* and we are anxious to show the world how Moscow has been taking it and how Moscow, too, is unafraid. I have spoken with Sergei Eisenstein and he is anxious to work with you."

It was difficult not to blurt out, "My God, yes. Anyone would be glad of the privilege of working with Eisenstein."

"I'd love to do it," I told Lozovsky, "but I'm so busy. As you know, I'm desperately anxious to interview Stalin. Both

Beaverbrook and Harriman think it would be a great idea to get a good human interest story about him across to Britain and America." (This was of course a downright lie; neither Beaverbrook nor Harriman cared whether or not I got a story from Stalin.) "So, Mr. Vice-Commissar, I am spending all my time trying to arrange an interview with Stalin. Of course, if I could get it, I would have plenty of time then to work on the picture."

Lozovsky smiled politely, and I thought he was going to say, "Touché." He knew what I meant, all right. The Russians are very fine traders. They have the bargaining instinct to a very great degree. My colleagues had taught me that.

"We would be glad to pay you well for making the picture," Lozovsky ventured.

"I don't make pictures for money," I told him. "I wouldn't take anything for *London Can Take It*. I'd be glad to be able to present Moscow as she is today if only to show my admiration for your wonderful people. It is merely that I am so busy. But if I could see Stalin . . ."

"Well, we'll see what we can do," Lozovsky said. "I can't promise. However, I will do my best. And so, Eisenstein will phone you tomorrow. Will you talk it over with him?"

"As long as you have promised to do what you can to get me that interview," I said, "I'll stop all work that I'm doing and spend all my time with Eisenstein. I'll be glad to make the picture. Suppose we call it *Moscow Fights Back*?"

"Fine, fine." Lozovsky was very pleased and so was I. I'd always wanted to meet Eisenstein. I'd seen lots of his pictures and I'd heard his pupils talk about him with awe. He did very little directing, but he headed the Academy in Moscow where directors were made. Herbert Marshall, not the actor but the British director, had told me that he had gone through Eisenstein's three-year course. Eisenstein began by telling his pupils that they couldn't make pictures unless they were familiar with the literature of Shakespeare, Dostoyevsky and other great writers; unless they were familiar with Beethoven, Tchaikowsky, and Rimsky-Korsokoff. When a director emerged with his degree from Eisenstein's Academy, he was as much at home in a concert hall as he was in a cutting-room, and he knew the philosophy of Marx as well as he knew his way around a dolly or a make-up box.

The next day Eisenstein phoned and I went to see him at his Moscow studio. Eisenstein is a man you like at first sight. He is huge, vigorous, full of robust laughter. He had an hour of film taken of Moscow and the Moscow defenses. It seemed pretty flat to me, but my awe of Eisenstein was such that I hated to say it. But he said it for me.

"Maybe you could cut this down to about 1,500 feet," he suggested. "Write a commentary to fit it and then that'll be all. Have you any ideas about adding anything?"

"Yes," I said a bit reluctantly. I wanted to learn from the master; not to have to display my ignorance to him. "There's no music in the picture. Every night recruits go through the square, presumably on the way to the front. They are always singing. Usually they sing "Moskva, Moskva," a good song with plenty of melody. That'll appeal in Britain and America."

"Good, good," Eisenstein beamed. "Now I'm giving you my assistant and she'll work with you. You just tell her what you want. This isn't Hollywood, you know," he laughed. "We have no producers or supervisors to worry about. You just give orders, and she'll see that they're carried out."

"Of course you'll cut the film," I asked.

"No, this is your show," he said. "Cut anything you want; add anything you want. Throw this all away and start fresh if you want."

I tried in vain to explain that I was not a technical picture

112

man. He waved that aside. "That assistant I'm giving you is the best technical worker I've got. She'll do the actual work in the cutting-room; you just tell her what you like and what you don't like."

His assistant came to see me the next morning, a large, smiling, affable woman whose name I never did get. We went over the Russian script which she had translated into English. She agreed that it was too slow; the pace wouldn't do for Britain or America. I was getting excited about the film. In London, we work from a rigid and economical budget. It is difficult to get facilities from the Air Ministry or the Admiralty to take cameras into operational zones. Here in Moscow we were the State; we could do what we wished. I could take a crew into the Kremlin if I wanted to, and I had resolved to do just that. A sequence showing Stalin at work would be something; a few shots showing the Kremlin grounds and the beautiful interiors would present something never shown before. I decided to write my commentary first and then make the film fit it. Harry Watt and I had worked it that way when making *London Can Take It*. How I wished Harry was with me in Moscow! I could only think of the magnificent picture he would make unhampered by budgets or government regulations. I tried hard to remember some of the technique I'd picked up from Harry and Humphrey Jennings when we worked together. You couldn't work with a man like Harry Watt without learning something about the making of documentary films.

"People are more interesting than machines. . . . Landscapes without action are dull. . . . Don't have any static stuff at all in a 1,000-foot film. . . . Underplay rather than overplay a tear-jerker scene. . . . Hint at gruesome details. . . . It's more effective than actually showing bodies and death. . . . Don't mix your commentary and music so that the effectiveness of both is lost. . . . Sometimes let the music carry the whole thing by itself. . . . Don't be afraid to show a sequence without either music or commentary. . . . Have one central theme all the way through. . . . Don't harp on it, but every now and then come back to it as though it were the main melody.

Phrases of Harry's came back to me as I worked over the commentary. The theme would be not *Moscow Can Take It* but *Moscow Fights Back*.

10

Reds in White

COMMANDER IRWIN L. NORMAN, M. C., won me over temporarily from the making of the picture to a new interest in hospitals. He had come to Moscow with us as a member of the Harriman mission and he had remained behind to take care of the health of the American Embassy staff pending the arrival of an army doctor who was en route. Dr. Norman eventually became very fond of me. Before I had left Russia, I picked up about every Soviet ailment that was available, and I became Dr. Norman's most regular customer and private guinea pig. I began with a cute little number called "scabies." Very small bugs dig under your skin and lay eggs. Then the little scabies come out of the eggs, look around, say, "The hell with this," and start to burrow their way toward freedom. They raise great scabs on your body and they itch so that only a very liberal dose of sleeping pills will get you into slumber. It is the most annoying disease I ever had.

"You get this thing," Norman explained, "from sleeping with someone who has it."

"I've been sleeping with a ghost called Trotsky for the past few weeks," I reminded him. "I've got his suite and his bed. Do you think I caught it from him?"

"You misunderstood," Norman said. "Scabies is a common complaint at the front. Apparently some soldier on leave had your room before you arrived and left the bed infected. That's how you caught it."

The best way to cure scabies, he told me, was hot sulphur baths. However, there was no sulphur in Moscow of the type needed. But he did find some sulphur ointment and he lathered me from head to foot with it. I hated living with myself for a few days, but it killed the little brats and, within a week, the enormous scabs I had all over my body disappeared. The lot of a foreign correspondent is not entirely champagne and caviar, dining with ambassadors and knowing diplomats and cabinet ministers by first names. The first thing any foreign correspondent does in Europe (except Britain) is to contract the well-known, so-called "diplomatic fever," or—to give it the medical name under which it goes—dysentery. From there on, you usually pick up whatever assorted diseases the country you are in has to offer.

Norman injected all of us (correspondents included) for typhus, typhoid and tetanus. None of us liked the idea and we tried to duck his injections at first. But when a few of the Embassy staff reported that Norman's touch with the needle was so light that you never felt the prick of it, we hurried to him.

Norman was only thirty-five and he was bright-eyed and eager about anything new. He spent a great deal of time in Moscow hospitals watching operations, his fingers, I am sure, itching to get at a scalpel, although his primary interest was medicine not surgery. Because of his service in our Navy, he had, of necessity, become a specialist in venereal diseases. The realization that gonorrhea is about as common in our Army and Navy as sunburn in Florida, will not, I trust, come as a shock to anyone. Investigating conditions in the Russian armed forces, Norman was startled. Gonorrhea and syphilis

116

were virtually unknown. He made a serious study of the subject, and his conclusions were interesting.

It is like that in Russia. You mutter angrily about the strict censorship; you think darkly of the millions in jail and work camps; you hate the controlled press—and then you hit on one aspect of Communism that is so fine that you begin to get a glimmer of the whole. Then you begin to understand why it is that more than 100,000,000 people neither want nor think they need any religion other than the political philosophy under which they live and of which they are so willingly a part. Their faith in this political system is as natural and as strong and as honest as is the faith of a saint in the Holy Trinity.

"The real cause of venereal disease," Norman explained to me, "is prostitution. Ninety-nine out of a hundred cases of the disease come from contact with prostitutes who have it. Now, it is my belief that prostitution is almost entirely the result of unemployment. Women, except in a very few communities, are not brought up to prostitution as a profession. Get the story of a thousand girls in the ports of Europe, South America and the United States and you'll find that nearly all of them got into the racket because they couldn't earn a living any other way. Here in Russia I've found that there is no unemployment. Every man or woman in Russia who wants to work can find work. As far as I know, there are no stringent laws against prostitution; there are no penalties for it, and yet it is virtually non-existent. The reason is that women are given jobs. Look at our hotel—the National. The manager is a woman. Every floor clerk is a woman. The same is true of the Metropole. Go around to the hospitals. They're full of women, not only nurses, but doctors and scientists. Now, don't get me wrong. I'm not one of these tourists who come to Russia, spend as little time as you and I have spent here, and then start popping off about how wonderful it is or how horrible it is. I don't care about anything but medicine and, believe me, in medicine and surgery these people know their stuff as well as we do. Mind you, I have enough pride in American medicine to think it's the best in the world. But, in lots of ways, these people here are our equals. Read whatever social significance into it that you want, but give a thought to the fact that the Red Army and Air Force are virtually free from venereal disease. You can't say that about any other army in the world. As a doctor, that impresses me."

Well, it impressed me, too. From the viewpoint of thousands of American doctors who specialize in what used to be called the "social diseases" and make a handsome profit out of this practice, this might be an unhappy state of affairs. But from Dr. Norman's viewpoint—and mine—it was a conspicuous achievement as a medical, as well as a social, experiment.

I listened to Dr. Norman, and the more I listened the more I liked him and respected his views. Once, as a kid, I had a job as orderly in the operating room of a hospital, and the fascination of those days has never left me. I'm a sucker for doctors, and any time they're in a talking mood, I'm the perfect audience for them.

I made a list of the hospitals and clinics Norman suggested might be of interest to a layman. My Russian secretary wrote my request (in Russian), and then I brought it to Pulgonov. Pulgonov had to consult with Lozovsky. Lozovsky had to phone the hospital heads and make appointments. It took a week to do what I could have done in London in a half hour by three or four phone calls. But that is how it is in Moscow and, after all, Moscow makes no attempt to make London or Washington change their way of doing things so there seems no authority for us to ask Moscow to conform to the London or Washington methods. It was finally arranged. My Sophiana came with me, of course. In fact I seldom ventured ten steps away from the National Hotel without Sophiana. She had once been Erskine Caldwell's secretary; she had been the secretary to Vernon Bartlett, press attaché to the British Embassy. Years before that, she had been secretary to Spencer Williams, president of the American Chamber of Commerce in Moscow. Because of her work for him, she had been accused of being an American spy and was tossed into the clink. Joseph E. Davies, then American Ambassador to Russia, used his best offices to get the obviously innocent Sophiana out of the clutches of the OGPU. But this intervention merely proved their case against her.

"If the American Ambassador uses his influence to get her off," they cried triumphantly, "she must be an American spy. Otherwise he would not bother. The American millionaire and diplomat Davies would never worry about a mere secretary."

So off to the concentration camp went Sophiana, a happily married Russian woman with two young children. For seven years she worked as a laborer on farms. Then she was released. She emerged from those seven years of agony without one drop of bitterness in her soul. Oh, they had been wrong she admitted, but they had made a natural mistake. She came out of her imprisonment in perfect health, mentally and physically. She came out of it a more fervent Russian patriot than she had been when she went in. She took a risk working for me or working for any foreigner, but she was willing to take it. She had great faith in her country and she was 100 per cent loyal to the Marxist ideal. It has been my good fortune to have good secretaries. Sophiana was one of the best. She was big, strong, perhaps thirty-six, and attractive. Her English was excellent; so was her French and German. I admired the way she fought with the hated Pulgonov. In fact, I loved every-

119

thing about my Sophiana. Lest anyone think I am hinting at a romantic interlude, let me hasten to add that I am sure that anyone who might have had the temerity to make even the conventional pass at her would have been hit very hard in a vulnerable spot by a dull blunt instrument. Sophiana impressed you that way. She was invaluable to me and well worth the forty dollars a week *Collier's* (all unknowing) paid her for her services.

It was Caldwell and his wife, Margaret Bourke-White, impressed by her ability and loyalty, who had set that figure on her services and, like the Hollywood star, who will not lower her price, Sophiana would henceforth never labor for less. Happily, Erskine Caldwell, during his stay in Moscow, had trained her to work odd hours. I work odd hours. My first order to Sophiana was to wake me every morning at ten-thirty with four cups of tea and a pack of either British or American cigarettes. Four cups of tea and about ten cigarettes is my idea of the perfect way to start the day. Russian cigarettes weren't bad, but there was only about an inch of tobacco in them; the rest was a sort of cardboard holder. You took five puffs and the damn thing was finished.

I'll never forget Sophiana's first day on the job. I was awakened, not by the brutal, horrid rays of the morning sun let into the bedroom by the imbecilic hand of one whose idea of a cheery good-morning was to pull aside the blackout curtains and raise the shade, but by the soft electric light coming from the chandelier upon which Trotsky once gazed. Half awake, I heard Sophiana whispering in Russian to a waiter, and finally, when I opened both eyes there on the table at my bedside was a huge pot of tea, a pack of Players and a pack of Chesterfields. I looked in amazement and delight at Sophiana, who stood there sturdy, rocklike, placid, not looking for praise; just a good craftsman who had pride in her job and who knew she had done well.

I looked again at the Players and at the Chesterfields. You couldn't get either British or American cigarettes in Moscow then. Even the British Embassy didn't have British cigarettes, chiefly because Sir Stafford Cripps, the Ambassador, liked Russian cigarettes himself and saw no reason why his staff should ask that Players be sent from London. Only the American Embassy had American cigarettes, and members of the staff were very decent about selling us an occasional carton. But we all knew that supplies from home had about stopped, so we didn't like to try our pals at the Embassy too far. I looked from the cigarettes to Sophiana.

"Why the hell don't you marry me?" I said. "You're the only sensible woman I ever met in my life. And where did you get the cigarettes?"

"I got the Players from Mr. Jordan," she said.

Philip Jordan from the *News Chronicle* lived at the Metropole a couple of blocks away. Jordan, too, had peculiar working hours. He had a secretary who woke him at noon every day, and I had heard him threaten to fire her if she ever woke him earlier. Usually Jordan worked well into the night (and worked well, too).

"You never saw Jordan this morning," I told Sophiana.

"I went to the Metropole and found his door open," she said, as though house-breaking were an every-day affair with her. "I knew he had some Players. I didn't bother waking him. Then I went to Miss Moats' room, in the Metropole. Her door was unlocked too. I went in and found the Chesterfields. I didn't think she'd mind."

I looked at Sophiana as Balboa must have looked at the Pacific Ocean. She was indeed a jewel of rare price.

"You and I are going to get along, sweetheart," I said,

completely immersed in hot tea and cigarettes and happiness.

"Your bath is ready," Sophiana said. Wonderful Sophiana! Marvelous Sophiana! I couldn't wait to get back to London to tell Betty Marais all about the wonderful secretary I had found who was so superior in every way to every secretary who had ever lived. I loved everything about Sophiana, except one thing. She insisted upon calling me "Mr. Reynolds." I can't stand a secretary or an office boy who calls me "mister." The title "mister" should, I feel, be reserved for cabinet ministers alone. Anyone who gets you hot tea, cigarettes, and wakes you gently without the aid of the artificial glare of sunlight; anyone who hears you talking and swearing to yourself while you're working on a story which doesn't jell; anyone who acts as buffer between you and people you don't want to see and who arranges that you talk to and see those you should see; anyone who gives you 100 per cent loyalty and exercises the slight discipline that one needs to get things done that must be done—that person is too close to you to have to stumble over that horribly formal, unnatural barrier of "mister." But I could never convert Sophiana.

Bright and early one morning, Sophiana and I went to the Central Institute of Experimental Medicine. It was a big, gloomy-looking building from the outside. Inside it was cheerful, with the exciting smell of ether. We were expected. Before we went upstairs to the office of the head man, we had to put on white robes and caps. Sophiana had quite a job finding a white sterilized robe that fitted me. She spoke very sharply in Russian to the two attendants, and they laid out all of their stock for me. They found one that fit, smoothed out the wrinkles, and looked at me with great respect.

"What the hell did you tell these two monkeys?" I asked Sophiana.

"I told them you were the head of the Rockefeller Institute, the greatest brain surgeon in America, and that you had come all the way just to see this hospital and to watch Grastchenkov operate."

"You can lie better than I can," I said, looking at placid-faced Sophiana with real admiration.

"Oh, I don't know. I've heard you on the phone," Sophiana said indifferently, and that was the only subtlety I ever heard her perpetrate.

The next hour passed quickly. Doctors showed us around and we spent some time watching Grastchenkov operate. We watched him taking shrapnel and bullets out of the brains of Soviet soldiers. We sat in the theatre of the operating room and consequently couldn't see much because the operational surface is small in such cases. Then I met Grastchenkov. I fell for him completely, as Norman had told me I would, and we went around to see patients to whom he was giving post-operative treatments. Grastchenkov talked perfect English.

"Come in, and let's see how Alexis is getting on." He smiled, and we went into one of the quite cheerful hospital rooms. Alexis Matveev lay on his side. An intern had just taken twenty-five grams of fluid from his spinal column. When the brain has been injured, the spinal column generates an overproduction of fluid and this has to be removed. Alexis was breathing easily and no fear showed in his large gray eyes. Two weeks before, he had been found in the mud outside Bryansk with a large piece of shrapnel in his brain and one chance in a thousand of living. Now he was in the hospital under the care of one of the world's greatest brain surgeons, Dr. Nikolai Ivanovitch Grastchenkov.

The doctor talked soothingly to the young soldier. Then

he removed the dressing from the boy's skull. It is easy to look at a bullet wound because the skin, as though ashamed of its weakness, closes quickly over the hole. It is not easy to look at a shrapnel wound because the shrapnel, being jagged and dull, tears as well as cuts. Alexis had been operated on three days before. The wound was ugly and nearly half the brain lay exposed outside the skull. But the wound wasn't ugly to Grastchenkov. He smiled as he looked at it; he took a probe and touched the brain and, surprisingly, the boy did not even wince. But I did.

"The brain is a wonderful organ," the doctor said, seeing the look on my face. "It is so wonderful that it is not capable of feeling pain. Skin, muscles, bones—these give pain but not the brain."

He put the dressing back with quick, deft fingers, told Alexis that he'd be back fighting in a month or two. Then he left.

Grastchenkov, who studied in Cambridge and later at the Rockefeller Institute in New York, performs miracles every day at the hospital which is part of the Central Institute of Experimental Medicine. The brain and the spinal column are his special provinces. In Russia he is acknowledged master in these fields. He is blond, looks younger than his forty years, and his hands are large and capable. Though his eyes are grave he has a quick smile. He looks like Spencer Tracy.

Only serious cases are brought to him. Day after day he removes shrapnel and bullets from brains or spinal columns. Then he supervises the long convalescence necessary to final recovery.

"Here's the bit I took from the brain of Alexis," he said when we were back in his office. "Pretty big, isn't it? Weighs about seven grams. But he will be all right. The shrapnel lodged in the left lobe of the brain. It affects his speech. It also paralyzes his right side. But once his wound is healed we'll go to work on that. I have a few men here who had exactly the same type of wounds. They're learning to talk and to walk and to write again."

There are no wards in the hospital run by Grastchenkov. He does not think a crowded ward is conducive to mental recovery. The neat, clean rooms held four patients. We went into a room where four were learning again to talk and to read and to walk. They took turns reading aloud, laughing at one another's mistakes, and they laughed, too, when one stumbled as he tried, with the pride of the wounded, to show the doctor that he could walk the length of the room. Here was Captain Kafelev, who had been wounded in the fighting near Mogilev. He sat in a wheel-chair, looking small and schoolmasterish with his neatly trimmed black beard. But within two months he will be almost recovered and able to do light work. Sergeant Peter Zinchenko, who was brought in with a large bit of steel helmet lodged in his brain, talked normally, but his left side was still paralyzed. He was wounded outside of Smolensk.

"Was it bad there?" I asked him.

"It was bad," he nodded gently. "We fought for eight days. I killed many Germans before they got me."

One room after another showed its quota of men who had been brought back to life by the genius of Grastchenkov.

In the last war, mortality from brain wounds was 35 per cent in this hospital. It is now less than 5 per cent. This is chiefly due to the efficiency of sulfanilamide as a deterrent to infection. Grastchenkov says his main problems come from bullets and shrapnel lodged in the spinal column. These are much more serious wounds than brain injuries.

Grastchenkov is only one of many thousands mobilized to fight wounds and diseases in Russia. The whole army of surgery, medicine and research has been thrown into the battle.

In many cases the civilian population has come to the aid of the men and women of science.

Then Sophiana and I went to another clinic. The Soviet Central Institute of Blood Transfusion is presided over by brilliant Andrei Bogdassarov, dark and eager-eyed. The Institute has three additional branches. There are 100 nurses and doctors working at the clinic. Only ten are men, another proof of Norman's thesis. Every day from 1,500 to 2,000 civilians go to these clinics and offer their blood. Blood is a precious commodity in time of war. Nine-tenths of the donors are young girls and women—mothers, wives and sisters of men at the front. Nearly all of them decline pay for their services, but, after each blood donation, the donors are given a good meal and an extra ration coupon. A steady stream of blood from Russian women flows to the front.

"We have three times as many donors as we need," Bogdassarov laughs. "Everyone wants to do his or her part in beating the Germans. Those who come here feel that in giving their blood they are saving the lives of soldiers and, of course, they are right."

Only those above eighteen are taken. Dressed in white gowns, they sit on benches in the long halls of the clinic, waiting their turn. They chat and laugh and, now and then, one proudly displays a letter from the man who was helped to recovery by her blood. Each has the privilege of sending a note with the ampule of her blood which goes to the front. The recipient often writes his thanks, correspondence springs up and Cupid thus finds himself with one more arrow to his bow.

Russia has for a long time been a leader in the conservation of liquid blood for the purpose of transfusion. Thousands of damaged lives have been repaired since the war began by methods either introduced or developed by Bogdassarov.

Blood which he and his small army of assistants gather at the clinic can be kept "alive" for more than thirty days. Only as recently as the Spanish Civil War, blood was considered to be usable only if it had been drawn ten days before.

Bogdassarov keeps the blood alive and preserved by the addition of sodium citrate and glucose. It is packed in air-tight ampules and kept at a constant low temperature. Bogdassarov has done a great deal of experimenting with cadaver blood, but he believes in its use only in emergency. Cadaver blood is efficacious only if used within twenty minutes after it is taken from a dead person. Two years ago, this explorer in the dark red streams of the blood took up the study of plasma, or dried blood. There is a quantity of this at every front-line operating station, but it is only for emergency use. Plasma is usable for eighteen months or so, but Russian doctors are not completely sold on it.

This discussion of blood and its use in reviving those on the borderline of death is hardly pleasant talk, but it is war talk, and it concerns the conduct of the war and is an important item in the saving of lives.

It is interesting to talk to the girls in Bogdassarov's clinic as they lie, white-clad, on the tables giving their blood so that some soldier may live to fight again. There are five tables in each room with a doctor in charge and five nurses assisting. First, the nurses cleanse the arm with disinfectant; then the doctor gently inserts a needle filled with novocain. The donor feels absolutely no pain. She has just had a cup of highly sweetened tea and she has had a fine gossip with her friends in the corridor, and now she lies there unafraid and content. The doctor inserts the needle, which has a long tube attached, and within a few seconds the blood begins to flow into a glass jar. No one donor is allowed to give more than a pint of blood. I have heard them plead with the doctor in charge to be allowed the privilege of giving twice that amount. "Come back in six weeks," the doctor laughs, "and we'll take the rest."

There is another clinic which has no patients. It houses 600 horses, 2,000 guinea pigs and thousands of white mice. This is the Bacteriological Institute, where serums and vaccine are prepared. Scarlet fever, dysentery, diphtheria, typhus, tetanus and gas gangrene are the enemies that the scientists of the Institute battle. Dr. Vladimir Pavlov, young and dynamic, leads these microbe hunters. By law, all children in the Soviet Union have to be immunized against smallpox, scarlet fever and diphtheria. Soldiers must be made immune to typhus, tetanus and typhoid. Pavlov showed me through the immaculate but evil-smelling clinic from attic to cellar, from largest horse to smallest guinea pig. Here some of the greatest research men and women in Russia are making serum and vaccines, experimenting with animals, trying to help the human race in its war against disease.

"Our production has tripled since the war," Pavlov explained. "No matter what the needs at the front, we are ready to supply them. We have a surplus of everything and are continuing to produce serum and vaccines at top speed."

Once more the women outnumbered the men by five to one in this clinic. In one room, a woman was performing the unique operation of injecting a louse with serum. The louse was merely a tiny black spot on the slide of the microscope. But she motioned to me to fix my eye to the microscope and when I had adjusted it, the louse was no longer a harmless black spot. It was a huge, malignant-looking monster seeming to snarl angrily at mankind which he plagued and now unknowingly was helping. Then the woman doctor inserted an incredibly thin needle into the intestines of the louse. The insect, enormous under the microscope, turned darkly purple

128

as the serum penetrated to every part of his anatomy. He twitched ominously and looked, under the microscope, uglier and fiercer than ever, and I had a momentary doubt as to the sanity of St. Francis of Assisi who had called lice—"celestial pearls."

The clinic, about fifteen miles from Moscow, was in an area that had been fairly heavily bombed. Often, Nazi bombers, frustrated in their attempts to pierce the barrage that protected Moscow, would drop their bombs on the outskirts. Bombs had landed within a hundred yards of the Institute. Some of the doors leading to rooms where dangerous, infectious serums of poison were kept, had red and white disks displayed. In case of a direct hit, these rooms were to be locked and the personnel was to stay away from these danger spots. But work went on at the clinic twenty-four hours a day. No one paid attention to the bombs which fell close. These intent, brilliant men and women heard only one voice: the voice of their master—science.

11

City of Courage

THERE WAS VERY LITTLE EXCUSE for gayety in Moscow during October, 1941. The encircling pincers of Von Bock's army crept closer to the capital. One city after another fell, and it looked as though there was little hope for the capital. You can't live in a city for any length of time without either hating it or loving it. I began to have a real affection for Moscow. I didn't love it as I loved London, but after all—there is only one London. But the bravery of the city, in the face of what looked to be certain capture, could not but arouse one's admiration.

Because the official communiqués gave us so little news, we arranged frequent press conferences with the military experts attached to the American and British Embassies. The British correspondents saw General Mason MacFarlene, head of the British Military Mission, every day. Because I represented the *Daily Express* as well as *Collier's Weekly,* I had two strings to my bow. I got any facilities which might be handed out to both groups. MacFarlene is a tall, slightly-stooped but youthful-looking man. He was full of charm, but not so full of information. This wasn't his fault; the Russians didn't tell him much. But he could analyze the situation for us, so we wouldn't go entirely wrong in making any comments or prophecies based on the communiqués. Mason Mac,

130

as we all called him, had a lovely expression. He would usually open his conference by saying apologetically, "I haven't much information. And please remember that anything I say is 'off the rocker.' "

Where he had picked up that expression, I never learned. It was a variation of the "off the record" which we heard so often. Mason Mac wasn't very optimistic. Neither was the American Military Attaché, Colonel Ivan Yeaton, whom we saw quite often. Yeaton and his assistant, Major Michella, were both very good poker players and grand chaps to sit up late with. Yeaton was even more pessimistic than Mason Mac.

"They'll be in Moscow within two weeks," he said, with complete finality. "Hitler swore he'd review his troops in Red Square on November 7th, and believe me he'll do it."

Tired of the pessimistic (but well-founded) views of friend Ivan, I bet him ten dollars that the Germans wouldn't be in Moscow by November 7th. I bet him another ten they wouldn't be in Moscow by Christmas, and he thought I was crazy. He was equally pessimistic about England's chances of withstanding an invasion. Colonel Yeaton, like most American Army officers, had spent his life fighting theoretical battles on blueprints. Even as late as the fall of 1941, American Army officers had, to me, the quaint idea that armies won wars. Britain's experience had taught me that people win wars. The civilian army of England had won the Battle of Britain—the ARP wardens, the fire fighters, the police, the volunteer relief organizations. The RAF had helped, but it was the magnificent civilian resistance which turned the tide.

Any army officer well versed in tactics could easily concoct a plan by which Hitler could successfully invade Britain. Yeaton had one figured out beautifully. It could be done in a single day. I knew nothing about military tactics, but I knew the civilians of Britain. I had seen housewives in Kent making "Molotov cocktails," home-made bombs to throw at enemy tanks in case the invader came; I had seen housewives so arrange things that if the invader came, their homes could immediately be set on fire and all food in them burned; I had seen the Home Guard at maneuvers and had seen the result of their long training at marksmanship. I knew the civilians of Britain as well as I knew the back of my hand. They never could be invaded successfully, and I would have bet my life on it. But army officers never think of civilians as combatants. Even the Spanish war, in which a civilian army, ragged, poorly-equipped, held out for years against the might of the murderer Franco and his Italian and German allies, taught the military experts of the world nothing. The War Office in London certainly failed to profit by that lesson, and no American observer I met in London or Moscow or Teheran or Cairo even considered the Spanish war worth discussing.

"I'll bet you a hundred to one, they'll never invade Britain successfully," I told Ivan.

"I haven't the heart to take your money," he laughed, and he meant it. Ivan Yeaton was a fine, generous, grand person, and he really thought he would be taking advantage of me.

"All right, I'll give you ten to one they won't successfully invade Britain during the duration of the war," I insisted.

He took the bet reluctantly. I bet him a hundred dollars to ten, and it will give me delight to collect it. Of course, he'll only take it right back from me at poker, but that'll be all right.

There was only one man in Moscow who was not pessimistic. He was Colonel Philip Faymonville, the type of officer who makes you think that our Army must be a very great one. Faymonville had come to Moscow with the Harriman mission and had remained behind with his two bright young assistants, Lieutenant Clinton Olson and Lieutenant John J.

Cook, to tie up any loose ends. Faymonville had worked in Russia before. He spoke the language, and the Russians, I think, had more respect for him than they had for any foreign diplomat or military expert in Moscow. Faymonville was a realist like themselves; he was a one-hundred-percent soldier caring nothing for politics or anything else outside of his own particular sphere. I saw him as frequently as possible and took my line from him.

"They'll never take Moscow," he would say quite casually, but emphatically, and then he would explain in convincing military language his reasons. That was good enough for me. Philip Jordan and I were completely sold on Colonel Faymonville. Of course we couldn't quote him, for he only talked to us "off the record," but in our stories we could take an optimistic line. I did that in my daily stories to the *Express* and in my *Collier's* articles. Our colleagues thought we were out of our minds to go out on a limb as we had done. They were sure the German advance would, within a week or two, cut that limb off and drop us with dull thuds. But Philip and I, made more optimistic by their pessimism, kept it up. Circumstances proved Faymonville to have been absolutely right.

I roamed around the city a great deal with Sophiana as my guide. People didn't look very happy, but neither did they look discouraged or panicky. This, I felt, would be London all over again. Jordan agreed with me. I enjoyed working with Jordan. In addition to being one of the finest reporters in the craft, he was a fascinating conversationalist. He would talk on any subject in the world. It was a treat to listen while Jordan, Chollerton, who always plucked excitedly at his red beard, and Alice Moats argued. Moats (never called anything but Moats, even by ambassadors) has a keen, biting wit, in the Dorothy Parker manner. She also had a fur coat, and she was very proud of the fact that she had bought it in Moscow

133

at only about double New York prices. Had there been more news for us and better facilities for our work, Moscow would have been a pleasant place, even during October. We played poker frequently at the American Embassy, but found it difficult to hook Ambassador Laurence Steinhardt or Yeaton or Second Secretary Llewelyn Thompson, one of the shrewdest of all poker players. I tried to make a bet in Moscow that Thompson would end up as a minister within five years. No one would take it. Our State Department, quite properly I suppose, cloaks our brilliant young diplomats abroad with anonymity, and I trust I do Thompson and others I mention no harm by dragging them out into the open. For the most part the career men I have met in Britain and Russia and Iran and Cairo and, years ago, in Germany and France, are excellent. Thompson was one of the best, but all of them, diplomats and correspondents, kept saying, "Wait until you meet Dickerson." Charles Dickerson was the First Secretary of the American Embassy. Steinhardt, with more foresight than any of the other ambassadors, had sent Dickerson to Kazan with plenty of food and important Embassy documents. If Moscow were to be evacuated, Kazan on the Volga would in all probability be the war capital.

Meanwhile there was the zoo. Sophiana and I went there one morning to see the animals. I always go to the zoo. Professor Huxley, who once showed me through the London zoo, seemed to be on intimate terms with every animal under his charge. During the blitz of 1940, the London zoo was hit several times. Huxley discovered that the bravest of all animals was the giraffe. The lions roared nervously when bombs fell close; the zebras squealed; the camels became panicky; the giraffes merely stuck out their necks a bit farther to show their contempt for the bombs. Once the zebra house was hit and the animals streaked out of it and out of the park. Late

134

that night, dock workers in the East End were surprised to see a half dozen zebras walking slowly down the streets. Many a man took the pledge in the East End that night.

The Moscow zoo was excellent, although most of the lions and tigers had been removed. However, there were a few left. We walked into the lion house in front of which stood a bust of Darwin. The house was deserted. I walked down to the last cage and saw a sight which froze me with horror. There an enormous striped tiger crouched and in the corner of the cage was a small dog. The tiger was growling menacingly and inching toward the dog. I yelled to Sophiana, "Get the keeper before that dog gets killed." Surprisingly, the dog showed no fear. Instead, she too growled a dainty, ladylike growl and started to walk toward the tiger. Then she leaped at him, bit his ear and scurried away only to return and nip his flank. The tiger roared and sprang toward her. She was cornered. Slowly the tiger stuck out his huge paw. I expected to see a lifeless dog in a moment and yelled again for Sophiana to call the keeper. But Sophiana just stood there. The paw of the tiger reached the dog—and then the dog began to lick it.

"They are only playing," Sophiana said in her monotone. "They live together. They always have."

Then she told me the story. This tiger was five years old. Its mother had died bearing it. The tiger cub was very sickly, and the keeper conceived the idea of getting a dog to nurse it. A girl living in Moscow had a dog named Lilli which had just given birth to pups and was therefore in the right condition to act as a nursing mother. The feeble tiger cub was brought to the girl's home and took to its foster mother immediately. Needless to say, the cub became mamma's pet. The cub grew healthy feeding at its foster mother's breast (if dogs have breasts) and also developed a passion for Lilli. When the cub became too big for the house, he was shunted back to the zoo. But he grew morose, surly, refused his food. He was obviously missing Lilli. Lilli, too, the woman reported, seemed heartbroken. As long as the tiger was too big to live with Lilli, she would have to live with him. So for nearly five years Lilli and the now fully grown tiger had lived happily together.

I wouldn't have believed it had I not stood there for an hour watching the two play. Lilli wasn't a large dog; she looked like an overgrown Pekingese, but her hair was too short for that. I imagine her ancestry was uncertain and one of those things it would be tactful to leave uninvestigated. It was amazing how the tiger would fondle and cuff the little thing around yet never hurt her.

If you looked, you could find things like that in Moscow—but it took some looking. You were, of course, cut off from contact with all Russian citizens. The authorities still forbade Soviet citizens from fraternizing with foreigners, and the only Russians we ever met were government officials. Lepeshinskaya was the most beautiful of all ballerinas. She was the head girl of the Bolshoi Ballet—no doubt the best ballet in the world. She was only twenty-five and beautiful according to any standards. Half of Russia and all of us were in love with her. Lozovsky arranged a cocktail party so that we could meet her.

Happily, she spoke French. She was as lovely and as charming lifting a vodka glass as she was fleeing from the bad sorcerer in *Swan Lake,* nicest of all ballets—it even has a happy ending. One of the young secretaries to the British Embassy said that the Embassy was having a cocktail party in a few days. He asked Lepeshinskaya if she would come.

"I'll have to ask Mr. Lozovsky," she said doubtfully. "I'd love to attend."

Lozovsky in turn had to ask Vyshinsky. Vyshinsky said "No," so we were never able to better our acquaintance with

136

this vision. Any Soviet citizen running around with a foreigner or even seen talking to one automatically comes under suspicion unless he can explain his foreign contacts satisfactorily.

We could, however, talk to the waiters and the barbers at our hotel, which wasn't much help because few of them talked anything but Russian. One morning I went to the barber's for a haircut. He was one of the few who did talk English. He even had the conventional talkativeness of the American or British barber. The greatest and most uninteresting talkers in the world are barbers and Washington taxicab drivers. I've never gotten into a Washington taxicab without having to listen to political gossip, the chances of the Washington baseball club and a dissertation on the right-hand punch as exhibited by Joe Louis. But this little Russian barber wasn't quite as bad as that.

The little barber was very proud of his English. He was the only barber in Moscow who spoke any English. He was stropping his razor slowly and, as he skillfully turned the blade over and ran it smoothly over the leather, he talked.

"The Germans have started a big offensive against Moscow," he said. "I read it in *Pravda* this morning. The wireless says they are throwing thousands and thousands of new men into the attack. Well," he chuckled, "if they have a lot of men they want killed we will be glad to help."

"It's nothing to laugh about," I reminded him. The stropping became faster and his face became grim. "Let them come. We will fight."

The razor flashed backward and forward with quick, sure strokes. There was nothing hesitant or uncertain about its firm, steady motion. The hand that wielded it was steady. There was something symbolic about the way this little barber grimly stropped his razor. Charlie Chaplin was wise when he picked a barber to be the prototype of the Little Man in *The*

137

Great Dictator. This little man with his razor was speaking for Moscow. Moscow was a city unafraid, and the people of Moscow, knowing their danger, knowing the might of the German war machine, remained calm, ready for whatever might come. This was the Moscow I saw in October, 1941.

Moscow was far different from the Paris of June, 1940. Paris was apathetic, indifferent. Thousands then mumbled this false, self-deceiving phrase: "They'll never take Paris." Moscow read the war news carefully, consulted its maps and was grave, but not gray with fear. Moscow was confident of the ultimate triumph, but Moscow knew that months, maybe years, of suffering lay ahead. Moscow was a city of realists taking their cue from Stalin, the greatest realist of them all. She tasted the cordite flavor of German bombs; she saw her buildings wrecked; she buried her dead, and her heart was made heavy by the news that thousands of her fathers and sons had been killed at the front. She hid her pain and wore a look of grim determination. The germs of hatred dropped by the Nazi bombs had spread over the streets of Moscow, as they had done in London on that memorable May 10th, infecting the people, and one saw the grim hatred of Germany showing on the faces of those who passed on the streets. Moscow knew that her suffering so far had not been particularly heavy. She had not taken the beating that the people of Kiev and Odessa and Leningrad had taken, but she expected that the full force of the Luftwaffe would soon be hurled against her and she was ready.

Meanwhile, life went on with some semblance of normalcy. That is, during the daytime. The ballet was open and crowds argued as to the relative merits of Ulanova and Lepeshinskaya. Some time before, both had appeared in *Swan Lake,* and opinion was divided as to which cast the more potent spell over the audience. Lord Beaverbrook and Averell

Harriman, when they were there for the Moscow conference, attended a special performance of *Swan Lake,* and both were captivated by the twinkling toes and artful grace of Ballerina Ulanova. Admirers of her rival scoffed and told them, "But wait until you see Lepeshinskaya."

The opera was open, too; the motion-picture houses showing the Russian-made *Masquerade* were crowded; and the picture *London Can Take It* was being shown there for the first time. True, the audiences were usually 80 per cent feminine. The men of Moscow were at the front.

One day Moscow took a holiday from the war to watch its own world series. At the big Dynamo Stadium the two best soccer teams in Russia met for the championship. It was Dynamo against Spartak, and the spectators behaved just as our own football fans behave. They yelled encouragement to the team of their choice; they groaned when Alexis or Ivan missed what seemed certain goals. Airplanes swooped lazily overhead, on the alert against possible daylight raiders, for it was an overcast day, the kind the Nazis like for dive-bombing.

The football was not quite up to that displayed by the leading English professional teams, but it was spirited and hard-fought. Now and then Nikolai, star forward of the Dynamo team, was very wide with his poorly aimed shots at the goal. I'd been told to watch him, for Nikolai is considered to be the Big Bertha of Russian football. The reason for his poor timing was soon forthcoming.

"No wonder he is off today," a man from the British Embassy said. "He only got back from the front yesterday. They gave him leave just for this game."

Nearly all of the players were in one service or another. Those who were not Army or Air Force men worked in factories and had been given the Sunday afternoon off to play.

They made 15,000 citizens of Moscow (and this temporary citizen) forget the war for the afternoon.

Then there was the circus. The news had just been announced that Orel had fallen. The press room at the Narkomindel (the Foreign Office) was in a turmoil. My colleagues were grave and discouraged. The gloom was thick in this press room, where we brought our stories to be censored and where, while waiting for the process of censorship, we shared gossip. To escape the depressing atmosphere, I went to the circus. It was a good circus, but then all circuses are good. Instead of three rings there was only one. There was the same provocative smell of sawdust and the exciting, vibrant atmosphere of the circus as we know it. The arena was crowded and the clowns were even funnier than our clowns. The bareback riders were just as thrilling and the ringmaster just as stentorian in his introduction to this death-defying act or that.

There was a magician who made everyone but the audience disappear and the shrieks of laughter which rang out from the crowded arena were the same shrieks one would hear in Stamford, Connecticut, or Orlando, Florida, or Portland, Oregon, when the circus comes to town. There wasn't an empty seat in the huge stadium. Laughter is a defensive weapon the Germans have never learned to combat. Hitler cannot kill laughter with bombs.

"And now," the urbane ringmaster said, "we come to the finale. I know you have enjoyed this performance, people of Moscow. I hear your laughter. That is good. Moscow does not wear a frown upon her face, despite her trouble. Moscow laughs."

It is impossible to live in Moscow long without coming to love the people of Russia. They are decent, home-loving people, and you could take a slice of them and drop them in our Midwest, and within a few weeks you wouldn't be able to distinguish them from our own decent, law-abiding citizens. I hadn't been in Russia long before I found out that these were our kind of people. The other American and British correspondents felt as I did.

I am no nearer to being a Communist than are you who read this, but I defy anyone to remain objective and impersonal when he has been with the people of this city. No matter what your political convictions, these are people who only wanted to go their own way; who only wanted to solve their own problems. But now they found themselves in the most horrible battle of the ages. I found it impossible to be neutral in this struggle.

Food rationing in Moscow was not severe. One could get as good a meal in a factory kitchen as one could get in a London West End hotel. There was no clothing rationing, but most of the mills were busy making uniforms and the shops had not a great variety of goods in them. But the people of Moscow were not clothes-conscious. As long as clothes were warm, they needed to serve no such frivolous subsidiary purpose as to be ornamental. One could still buy furs, and there were tailors who would make you fur coats or wraps at London and New York prices.

Except for the uniforms one saw on the streets during the day and some queues in front of food shops, one might forget that the most terrible war in history was being fought less than an hour's flying time away. Occasionally, muddy uniforms and bandaged heads reminded one that Moscow was at war. It was at night that the war came to Moscow. Black-out was at six o'clock. It was a more severe black-out than we knew in England. The buses and tramcars kept going. To one accustomed to the London black-out, their lights and the occasional flashes from their overhead charged electric wires, as well as the headlights from automobiles and the street lights, there was reason to be a bit dubious as to the effect the Moscow black-out might have. But when the sirens screamed even these lights faded. The buses and trams crawled back into their barns. Automobile headlights were extinguished. Traffic and street lighting died and Moscow prepared a black face to welcome her uninvited visitors. Once the raid commenced one didn't see a single light in the center of the city.

Although up to that time Moscow had not had one raid which would compare in severity to any one of fifty London raids, the city took raids far more seriously and perhaps more intelligently than London did. When the sirens sounded the two best hotels in Moscow and the restaurants immediately stopped serving food. Guests were ordered, not asked, to go into shelters. The city fathers knew that foolish courage is a cheap commodity; people were beginning to have a dangerous contempt for bombs. The Soviet rulers are fiercely realistic. If citizens wish to get themselves killed by their own foolishness, well and good. But the more people injured and killed the more work for air-raid wardens and firemen. There were only a limited number of these, and they had more important things to do than to attend the wounds of citizens who had no business being out of doors. No casual pedestrians walked through the Moscow night when a raid was on.

There was a twelve-o'clock curfew even on raidless nights, and only those with special permits were allowed out after that hour. The correspondents received the precious nocturnal freedom of movement. But then there was nothing for even the most indomitable stayer-up-late to stay up for in Moscow. Even on quiet nights the hotels and restaurants closed at ten. There were no night clubs and no hideaways where the convivial could gather. Fleet Street would have been shocked to see some of its former celebrated night hawks retiring meekly to bed each night at ten. Life for the correspondents was fairly endurable until the day that both the Metropole and National hotels announced that there was no more vodka. Whisky, of course, could be obtained only if one had a very special friend at an embassy. Beer was non-existent, nor were there any British or American cigarettes to be had. It looked as if circumstances, having already forced the correspondents to what was virtually a compulsory early-to-bed policy, would now force them to become teetotalers and non-smokers.

But Moscow was girding for battle. The tastes and feelings of individuals did not count. The invader was not far away and Moscow, so far as was humanly possible, would be ready. Moscow had a great example to lend her courage. For a year she had watched London going through her Gethsemane. London was equal to her destiny. My guess then was that Moscow, too, would not be found wanting. I was right.

12

Retreat from Moscow

WHEN SOPHIANA WOKE ME at nine in the morning on October 15, I should have known that it was going to be a bad day. Any day that starts as early as that is bound to be a bad day. She had a depressing message to give me. Eisenstein had phoned to say that the whole film industry had been evacuated from Moscow, was leaving that morning, in fact. He didn't know where they were going, but he would let me know later. Meanwhile we would have to hold up work on the picture. This was discouraging because I had finished the commentary and Eisenstein had been delighted with it. A camera crew was working on it, and I thought I had something that would be as good as *London Can Take It*.

My interview with Stalin was almost clinched. Lozovsky had seen Molotov and Vyshinsky; had told them of the picture I was making; had told them I'd refused payment and had told them what I wanted. They had already agreed to give me the same privilege accorded a few months before to Ralph Ingersoll, publisher of *PM*. That is, I could spend some time with Stalin, talk with him, ask him anything I wished, but with the understanding that anything Stalin said would be considered "off the record." This I had turned down flatly. I had once interviewed De Valera in Dublin on those terms and had always regretted it. He said many vitally important things that would have made great news at the time, but not a word of it could I use. You have to obey that "off the record" pledge. I don't know one correspondent of any standing who ever broke it. I had another reason for not wishing to duplicate Ingersoll's stunt. I hadn't seen his story, but I knew Ingersoll and I knew how capable he was and I knew he could write like a streak and my story at best would be but a pale imitation of his—and it would appear months later.

So I told Lozovsky I wasn't interested. He was decent enough to see my point and he went back to Vyshinsky again. Meanwhile, I had Oumansky trying to induce Vyshinsky and Steinhardt trying to influence Oumansky. I wanted an "on the record" interview with Stalin and wouldn't be satisfied with anything else. Now with the picture delayed, the slight club I held over Lozovsky didn't bear much weight. But he had seen my commentary and had heard Eisenstein's enthusiasm about the progress of the picture and he was very anxious to see it finished. I really felt that he was doing his best to get me my interview. Weeks later in Kuibyshev, Vyshinsky told me that I was right. The whole thing was virtually arranged when October 15th came along.

That morning Jordan and I had a date to buy a car. Taxicabs had long since disappeared from the streets and now it was impossible to hire Intourist cars. Sophiana had heard of a Ford owned by the Afghan Embassy that was on the market. We went and looked at it. Jordan drove it around the block. It was in fine shape and it had five new tires. The price was four hundred dollars—reasonable enough when cars were so scarce. We decided to buy it. There was one hitch. The First Secretary of the Embassy, who owned it, wanted dollars for it. We could give him rubles or pounds, and I offered him a check in dollars but he wanted the cash. We decided to scout around and see if there were four hundred dollars in Moscow. I phoned the American Embassy and Steinhardt said he could spare four hundred dollars. Then Jordan and I had lunch.

We had a good lunch to celebrate our imminent entrance into the plutocratic ranks of car owners. We had caviar and vodka and broiled chicken and a wonderful salad and excellent cheese. We felt so good that we had a bottle of champagne; Russian champagne is a bit sweet but palatable enough. We were fortunate in having had that good lunch. We didn't know it at the time but it would be some days before we would have another decent meal. I was called away by a phone call. It was Steinhardt. "Come to the Embassy at once," he said. "This is urgent."

I got Moats and we scurried to the Embassy, wondering what it was all about. We knew that the military situation was serious. I didn't believe that it was critical. For weeks we had seen the railroad stations jammed with people trying to get out of Moscow, but the sight had become so familiar that we no longer attached any significance to it. We had seen tanks trundling through the streets en route to the front and we had seen loads of wounded brought back. But I was still saying, "They'll never take Moscow," occasionally recollecting that in June, 1940, I had been saying the same thing in France about Paris.

My colleague Moats had her special sources of information. General Vladislas Anders, in command of the Polish Army in Russia, and Mohammed Saed, the Persian Ambassador, dean of the diplomatic corps, were extremely helpful to her. All agreed that Moscow could not long be defended. But Moscow was fairly comfortable. True, the vodka had almost run out and cigarettes were virtually unattainable and the Nazi bombers came over every night, but this was routine to those of us who had been in London the past year.

146

Then, on the afternoon of October 15th, there was the phone call from Steinhardt. Bluntly he told us, "The balloon has gone up. Cripps and I were summoned by Molotov this morning. He told us that a train would be waiting at the Kazan station at seven o'clock tonight for the diplomatic corps. He said that you could, in fact must, go along."

"Suppose we want to stay?" I asked Steinhardt.

"You have no discretion in the matter," the Ambassador said. "The Government is going, the Press Bureau and the censors are going. Stay here, and you won't be able to send anything. There will be no further communications out of Moscow. Report here at five-thirty with what baggage you can carry and if you have any food, bring it along. I don't know where we're going, but it'll probably be a long trip."

If you are accustomed to making hurried evacuations, it doesn't take you long to pack. Some warm clothing, a blanket, a couple of bottles of whisky, some bread and canned food, if you have it, toilet articles, your typewriter, and you're ready.

The snow fell hard at dusk. It swirled down in large dry flakes only to turn into slush as it hit the pavements. The huge Kazan station was packed with refugees trying to leave what they thought to be a doomed city. More than ten thousand apathetic-looking women, grim-faced men, and bewildered, sleepy-eyed children lay on the cement floors waiting for trains to take them east. The Nazi pincers had closed in on three sides; the railroad line to the east remained the one lifeline to safety and there were reports that it too had been heavily bombed and machine-gunned.

The various ambassadors and ministers trudged in from the snowstorm. A huge dining room was reserved for the diplomatic and journalistic corps. Haidar Atkar, the Turkish Ambassador, came in. Anxious-eyed Vladimir Kot, once a college professor but now Polish Ambassador, appeared. *"Bon soir, Excellence,"* we murmured, as these exquisitely polite diplomats shook hands quite formally with us. Genial Shao Li-Tze, one of the best-liked men in the capital, came in smiling with his aides. Shriveled, apple-faced General Tatekawa, Japanese Ambassador, brushed the snow from his uniform and took a seat at a table.

Our train was not to leave for three hours. Meanwhile, there was beer. We drank beer and none of us felt very good. We felt resentful because we were being forced to leave the best story of the year. We were annoyed with Molotov for making us leave. Moscow was in no immediate danger, we felt. The room began to fill.

"Bon soir, Excellence." Here was Greek Minister Pipinellis and Milan Gavrilovitch, the Jugoslav Minister. Fierlinger, the Czech, came in and looked around with tired eyes. Evacuations were old stories to him. *"Bon soir, Excellence . . ."* Roly-poly Mohammed Saed walked in smiling, for it is his nature to smile even though empires totter. Steinhardt and the most faithful aides any ambassador ever had entered. Llewelyn Thompson, Second Secretary, Charlie Thayer, Third Secretary, Counselor Walter Thurston and his huge brown German boxer, Sully, all kept anxious eyes on the crates of food they had brought. Only Steinhardt, of all the ambassadors, had foreseen the possibility of a quick getaway and had prepared. Sir Stafford Cripps, the British Ambassador, brushed the snow from his black foreign-office hat and sat down alone. He looked suddenly old as he sat there tight-lipped and sad, occasionally stroking the head of his Airedale, Joe, best known dog-about-town in Moscow.

The dining room was crowded with diplomats from a dozen countries and their innumerable aides. The British Economic Mission, headed by Sir Walter Citrine, sat together, frankly angry because their work had been interrupted. Gradually the smoke from a hundred cigarettes filled the room. Gradually individuals disappeared to be merged into a mass of humanity—unmistakably a mass of refugees. A hurried evacuation is a great leveler, and by now it was impossible to tell an ambassador from a porter.

Then came word that our train was standing at a siding, waiting for us. Thayer and Jack Morgan, of the American Embassy, had already taken our baggage in, and it was waiting on the platform for us. The others, even ambassadors, carried their own. Correspondents will never forget the magnificent job done by the Embassy staff that difficult night. The snow had thickened outside, as though to hide the shame of the most ignominious diplomatic and journalistic flight in history. There was absolutely no reason for any of us to leave this city. Through the heavy blanket of snow came the muffled sound of the guns, and now and then their flashes penetrated the white opaqueness of the night.

Somewhere above there were Nazi airplanes. Not even the first snowstorm of the winter could stop them. We looked up and swore softly and hoped that they'd never make their landing. A year and a half of bombing will rub the ridiculous veneer of neutrality off any hitherto objective reporter.

We found our baggage in the pitch blackness of the night and slipped and slid through the heavy slush into the train. We said reluctant good-byes to Thompson and to Freddie Reinhart of the Embassy staff who were remaining in Moscow, and then looked at what was to be our home for the next five nights and four days.

You travel either "soft" or "hard" on Russian trains. The "soft" coaches are every bit as good as the best luxury American trains. There is nothing in America as uncomfortable as the "hard" Russian coaches. With Cy Sulzberger, Henry Cassidy and Robert Magidoff of the Associated Press, I shared a "hard" compartment. There were four wooden bunks in it and no heat. The train pulled out of Moscow at 1:30 A.M. We tried to sleep. The cold filtered through the windows and caught us in its terrible grasp. It got under our skin and into our bones and we breathed it into our bloodstream and somehow it got into our brains, so that from head to foot we were one numbed mass. Bitter cold is not an anesthetic. When we moved, our joints screamed in protest. Sleep was impossible.

The night passed. Dawn found us in a region of small villages. We passed one such, Lida, a mass of smoking ruins. The Germans had paid it a visit only a few hours before. There were interminable stops. We were detained on the tracks at Ryazan for seven hours, not at all cheered by the sight of a long, bomb-and-machine-bullet-scarred troop train that stood on the next track. The incredible Thayer had a breakfast of parts ready for us two coaches ahead, and when we groped our way there and breathed the blessed air of this heated car, we flatly refused to return to our air-cooled accommodations. Alice Moats, the only woman correspondent traveling with us, had a compartment with four bunks in it. Sulzberger, Cassidy and I laid claim to them and, during the rest of the retreat, Moats, with great good nature, had to put up with us as boarders.

It was not a pleasant trip. There was no hot water at all. There was no drinking water after the first day and we had to depend upon tap water from railroad stations, a precarious method of quenching one's thirst. No one drinks tap water in Russia unless it is boiled. Thayer had a few cans of beans and some tinned salmon which we ate cold. Sometimes a station restaurant yielded black bread and sausage and one morning at 5 A.M., we found a hot meal of cabbage soup, fried eggs and hot beef waiting for us. That meal lasted us for two days.

The train crawled with paralyzing slowness. Often we stopped for six and seven hours waiting for trains laden with troops and guns to pass en route to Moscow. We were a long train, thirty-three coaches, and our one locomotive seemed tired with the task of pulling us all. Occasionally, looking out of the window, we would see airplanes approaching and we would grow very quiet and just watch until we saw the red star on the fuselage of the planes. Then we would laugh and say that we knew they were "our planes" all the time. So it went —a dreary odyssey—and to our physical misery was added the mental torment that we were running away. One hundred and twenty-nine years ago Napoleon retreated from Moscow, but with far better cause than we had. In vain we told ourselves that we had been offered no alternative. The fact remained that the story we had come to cover was receding further and further as we steamed east. By now we had been told that we had an appointment in Samara or, as it is now called, Kuibyshev.

One day was like another. We played poker all day, but there was no light at night so we had to stop early. Once we persuaded Steinhardt to join us, and we were extremely happy to plunge him a thousand rubles in the red. But this changed to gloom when he came back to recoup his losses and win a little besides. We had forgotten that Steinhardt had once been a shrewd New York lawyer.

We slept in our clothes with our coats wrapped around us. By now our clothes seemed part of us, and it was difficult to know where the clothes ended and we began. Our female traveling companion, with amazing fortitude and with a commendable lack of the usual feminine insistence upon cleanliness and tidiness, earned our undying admiration. Her

151

philosophical acceptance of a difficult situation and her refusal to trade on her sex for special privileges is something none of us will ever forget. She balked only once.

Early on the fifth morning, she awoke us. Sleep was precious, and to have had it stolen from one so unceremoniously did not make our awakening any the more cheerful.

"You three have been snoring very loudly," she announced, from her upper bunk.

"You ought to be used to it by now," Cassidy grumbled.

"Yes, I am," Moats said coldly. "And I don't mind ordinary snoring but tonight you switched. Tonight you've been yodeling. Anyhow, there's a big city ahead. It might be Kuibyshev."

We looked out of the window into a thin dawn and, sure enough, a few miles ahead and to the left there was a lighted city. It was a beautiful sight. It was a beautiful sight of course only if you have lived month after month in blacked-out cities. This was Kuibyshev, and it was so far from the war zone that it was not even blacked-out. The lights twinkled in friendly fashion and the train moved slowly on. We approached the lights and then the train rumbled across a bridge. We looked below into the sluggish waters of the Volga. Its banks were snow encrusted and masses of ice and snow drifted lazily along with the current.

"I'll shoot the first one," Moats said, "who sings the 'Song of the Volga Boatmen.' "

Morning came quickly, and we had coffee which tasted as though it had come from heaven and we had black bread and jam and reveled in the thought that soon we would be in a hotel and in a hot bath and we'd be shaved and separated from these clothes that by now had grown on us. We stepped from the train into clean crisp air. The ambassadors alighted

152

and now once more they had contrived to look like ambassadors. Once more it was *"Bon jour, Excellence."*

On the station platform there was a sign-post telling the mileage to Moscow. It read "630 miles." We had taken exactly 105 hours to make the trip. In short, our average speed had been six miles an hour. It had been a slow and reluctant retreat.

We waited there on the station platform for an hour but nothing happened. We had been told that the correspondents were to be put up at the Grand Hotel. Clever Moatsie suggested that Henry Shapiro of the United Press and I go on ahead to see that no one stole our rooms. We managed to get one of the "Y.M.C.A." boys (we had a platoon of them with us by now) to drive us to the hotel. It didn't look too bad from the outside. It was on the main street. We went in and discovered that there were three single rooms and four double rooms waiting for us. There were eleven of us.

"It would only be reasonable," Shapiro said smoothly, "to give the three press associations' representatives the single rooms. After all, we work late hours and . . ."

"We will draw lots for the single rooms," I said very firmly. "In fact we might even let Moats have a room to herself without drawing."

Shapiro shrugged his shoulders. He couldn't be killed for trying. He decided to go back and let our colleagues know about the room situation. I told him to let Moats draw for me. I'd stay behind. The rooms wouldn't be ready for half an hour or so, the woman in charge told me. Meanwhile, there was a barber shop. I hadn't shaved, of course, since we left Moscow. None of us had. Nor had I washed. A barber shop, then a bath would be the procedure. I got a haircut and a shampoo and nothing ever felt as lovely as that hot water running down my neck. When it dropped back into the sink, it was black. I had a shave and while I was at it, I had a manicure. The buxom girl who was the manicurist shuddered when she saw my hands, but she did her best. I came out of the barber's still filthy, of course, but feeling fine. A shave does wonders to you. Now for that steaming hot bath and everything would be lovely.

"Give me the key to any of our rooms," I asked the woman in charge who spoke a little English. "We'll sort out the rooms when my colleagues arrive. I just want to have a bath."

"A bath?" Her eyes expressed wonderment. "But we have no baths in the hotel!"

I went into the restaurant, ordered a bottle of vodka and sat down, waiting to break the news to my bath-minded pals. When they arrived and heard it, they, too, sat down and ordered bottles of vodka. We felt very sorry for ourselves. It was hardly an auspicious introduction to Kuibyshev.

13

The Kuibyshev Blues

KUIBYSHEV WAS A LARGE, middle-aged city sprawling on the eastern bank of the Volga. The city wore a rather tired look, as though it had been through a lot. Nevertheless, Kuibyshev was the wartime capital of Soviet Russia, the news center of the German-Russian campaign and headquarters for most of the government figures.

Stalin remained in the Kremlin, but nearly all his aides were in this city of unpaved streets and ankle-deep mud, where personal hygiene and comfort were at a minimum. There was a time when the city was known as Samara. Samara is a lovely name, hardly suited to the bleak ugliness of this Volga city.

In 1937 it was renamed Kuibyshev. It was named after Valerian Kuibyshev, the genius behind the recapture of the city from the Czechs, who occupied it in 1918. A statue of this hardy revolutionist, great engineer and city planner stands in the huge public square.

In the summer, when the warm breezes from the Volga blow over it, Kuibyshev is undoubtedly a clean, tidy-looking place; but when winter comes and a warm spell melts the snow, one realized that Kuibyshev had only four paved streets and that life there was more primitive than in any city or village in the United States. Rivers of mud slopped down the streets into the Volga. Sleighs, ox-drawn wagons and automobiles became mired in the cloying combination of mud and snow; sewers backed up and water refused to run out of sinks and the very few bathtubs in town. Nature grabbed Kuibyshev by the nape of the neck and shook her, and we mortals unfortunate enough to be living there bore the brunt of her fury.

In 1935, when the last census was taken, Kuibyshev had a population of 200,000. But where once there had only been grain elevators, factories appeared, and the population almost doubled. Today it was swollen with the thousands of refugees who came there, fleeing from the scream of Nazi bombs and the terror of Nazi guns. At least a million people were in this dreary city when we arrived.

There were two hotels in Kuibyshev: the National, which was reserved for Russians, and the Grand, which was taken over by the correspondents, a few high-ranking Soviet dignitaries and an overflow of refugees. There were no bathtubs at the Grand and, to put it mildly, personal hygiene was almost non-existent. There was no heat in the Grand, and we huddled together in the room of one of us lucky enough to have found a small electric heater. In many ways Kuibyshev (except for the virtual absence of beautiful women) would be a fine setting for an Oppenheim novel. Oumansky, deposed Ambassador to Washington, lived across the hall from me, sharing his cheerless room with three others. The great Vyshinsky lived down the hall, and day and night four NKVD men mounted guard at his door. Vyshinsky smiled readily when we passed in the hall. He looked like a genial dean of freshmen at any small college, except that occasionally one noticed that hint of winter in his eyes.

Foreign Minister Molotov commuted between Kuibyshev and Moscow, and his chunky figure and bespectacled face were familiar in the main street of this town. Before he left for America, genial, smiling Litvinov was a familiar of the Grand. By far the most popular of all Russian diplomats, his appointment as Ambassador to Washington was hailed with joy by all of us. The dining room at the Grand was usually filled with correspondents, diplomats and uniforms, all waiting very impatiently for vodka, cabbage soup and the monotonous but filling food we were given. There had been no fresh vegetables for weeks, but there was plenty of butter and occasionally a sort of French pastry. We could buy five eggs a week at the local food store and a half pound of cheese.

In the dining room there were Russian, British, Czech and Polish uniforms. Bald-headed General Vladislas Anders, Commander in Chief of the Polish Army in Russia, usually dined with us, his ready smile and quick wit quite disguising the fact that only three months ago he had emerged from a rather horrible two years' imprisonment in Russian concentration camps and prisons.

General Anders had an army of 150,000 Poles, all of whom hated Germans so much that they were willing to forget the past two years they had spent in Russian work camps or prisons after the 1939 partition of Poland. One felt like taking off one's hat in the presence of any Pole. Such magnificence of spirit, such fortitude under adversity and such insistence upon vengeance against the Nazi spoilers of their home were inspiring. The Poles were very wonderful.

In the dingy dining room of this dreary hotel were, usually, three or four ambassadors and smart-looking RAF officers, and sometimes Colonel (now General) Faymonville.

The Soviet insistence that Russians (except officially) should not mingle with foreigners precluded any kind of social life, except that which we made ourselves. At least four nights a week we played poker at the Grand or the

American Embassy. If the expense accounts of foreign correspondents seemed high those days it was due chiefly to the skill at cards of Charlie Dickerson, First Secretary of the American Embassy, and Major Joseph Michella, acting Military Attaché. Lest one think that the Embassy staff spent its time in riotous gambling I have to add that we played for the same stakes that the boys around the firehouse in any town play for. If it had not been for poker there is no doubt that many of us would have gone crazy.

The British Embassy was the best and by far the most uncomfortable building in town. It is an imposing marble structure with large rooms. They were too large. The Embassy staff slept eighteen in a room. Ambassador Steinhardt had secured a former schoolhouse for his staff. From the outside it was a drab, three-story building facing an unpaved street that was perpetually mud-filled. But there were forty small rooms in the building and no one had to share his room with more than one other. So dependent were we on small bits of gossip to keep us from becoming intellectually moribund that a new chair or a curtain wangled somehow by an Embassy staff member was excuse enough for a party with vodka, salami and bologna to add to our gayety.

The streets of Kuibyshev were filled with uniforms, and at dusk each day new recruits drilled in the big square, with searchlights atop the magnificent palace of culture bathing them in pale light. Children, quite unaware that their country was fighting for her life, still learned their ABC's in the elementary schools. One of the most interesting features of Kuibyshev was the *Detsky Saf* on our main street, a nursery kindergarten where children of workingwomen were brought in the morning and where they remained under skilled supervision until the mothers called for them at the end of the day's work. Seen through big plate-glass windows, the sight

158

of fifty clean, happy youngsters playing with dolls or toys was an antidote for less pleasant sights.

I have mentioned the virtual lack of bathtubs in Kuibyshev. The British Embassy had two and the American Embassy four, two of which worked. But there were the public baths. You had to wait in line for a long time to be accommodated there, for 5,000 people a day used them. We never bothered. We found that the daily baths we were once accustomed to, though a pleasant habit and a rather over-rated luxury, were neither necessary to health or comfort. One gets quite used to going two weeks without a bath.

The public baths afforded us some amusement. One day I saw three Ambassadors (Mohammed Saed of Persia, Haidar Atkar of Turkey, General Tatekawa of Japan) and three Ministers (Pipinellis of Greece, Fierlinger of Czechoslovakia and Gavrilovitch of Jugoslavia) standing forlornly in line waiting for their turn to dip into the communal tub.

Kuibyshev was so crowded with unexpected visitors that we walked in the streets as a matter of course, trying hard to keep up a pretense of normalcy. Twice weekly there was a musical comedy at the local theatre, and the Kuibyshev ballet company, inferior to the great Bolshoi Ballet of Moscow but still perhaps better than any ballet in America or Britain, performed *Don Quixote,* gayest of all ballets.

Such diversions took our minds off the slaughter going on 700 miles west of us; they took our minds off the constant battle with the Press Bureau, by far the toughest censorship in the world. We tried desperately to get to the front and, failing that, to Moscow, but had no success. We almost made it, though. We persuaded a Russian playwright, Afinogenov, to intercede for us. He obtained permission to go to Moscow, where he was to see military authorities who might grant us permission to get out of what amounted to exile. He left,

159

despite the fact that his new play, *Mashenka,* was to open the next night. When the curtain went up on *Mashenka* at eight-thirty, he had an appointment somewhere else. At eighty-thirty that night he was killed by a bomb in Moscow.

The main street of Kuibyshev was pleasant enough. It was wide and well-paved and, until the black-out was ordered, well-lighted. It was Main Street in the only city for fifty miles around. Rather incredibly, a dozen manicure and hairdressing establishments were located on Main Street and they did a land-office business until midnight. Sometimes there was a line of a hundred women waiting their turn. Even the ancient waitresses who served us at the Grand had immaculately manicured nails and waved coiffures. Twenty-five years ago, only 10 per cent of the people of Russia wore shoes. Now, except for refugees from ruined cities, they were warmly and well enough dressed, and they yearned for the minor luxuries denied them for so many generations. The crowded hairdressing rooms reflected this feeling.

Kuibyshev, hitherto obscure, really came into glory last November 7th, on Soviet Russia's most important anniversary. The Soviet Union was twenty-four years old on that day and, although Stalin remained in the Kremlin and reviewed troops in Red Square, the main celebration took place in Kuibyshev. The day was cold. Clouds too numb to move hung low against a dull, sullen sky. Twenty thousand troops massed in Kuibyshev Square and prominent Russian officials appeared on the platform to review them as they marched by. Little Kalinin, President of the USSR, was there, plucking at his thin beard with cold hands. Vyshinsky, Oumansky and Litvinov were there, and even the great Marshal Voroshilov had come from the front to review the Red Army.

They paraded by with their tanks and their artillery, and you didn't have to be Russian to feel a pride in these grim-

160

faced fighting men. They did not look like men who had been beaten. They did not look like men who would ever be beaten.

The river boats still tied up to the docks on the banks of the Volga. Once they brought grain and traders who bartered shawls and shoes for food or kopeks. Now they were unloading pitiful groups of refugees, and it was difficult to spend more than an hour watching them emerge from the badly overcrowded boats. The misery in the hearts of these elderly men and women who had come from destroyed front-line towns, showed in their dull, lusterless eyes. Nearly all of them had lost sons or relatives at the front and to them life is over. They squatted apathetically near their belongings, mud oozing through their broken shoes, and when it snowed they neither moved nor sought cover.

Now and then one would talk. One who had come from the South cried a little as she told of the nights of bombing which preceded the German occupation of her village. The bombing killed her daughter; her two sons had already been killed at the front. Her house on fire, she rescued what she could and waited outside. She couldn't run; she was too numb. The Germans came. Only the very old like herself were left. The Germans had no use for them. According to their well-established custom, they had immediately searched every house in the town for food and had then fixed up the biggest house for use as a brothel. By now the front had advanced further toward Moscow, and this was a second-line village. Then came the miserable Polish and Czech women who had been used by the German army ever since the occupation of those countries. The Nazi high command wanted its soldiers to be happy.

It was an old tale heard a hundred times before. Its accuracy cannot be doubted. Hoping to win favor from the natives of occupied Russia, the Germans had left the Soviet women reasonably alone. Invariably, they bring in their female prisoners of war to amuse the troops. The stories of refugees from front-line towns varied very seldom, except in detail. But always, even though the towns were separated by 500 miles, there was the story of the enslaved women of Poland and Czechoslovakia. Army morale must be maintained. They didn't have bread and circuses to give their soldiers; they gave them women instead.

The stories told by recently freed Poles were not pretty either. I spoke to four one day: a doctor, a schoolmaster, an accountant and an engineer. All were pitifully thin but each, despite his two years of Russian prisons, had volunteered to join General Anders' army. Only one of them broke down while telling his story. The accountant, a wisp of a man with a thin beard, suddenly began to cry. I think it was because we—I was with a Polish general—gave him cigarettes and lit them and called him mister. Then he wiped his tears away with his tattered sleeve and apologized. "It is the first time in more than two years," he said, "that I have shown any weakness."

"And now?" I asked him.

"And now I hope I will live long enough to kill some Germans," he said grimly.

This, then, was Kuibyshev. There was boredom among the correspondents and the diplomats. There was almost unbelievable misery among the refugees. There was everything except a spirit of defeatism. Not even the most miserable refugee, waiting in line for hours to get a bowl of soup and a bit of bread, would admit that there is the slightest chance of Germany conquering this vast country. And there was

162

nothing but universal admiration for Stalin, the man who stayed in Moscow. Timoshenko and Budenny and Voroshilov were almost household deities, and every man, woman and child in this Volga city knew that they would eventually be victorious. Kuibyshev was magnificent in her shabbiness.

14

The Wounded Do Cry

LIVING IN KUIBYSHEV was absolutely fantastic. There were fourteen sovereign diplomatic missions quartered in the dreary city. In addition to the American and British Embassies, there were the Czechs, Poles, Greeks, Jugoslavs, Swedes, Norwegians, Iranians, Turks, Afghans, Chinese, Japanese and Bulgarian, although one had to stretch a point to lend the title "sovereign diplomatic mission" to the latter. The Bulgarian Mission consisted of one melancholy Bulgar who lived alone and unhappily at the Grand Hotel with two "Y.M.C.A." boys in constant attendance. Russia did not exactly consider Bulgaria to be a friendly neutral.

A week after we arrived, our secretaries followed. We hadn't been allowed to bring them on the train with us. My excellent Sophiana was so much in demand that I rented her out occasionally. Cy Sulzberger and Philip Jordan used her, and I took either whisky or cigarettes in payment. By now, the American Embassy, previously our source of supply, had rationed whisky, gin and cigarettes. Finally Steinhardt told us sadly that he could no longer help us out; the remaining supply would take care of the staff itself only eight more weeks.

The filth of the streets, the horrible sanitary conditions in the Grand and the lack of fresh vegetables, soon began to have their effect on us. Every one of us had dysentery, the very worst thing we could catch with conditions as they were in the Grand. Sulzberger was in bed for a week with it. Our lives began pretty much to be bound up with the rooms which, for the sake of delicacy, I will call the "bathrooms." There were two such "bathrooms" in the Grand to take care of about a hundred guests. On our floor, we had a dozen Mongols with their families. They were not clean, and unless one arose very early in the morning, one found their imprint in the "bathroom."

One day, Chollerton said, "You know these Mongols would never make good soldiers. Their aim is too bad." It was disgusting, but it was true. Three or four times a day, an old chambermaid would come into the "bathroom" quite oblivious as to whether it was engaged or not and throw buckets of hot water about the place. This kept it reasonably clean for perhaps half an hour. We thanked our stars for the presence of Dr. Norman. He kept dosing us with pills to help our dysentery. He gave us stringent and sensible orders.

"Wash your shoes every night," he said. "They are always full of mud and filth. Don't drag those germs into your bedroom with you."

He couldn't put any of us on diets, for there was only the one menu. No one starved, but the heavy cabbage soup and tasteless meat was not the healthiest food in the world. Moats distinguished herself by getting influenza twice in two weeks and then climaxing it with the conventional diplomatic fever plus something called conjunctivitis, which made her eyes run. But she bore up well. Her great friend, Ambassador Mohammed Saed, had rented a house, formerly the home of the late Maxim Gorky. In it there was a bathtub. Moats usually lunched at Saed's, and used his bathtub to the envy of all of us. We would shun her when she returned with stories of good luncheons and positively gleaming with cleanliness. Often, when she had eaten her fill of beautiful Persian rice, she would either beg or steal what was left in the bowl and bring it back to the Grand for Jordan and myself. Cigarettes remained a major problem. She even came back from Saed's with a carton of Camels one day and quite rightly shared them with us. Old Saed, he was well over sixty, loved the fresh humor of our Moats and loved her bitter criticism of his ambassadorial colleagues, none of whom she liked. He also liked the fact that she talked French and German as well as he did. In fact, after six months in Russia, Moats, who had an amazing gift for languages, spoke enough Russian to get around quite nicely.

With the arrival of Sophiana, life became more bearable. She haunted the Univermag, the local Gimbel Brothers, but several visits resulted in the purchase of nothing more startling than five bath towels and an electric stove. The latter served to take the chill out of the room, but it was a temperamental gadget that seemed to be at its worst in really cold weather. She tried hard to get me something to use for at least a cat-bath and finally succeeded in getting a second-hand wash basin for seventy-five rubles ($15). This would have been perhaps a dollar in London or New York.

During the first few weeks, food at the hotel was as dull as food can be. There would usually be a half dozen items on the menu, but when we asked for the more attractive dishes, the waitress would invariably shake her head sadly and murmur, *"Niet"* which meant "No." We would see *ikra y luk* (caviar and onions) on the menu, but nearly always the answer was *"Niet."* Niet and *nitchevo* were the two Russian words we heard most. *Nitchevo* would mean, "Maybe tomorrow." The two words haunted us so that we composed a song and sang it to the tune of the "Song of the Volga Boat-men."

> *Nitchevo niet, vodka niet*
> *Nitchevo luk, coffee niet*
> *Butter niet, ham and eggs niet*
> *Nitchevo ikra,*
> *We haven't got it yet.*

Oh, well, we thought it very good and sang it quite lustily. After a few weeks of this, the local people who ran the hotel were tossed out and the experienced Intourist group from Moscow took over. Things were a little better. Then a food store for foreigners was opened. Now we could get an occasional quarter pound of butter; four eggs a week; two chocolate bars a week and pressed tea which came in black cakes. By dint of some shrewd wangling, Sophiana usually had eggs for Moats, Jordan and myself. There was also Russian champagne and Russian beer which tasted a little like soaped ginger ale. When the Narzan, a fine bottled mineral water, ran out, we switched to champagne. It cost four dollars a quart but we were all afraid of the tap water, although Norman had tested it and found it pure.

We had to make our own social life. Charlie Dickerson had arrived from Kazan, and his poker was all that the others had predicted. When we weren't playing at the American Embassy, Jordan and I were at the British Embassy with the Guinea Pigs. Colonel Robert Guiness, only thirty-six, headed a British Military Commission of four men and these four inseparables were soon termed the Guinea Pigs. They had a large room at the British Embassy, had engaged a cook and ran their own mess all in the one room. Of course, they slept there too. On the door of the room, which was called "The Hutch," was a large sign proclaiming, "The animals

167

may not be fed but may freely be offered liquor." Colonel Hill, who was the Number Two man of the outfit, was a remarkable person. He had been a spy in the last war. In fact his book, *Spy Out the Land* is perhaps the only authentic book on spying ever written. Hill had organized Trotsky's air force in the early 1920's. He was bilingual and Russians often thought him one of their own. He had all sorts of decorations from both the British and Russian governments. He had been wounded several times, but no trace of his incredibly hard and dangerous life showed on him. He was a plump, affable, smiling, middle-aged man, and it was hard to imagine him blowing up a bridge or laying a minefield. But he had done both of those things not once but many times.

One night, Jordan and I had dinner with the Guinea Pigs. Somehow or other Hill could always get caviar when there was none to be had. Jordan and I gorged ourselves on it. We were so sick of vodka that we had become practically teetotalers. As a steady diet, vodka leaves much to be desired. At its best it is only about half as strong as whisky. Vodka is a fraud. It tastes fiery and at first this gives it a slight distinction, but actually vodka is one of the weakest of alcoholic drinks. Members of the Red Air Force always carried vodka with them; the fighter pilots often took a generous drink before going up to fight because it had a warming effect. Colonel Hill had been doing research, trying to make vodka palatable, and he had come across a Russian equivalent of cherry brandy. It was heavy and sweet. On this night, he unveiled his creation—a cocktail composed of half vodka and half cherry brandy.

"You are a very fine character, Colonel," Jordan said gravely, approving the drink.

Hill had also gotten three or four kinds of cold meat and we dined well and happily, helped by Russian champagne.

168

The Guinea Pigs, who worked much closer with the Russian Army than did most of the military missions, had a Red Army captain to dinner that night. An old friend of Hill and Guiness, he really opened up. His views on the position of Moscow coincided with those of Colonel Faymonville, who still said stubbornly, "They'll never take Moscow." Everyone else in Kuibyshev looked for its momentary collapse.

The Russian Captain told us why we had been forced to leave on October 15th, and when he finished, we mentally apologized to Molotov for what, until then, we had thought to be his unfounded anxiety to get us out of Moscow.

"The Nazis had taken Mozhaisk," he said. "They had broken through and there was nothing between them and Moscow but a clear, undefended road. We got that news the morning of October 15th and honestly expected that they'd be in Moscow by nightfall. For some reason or other, the Hun suspected a trap. He thought we were trying to do what we had done in the South: let him rush ahead at one sector only to close our ranks behind him and cut him off. So he hesitated. He had his advance motor-cyclists there and his light tanks and, had he pushed on, nothing would have stopped him. But he delayed a day, and, by then, we had reinforcements up there. It snowed heavily that night too, you'll remember, and that threw him off, too. Seems funny to think that the Hun could quite easily have captured Moscow the night of October 15th if he had followed his usual course of rushing ahead every time he broke through. Moscow would have fallen; maybe—who knows?—Russia would have followed, and think what that would have meant to Britain and America."

The Captain, a chunky, darkly handsome man of thirty-six, talked English slowly but perfectly. He wanted to know why America didn't attack Japan. Japan? I hadn't thought of Japan for months.

"We have no quarrel with Japan," I said airily. "Why should we attack them?"

"Because," he said, "if you don't, they will attack you. They hate you very much. Now they are obeying the will of Hitler, who hates you very much, too. It puzzles me that Americans are not more aware of the Japanese threat . . ."

"There's one man aware of it," I said, and then I told the Captain of a half hour's talk I had with the President in March, only seven months before. I had been home for a vacation and, to my delight, received a command to meet the President at the White House. Previously, I had only met him at press conferences. For years I had been a member of the Roosevelt-and-Garbo-Can-Do-No-Wrong Club. I worshipped Roosevelt and I'd walk a mile to see a Garbo picture. I had just arrived from England and naturally thought that the President would talk of London. He was alone, sitting behind a desk in the second-floor office at the White House. He knew that I was a friend of his son, Franklin, and Averell Harriman, and we talked of them for awhile, and then he switched the talk to Japan. I was so full of Britain and the courage of the people of London that the Japs to me were merely a race of funny little men on the other side of the world. For half an hour the President, lighting one cigarette after another and sticking them into his holder, talked about Japan. I couldn't get a word in edgewise about Britain.

"They hate us," he said emphatically. "They come to me and they hiss between their teeth and they say, 'Mr. President, we are your friends. Japan wants nothing but friendship with America,' and then they hiss through their teeth again, and I know they're lying. Oh, they hate us. And sooner or later they'll come after us. Oh, yes, indeed. We can beat them, mind you. I think," he smiled, "that even my enemies will admit that I do know something about our Navy. My love for our Navy is no secret. We have a fine navy and when the present construction plans get fully under way, it will be even finer. But the Japanese have a good navy, too. Yes, we will beat them, but we will have to catch them first. It will take us six or seven months to do that, and it will take most of our fleet out of the Atlantic. When that happens, it will mean that we won't be able properly to protect American goods going to Britain. And that worries me. Yes, that worries me."

As I left, he asked one question about Britain. "What does Britain need most that we aren't giving her?"

Just before leaving London, I had asked A. V. Alexander, First Lord of the Admiralty, that very same question. The forthright A.V. had cried out, "In God's name, Quentin, we need one hundred more destroyers. If anyone at home asks you what we need, tell them that. One hundred destroyers and," he added with a smile, "if you could spare a few cruisers . . ."

I repeated that to the President, and he smiled grimly. "I know. I wish we could let them have what they want."

I left the White House that afternoon more fervently entrenched than ever in my one-man Roosevelt-Can-Do-No-Wrong Club. But at the time, I was puzzled about his preoccupation with Japan. Japan didn't seem important to me. I was a member of the deluded A-Company-of-Marines-Could-Wipe-Them-Out group, complacent in my ignorance. Although the President had not said that his talk with me was "off the record," I did feel that his freedom of expression implied that it was. So until now I've never written the story of that interview. But now Japan's attack upon us does, I think, release me from even that implied "off-the-record" ban.

I told all this to the Russian Captain that night in Kuibyshev. He nodded in agreement with everything the President had said. But he had one correction to make.

"Forgive me, if I offend," he said. "I don't mean to be discourteous, but I think your President underrates the Japanese Navy. I am afraid that it is a better navy than yours. Japan's heavy battleships carry more and heavier guns than yours do. Japanese gunnery is better than that of the American Navy. We have ways of finding those things out. I hope your President is right, but I cannot see how your Navy can destroy Japan's in six or seven months. It will, I think, take some years for your Navy to reach the proportions to enable it to destroy the Japanese Navy."

"I think you're nuts," I said bluntly, with the confidence we Americans have always had in our Navy.

"You see," he said gently, "your Navy has never been at war, unless you count that little thing with Spain in 1900. But perhaps I am wrong. I hope so."

We got to talking about what would happen after the war. We all had plenty of theories. Only the Captain remained silent. Finally, when we had exhausted all of the possibilities, Jordan remembered to ask him what he thought should be done.

"After the war," the Captain said mildly, "you Americans should keep out of it for awhile. You British stay away for awhile. Let us be the Army of Occupation for just one month, and things will adjust themselves."

Jordan and I were delighted with the Russian Captain. It was the first time we had really come close to a Russian who was not a government official. He was absolutely out of line in talking frankly with us, but we enjoyed it. We both resolved to forget his name for fear some Party bigwigs or powerful NKVD figures might use his frankness and friendship to foreigners as a weapon against him.

The Captain was a fervent Communist, a member of the Party since he was twenty-one. This was rather rare. The Communist Party in Russia is by far the most exclusive club in the world, and it is exceedingly difficult to obtain membership in it. There are only a million members with a waiting list of three million. For the first time, we heard a Russian talk frankly about Communism. With the Captain, it was admittedly his religion, his body and soul, his existence.

"You laugh at our love for Communism," he said in his soft, deliberate voice. "You know we have lost nearly 2,000,000 men during the past four months. You know they fought bravely until they died. Why? They fought because they were part of a new world they had helped to create, a world we think is worth dying for. My friend Colonel Hill was here in Russia in the Czarist days. He will tell you that only 10 per cent of our citizens owned shoes then. He will tell you that only 1 per cent of our people was literate. Now education—classical, scientific or industrial—is open to all. You have seen the worst conditions as well as the best since you arrived here. You have even seen the wretched refugees arriving here on the Volga boats. But, wretched as they are, they are clothed and they wear shoes and they are being taken care of as well as possible. Remember our world has only lasted twenty-four years. Yours in America has lasted since 1776. Yet, forgive me again, I think we have made more relative progress in our twenty-four years than you have in your—what is it?—hundred and sixty-five years."

"We haven't had to chuck religion overboard," I suggested.

"We have not chucked religion overboard," he smiled. "We've chucked overboard the religious abuses we suffered

173

from. Our people are naturally religious. You never heard of kidnappings or murder or organized gangs or political grafters here in Russia, except in isolated cases."

"We let our minority shout their heads off," I said. "We don't slap them into jail as you do."

"We only slap enemies of the State into jail," he said, reprovingly. "Enemies of the State are enemies of the people. And speaking of minorities, do you think the way the Negro minority is treated in America would be tolerated by us? Your Negroes are American citizens—are they not?—with the responsibilities of citizens. But you do not give them the privilege of citizens. Here, all citizens are alike. Each has his responsibilities but each, too, has his privileges."

Jordan and I left, elated that we had finally been able to get behind the official veil that hid the real Russia from us. We walked home discussing the Captain and agreeing that he was the highest type of Soviet citizen: the man who had first been convinced intellectually and had then been convinced emotionally. His love for Communism and for his country were one and the same. He would die happily (and probably will, too) to help his country drive out the invader. We walked along the dimly lit street toward the hotel. A light snow was falling, but it was dry and soft and the warmth of "The Hutch" and the warmth of the vodka kept the cold out.

"His arguments are good," I said to Philip. "He and millions like him love this system, and why shouldn't they? We certainly have no right to criticize."

"I agree," Jordan said. "Both your country and mine are too vulnerable for us to criticize anyone."

"We are vulnerable, but at one in the morning with the temperature at zero, you wouldn't see a scene like that anywhere in America."

I pointed across the street. Through the whirling snowflakes, we could see a line of patient women waiting in front of a food store. All day and most of the night, we saw these lines. There were only a few shops in Kuibyshev and food was not abundant. The rape of the South by the Nazis had put a severe tax on Russia's ability to feed everyone properly.

"No, we wouldn't see that," I repeated. "But then we're not at war. We haven't had 2,000,000 of our citizens killed, so perhaps that line of women really is no answer to the Captain's arguments."

"We must come back after the war and really learn something about Russia," Jordan said, and I agreed. Jordan and I remembered that night as one of the most pleasant we spent in the Volga city. We didn't have many really pleasant days. We wouldn't have minded, had we been in action, getting stories worth writing. Here we had only the brief communiqués to base our articles on. And always the discomfort of minor physical ailments.

In addition to the usual complaint, I caught myself two enormous carbuncles, and the pain from them was agonizing. I had to wait until they grew to maturity before Dr. Norman could cut them open. I will never forget the walk from the Grand Hotel to the American Embassy, which was only four blocks away, the day he plied his knife. No cars were available and I had to walk. Jordan came with me. The snow was ankle-deep, covering a layer of treacherous ice.

A thin snow fell through the dusk and we huddled into our coats and wished that our caracul hats were less picturesque and more warm. Carts drawn by oxen lumbered through the street. A group of recruits, looking very young but warm in their fine woolen coats, went by, singing, "Moskva, Moskva." Finally we reached the Embassy. To get to Norman's office we had to walk through the kitchen. He was waiting with young Major Phillipson, the doctor attached to the British Embassy. I rolled up my trouser-leg, and Norman and Phillipson looked with interest at the egg on my knee. Lieutenant Olsen, one of Faymonville's assistants, was there, too. Ollie was a grand fellow. The nicest thing about him was the fact that he didn't smoke. He drew his cigarettes from the Embassy and gave them to me.

"The doctor is letting me give the anaesthetic," Olsen said proudly.

The anaesthetic consisted of a tube of ethyl chloride. Norman got out his little knife. I had an idea he was merely going to stick a needle into the thing as one does into a boil, and that would be all. Ollie squirted the ethyl chloride. It felt cold. Then Norman said to me, "Look the other way." There was a searing pain in my knee and I screamed.

"It hurts! It hurts!"

I'd never felt pain like it in my life.

"You wrote a book once, *The Wounded Don't Cry*," Norman said dryly. "Where did you ever get that silly title?"

I started to tell him that I would change the title immediately, but I fainted instead. I came to, with my head between my legs and with both doctors, Olsen and Jordan, properly sympathetic. Ambassador Steinhardt, apparently attracted by my yells, came into the office. His eyes lit up.

"Brandy, that's what you need. I've got a bottle." He went and got the bottle of brandy and I took a good belt out of it.

"Never saw a neater cut," Phillipson said admiringly to Norman. "And that fine pus—laudable pus, isn't it, doctor?"

"Very laudable," Norman said gravely, smearing the inch-and-a-half cut with ointment and bandaging it properly.

176

"Who called that stuff an anaesthetic?" I growled to Norman.

"It really isn't," Norman admitted. "It freezes the surface of the skin and makes it much easier for the doctor in cutting."

"That's fine," I told him. "Give me more next time. I just want you to be happy in your work."

Now he had to cut open the one under my arm. He and Phillipson looked at it happily. It was, they thought, much riper than the one on the knee.

"Wish we could give you a shot of morphine," Norman said apologetically. "But you can't stick needles in things like this—too much danger of infection."

"I had those things once," Steinhardt said ghoulishly. "They come in sevens. You have five to go."

"In case you die, chum," Jordan said cheerfully, "I'll write a swell obit. And, incidentally, before this next operation, how about shooting *Collier's* a cable recommending me for your job? You know, just in case."

"Maybe Major Phillipson had better squirt the ethyl chloride on this time," Olsen said, but there was a disappointed look in his eye.

"No, Ollie, you do it. I just want you to be happy, too. Don't worry about me, any of you. Now we have the army represented, we have two doctors, we have a newspaperman, and the Ambassador is a lawyer. All we need is a priest. Isn't there one around?"

"Shut up," Norman said. "Give it the gun, Ollie."

Ollie squirted the freezing stuff on the eggplant under my arm and then once more came that knife-like pain. Norman was swabbing the wound and muttering soothing noises, and Steinhardt was insisting again that carbuncles came in sevens and in the midst of it, I fainted again, but was careful to keep one arm stretched out. When I felt the bottle of brandy

177

in it, I came to. I had a drink. It was wonderful brandy. For weeks we had seen nothing but that tiresome vodka and an occasional whisky and water. The brandy was fine.

"You look pale, Philip, better have a slug." Jordan admitted that he couldn't stand the sight of blood, and he took a healthy drink.

"You better have one more yourself." He handed the bottle back to me. Out of the corner of my eye, I saw an anxious expression in Steinhardt's eyes. This was probably the only bottle of brandy in Kuibyshev. When Norman was finished with his bandaging, Philip and I left. The one Embassy car had gone off somewhere and we had to walk. It wasn't much fun hobbling through the icy streets and now Kuibyshev was blacked-out, which made it worse. The knee was still on fire. I kept close to the buildings, feeling my way along. Suddenly, I stepped into nothingness. I fell with a crash and the fire in the knee flared up. I had stepped into an open grating. I lay there in too much pain to get up. Finally Philip helped me and we resumed our slow walk.

"How much money have you in your pocket?" Jordan asked suddenly.

"I don't know, about 1,500 rubles," I said.

"That's about a hundred dollars," he mused. "I have about that much, too. Yet here we are in a lousy snowstorm knee-deep in mud and slush and we can't get a cab. If we had all the money in the world we couldn't get a cab. We'll get to the hotel freezing and wet and you feeling pretty sick and a hot drink would do us both good. But with more than two hundred dollars between us, we won't be able to get a hot drink. Norman told you to eat fresh vegetables and fruit for the next few days, if you could get them. So with two hundred dollars between us, we can't buy an orange. When we get back to that hotel, you're going to bed. You'll have to stay in bed for a few days, anyhow. That would be a pleasure for you in London. You'd send out for a dozen detective stories and enjoy yourself. With two hundred dollars in our pockets we can't buy a sixpenny thriller, because there aren't any here. This is a great life we lead."

"It's a hell of a way to earn a living," I admitted, inching forward another few steps.

"And yet a lot of suckers think that ours is a glamorous profession," Jordan said in disgust. "Fleet Street is filled with men who'd give anything to be in our shoes."

"They can have my shoes," I said. "Especially the left one. That's full of blood now."

"I suppose there are fools in America who envy you," Jordan said. "Men who can finish work in an office at five o'clock and then go home to a family and a decent meal. Men who can say to the wife, 'Sweetheart, get me a martini, very dry and very cold,' and then sit back and read stories written by fools like us. People like that, well-off, able to sleep in beds that have no bugs in them; able to use bathrooms that aren't half-full of Mongols; men who can actually have a hot bath or a shower any time they want. I've met them in New York and in London and they envy us, the poor damn fools."

We had reached the main street. Another hundred yards and we'd be in our hotel. Of course, the hotel wasn't heated and at least twice a night the electricity went off, but it would be good to get out of this stinging snow that had frozen into millions of small knives that hurled themselves at us.

"It's our own fault, too," Jordan went on. "It began with Webb Miller. When he wrote *I Found No Peace,* he started to glorify our profession. Then Walter Duranty helped with *I Write as I Please.* Jimmy Sheean and Negley Farson and the rest of us followed suit. Everyone who read our books thought of us drinking with ambassadors and living backstage all the time. Sure, it was ourselves who made this lousy profession glamorous. What is glamorous about us right now? We haven't bathed or shaved for a week. We're filthy and tired and surly-tempered and, to make it worse, neither of us has written a story in a month worth the writing. We can't, with this awful censorship. There's no use in us working hard here; we can't send anything out. It's a lousy life and let's face it."

We reached the Grand. The small hall (the word "lobby" would give it a dignity it didn't deserve) poorly lit, was filled with smoke, the odor of bad cooking and the aroma of the downstairs "bathroom." I climbed the stairs very wearily, leaning on Philip's arm. We had to go up two very long flights. I made the room. Just.

"I've got something to tell you, Philip," I said, when he had helped me off with my shoes and I had let myself down very gingerly on the bed.

"You know that second time I fainted?"

Jordan nodded.

"Well, I didn't really faint then. That was just a gag to get the Ambassador's brandy." I laughed and Philip laughed and then Philip said, "I got some more news for you. When no one was looking, I went to the bathroom and stole a roll of toilet paper."

We shrieked with helpless laughter and then my hands were cold and I put them into the pockets of my coat which I still wore. My fingers encountered something unexpected. Then I pulled out four packs of Chesterfields.

"Olsen slipped them in there," Jordan said. "Pretty good guy—Ollie. They're all pretty good guys. Let's get Chollerton and Moats and eat here. Chollerton has some sausage and some bread. I know Moats has a can of peaches. Cassidy has a bottle of Scotch. I'll get them."

Half an hour later we were sitting in my room eating sausage and bread. Moats had given me a couple of pills that had stopped my pain. Sophiana had come in and had produced a pound of cheese. We ate and washed it down with Scotch and vodka, and the room was filled with smoke from my precious cigarettes, and now Chollerton was stalking up and down, plucking at his red beard, telling us of the days when he knew Trotsky; telling us a hundred stories, and who cared whether they were true or not? Little Mother Moats hovered over all, and when there was a lull she and Cassidy went to work beautifully on Lozovsky, on Pulgonov, on all censors and the mothers of censors and the families of censors.

I caught Jordan's eye. "How about those guys who get that 5:15 every night and who have to go home and be nice to some dame who has probably been out all afternoon with the iceman? How about them with their badly made martinis and having to get up early in the morning and be tied to a desk for eight hours? How about them?"

Jordan laughed. "The hell with them, chum. They can have it. This isn't such a bad racket after all."

15

Men at Work

THERE HAD BEEN a great deal of talk in Moscow and later in Kuibyshev about how Russian factories had been shifted from the front-line towns to the hinterland. Each time some Southern industrial city had fallen, Lozovsky had deprecated the importance of its loss by telling us that the production plants had been moved before the Germans had taken the town. We had seen no evidence of the fact in Moscow itself and since we were not allowed at that time to leave the city, we did not use the shifting of factories in our stories. By nature we are suspicious of "handouts." In justice to Lozovsky, I might say that we never received a "handout" which afterward proved to be untruthful. But our job was not to slap prepared statements on the cable; it was to write authenticated stories which we knew to be true. Lozovsky, at a press conference in Kuibyshev, said that he would arrange for us to see some factories which had actually been transplanted from cities now in German hands or threatened with capture. We were anxious to be shown. Some of these factories were right here in Kuibyshev.

There was a time when the Volga Valley was a lazy place with the song of boatmen towing barges echoing in the gentle hills beyond the Valley. It was different now. Today a song of industry was being sung on the banks of the old river. Just outside of the city there was an aviation parts factory. It had been evacuated from Kiev when that far-off place was threatened with capture. Bomb-rack instruments and mountings for airplane machine guns were being made there, and it was obvious that most of the machinery was in fresh mountings. It had certainly been moved from somewhere, and "Kiev" was stamped on many of the drills and presses. Due to the fact that these were precision instruments which were being made, only skilled labor experienced in the delicate working of the rather fragile machines could be employed. I asked the foreman in charge how he had trained Kuibyshev workers to this rather complicated task.

"When the machinery arrived from Kiev," he said, "600 skilled workers arrived with it. I was one of them. We worked eleven hours a day modernizing the factory and training local men and women to handle the machines. We drew a great many bright youngsters from the State Labor Reserve schools and they learned quickly. Within a month we had changed this eighteenth-century factory into a modern plant. You'll notice the concrete floors; they had been dirt floors. Notice the steel-girded ceilings. The brick walls are new, too. After a month of hard work the plant was ready to operate. Many of the workers who came with us returned to Kiev or to Moscow, but a great many of us remained behind."

I walked around the plant trailed by the inevitable and useful Sophiana.

"How much do these men make?" I asked Sophiana.

She turned to a good-looking young giant who was running a lathe. He seemed very willing to talk, and they jabbered away in Russian for five minutes. They laughed and seemed to be getting along fine.

"You're a married woman with two children," I growled

183

at her. "Stop flirting with this man. What has he been say-ing?"

"He makes one thousand rubles a month," she said. "That is twice what he made in peace time. He's very happy living here in Kuibyshev, and he likes the local ballet company very much. He also wants to know why Britain doesn't form a second front in France to worry the Germans, and he wants to know why America isn't in the war."

"Tell him I don't know the answers to those two myself."

About ten miles upstream, we found another factory. Six months earlier this one had been operating in Leningrad. Now it turned out 1,500 carburetors a day. It made carburetors for army trucks, for airplanes and for tanks. Somehow I'd never thought of a tank needing anything so puny as a carburetor. Before the Nazi air force had disrupted rail transportation around Leningrad this factory had been evacuated more than 1,500 miles to the Volga Valley. Four thousand men and women worked here nine hours or more each day. Anyone working more than nine hours received overtime pay.

"However," the director of the factory said, smiling, "our men don't count the hours. Our friends at the front don't fight by the clock, do they?"

It was rather incredible to think that these masses of machinery had traveled all the way from Leningrad. However, on our trip from Moscow to Kuibyshev we had seen dozens of trains, long lines of flat cars, loaded with machinery such as this all coming away from the front. There are very few concrete roads in Russia. Virtually all transportation is by rail. In rural districts the roads are only passable in the summer months. But transportation by rail was excellent; that is, if the train had military priority, and machine tools going away from the front had the same urgent priority as did ammunition and guns going toward the front.

Visits to these factories made me want to investigate the industrial and production problems a bit more thoroughly. I couldn't do it first-hand because we were not allowed to stray very far from Kuibyshev. The chief reason for this was lack of transportation. I couldn't go to the Urals because at the moment there was no way to get there. But I met a few factory heads and a few government representatives who supplied me with production figures. It was no secret that the Russian Army had left vast stores of guns, tanks and ammunition behind when it had retreated from the South during the bad summer months. Yet the retreat had not become a rout. Fresh equipment had come from somewhere. But where? I found that Soviet production had more than kept pace with Soviet losses. During the past eight months coal mines and steel factories had actually doubled their output. The huge Bakal mine had produced twice as much iron ore in October as it had in August. The Magnitorgorsk Mine, the largest in the Soviet Union, was working at red-hot speed and the coal mines of Kuznetsk, Kizel and Karaganda were producing 50 per cent more than they did before the Nazi invasion.

The entire Urals had become a vast arsenal supplying the factories, the farms and the front. Eighty-seven per cent of the lead, most of the zinc and nickel and 96 per cent of the copper produced by the Soviet Union came from the Urals. Huge aluminum, sulphur and magnesium industries had sprung up in this tremendous arsenal. The Soviet East also produced vast amounts of oil with new fields in the Bashkiria, Kazakstan, Molotov, Sverdlovsk and Kuibyshev regions leading production. The people, government and men back of the front realized that only super-production could balance the losses of the past and the possible losses in the future. The workers in mine and factory have a standing in the political and social life of the Soviet Union, difficult for British or Americans to understand. Workers in Russia cognizant of their responsibility in the war effort, took this responsibility solemnly. The front must be fed with finished products of their work. Wherever I went I saw nothing but a firm determination to fulfill this responsibility.

Arch Steele of the *Chicago Daily News* had heard of a huge factory some fifty miles away in the steppes and he thought we might persuade Lozovsky to fix a trip there for us. I had been fighting with Lozovsky so much lately that I doubted if he would arrange anything but a hanging for me, but Arch went to work on him and, to my surprise, the trip was arranged.

Steele could usually arrange things the rest of us found difficult or impossible to arrange. He had been considered the Number One man in the Far East, and now that he had been transferred to Russia, he already ranked with men like clever Henry Cassidy of the Associated Press and Shapiro of the UP as our stars. Steele was a terrifically hard worker. He would work a week if need be to verify one small item. It was typical of the *Chicago Daily News* to have an exceptional correspondent in Russia. In our craft, the *Chicago Daily News* is considered the best newspaper in the world. Naturally, working abroad, we never see the paper, but we see its representatives. We saw the inimitable Bob Casey in France, whose fat fingers had the lightest touch on a typewriter I ever saw. Casey was so far ahead of the rest of us not only in reportorial ability but in sheer writing that, instead of being jealous of him, we were merely proud that he was a member of our profession. In London, Bill Stoneman of the *Chicago News* had long been considered our top man with his assistant, Helen Kirkpatrick, not far behind him. Last summer we elected Stoneman president of our Association of American Correspondents. Despite two intensive weeks of bitter campaigning, during which time he buttonholed each one of us pleading for us to vote against him, when the election came, he could only muster one negative vote—his own. The vote was forty to one, and Stoneman henceforth had to represent us when we had complaints to make to the Ministry of Information or any other Ministry. I don't own any stock in the *Chicago Daily News;* never met any of the editors; never even saw the *News'* building and never met Colonel Knox, but the foreign staff that newspaper has gotten together is the crowning glory of the newspaper world.

Steele and I were put under the charge of a Russian Colonel. He ushered us into a car early one morning and off we went. It was a long trip. The country outside of Kuibyshev was dreary, and two days of warm rain had melted the snow and made the roads sticky mud tracks. A few miles outside of Kuibyshev we passed one of the big concentration camps reserved for political prisoners. Beyond that we saw a long line of them working on a new road. There were about 800 of them. They were swinging pickaxes and wielding shovels and, on their faces, there was no sign of hope. A few soldiers with rifles guarded them carelessly, for there was no place for them to run. Steele and I looked at each other and winced. Of course it wasn't as bad as the convict labor I'd seen in our own South, because these prisoners weren't shackled and they didn't wear stripes. We winced, I think, because these 800 prisoners were all women.

The steppes are definitely not Nature's masterpiece. They roll lazily, their good black earth turned upward toward the sun which neglects them for such long periods. For thirty miles we crawled along, slipping over the greasy road without meeting a single car or person. We were in the Russian equivalent of a Buick. Russia bought the plans of the 1936

Buick and modeled this car after it. They picked a great automobile to copy and did a good production job on it. This car took as much of a beating that muddy day as any American car could and yet it never let us down. Sometimes Steele and I held our breath as we slid down a muddy bank to cross a swiftly running stream, and then without trouble climbed up the other side. The 1936 Buick was the best car I ever drove, and its Russian twin seemed just as good.

Our first sign of life was an enormous airfield. Its runways stretched to the horizons. At least forty Russian fighters were either in the air, taking off or landing.

"Training field," our conducting Colonel said briefly. "We have them scattered all over this part of the country."

Another hour of driving brought us to an amazing industrial city hidden in the steppes. The Colonel said that so far it hadn't been bombed by the Nazis, and the authorities felt that the reason was that as yet its location was not known to them. So would we please refrain from mentioning the city by name. I hereby refrain.

The city was devoted entirely to war production. We looked in envy at the paved streets and the clean houses and wished that this place instead of Kuibyshev had been made the war capital. The population was 125,000, every one of whom was connected in some way with the production of guns, ammunition or other war equipment. Smoke poured briskly from a dozen tall chimneys. We drove through the city and came to a large wall. This was the factory we were to visit. The director of the factory, a young, good-looking Russian with the formidable name of Sergei Alexeivitch Chekotikhin was waiting for us. He explained that his factory finished shell cases, made TNT and other explosives, filled the shells, crated them, and sent them to the front. He had ten thousand men and women working under him. As we walked around the huge plant, about one mile square, Chekotikhin explained things to us. He talked about chemicals, machines and men. He was very proud of his workers and he wanted us to meet Peter Kashin, the pride of the factory. We went into a long low shed and there was Peter.

Peter Kashin looked like a more robust Jimmy Cagney. He picked up the 100-pound shell which came hurtling down the long bench on a cradle which had steel wheels. He deftly poured what seemed to be corn meal into the empty shell and then slipped it into a machine which packed the innocent-looking corn meal down tightly. He swung the shell onto another cradle and sent it spinning down the long bench where women polished the shell and then painted it. Kashin did this little job ten hours a day, six days a week. In this enormous shell factory Kashin was a hero. He had been decorated for his work and daily he did 100 per cent more work than he was required to do. Kashin was a Stakhanovite. In Russian factories, each worker is given a quota norm. This is determined by the production quota assigned to each factory and wages are paid on the basis of that norm. An ordinary worker receives about 600 rubles a month for doing his assigned job. A Stakhanovite like Kashin, who either saves man power by running several machines himself or who by his ingenuity increases his capacity for production, makes a great deal more. Kashin earned 1400 rubles a month. In addition he was a hero to his fellow workers.

This factory which made TNT and other explosives which are packed in shells and bombs, was almost a thousand miles from Moscow. Shells and trench mortars were shipped out of the city each night bound for the front. Our explosives factory which made such innocent-looking but hardly digestible corn meal was typical of the war production factories I saw in Soviet Russia.

We got Chekotikhin talking about himself. He was the son of a factory worker. At Military Engineering Academy he specialized in chemical engineering. He was decorated with the Order of Labor, as highly thought of in Russia as the D.F.C. in England, for some inventions of military value. He went to the factory two years ago as engineer. Today, at thirty-one, he was in complete charge of the big plant. "Doesn't this remind you of the du Pont plant in Wilmington?" he asked me as we toured the factory. I told him I'd never seen the du Pont factory.

He looked shocked. "Imagine having lived in America and not having visited that factory!" he said. "It's the first thing I'd want to see if I went to America. Several of our engineers have worked there, and before the war we sometimes had visitors from du Pont here. We use much the same methods in making explosives as they do."

An explosives factory is a smelly proposition, and to the layman both bewildering and alarming. The first process apparently is to cook the TNT in huge boilers. There were twenty of these in one building, all attended by women.

"Seven of these boilers came from Donbas," Chekotikhin said. "They are the result of our policy of transporting war production factories from front-line cities. We have shifted factories from Kiev, Smolensk, Odessa and other cities to the Volga region or further east. We move all important machinery and machine tools. These boilers were in action here three weeks after they were removed from Donbas."

One of the most amazing industrial feats in history is this rapid removal of essential machinery from threatened cities. Usually, when Germans enter a factory town, they find little left but brick walls and unimportant tools.

After the TNT is cooked, it resembles very muddy coffee. Then it is refined and put into powdered form. After that,

190

it is carried into the long, low sheds where thousands of shell cases made in neighboring sheds are waiting for it. The belt system is used, and the shells move rapidly down the line, with deft hands contributing something to what would eventually be the finished job. The last step is crating them. They put two hundred-pounders in one gray-painted box. The belt moves the crates out of the building and directly into waiting freight cars. We watched the crates piling into cars. I counted the boxes as they passed on the belt. During one minute by my watch, sixty-two crates, each holding two shells, went by. That is war production.

"We keep that up twenty-four hours a day," Chekotikhin smiled, because he saw me watching my wrist watch, "and nearly every month they raise our quota. We haven't failed to fill our new quotas once. And if we could get more chrome nickel and toluol from you people we'd do even better."

I had lunch in the workers' dining room. It was the best meal I had since leaving Moscow. In addition to *schi* (cabbage soup) with a piece of boiled beef, there was steak, fresh tomatoes, beans, fried potatoes, pastry and coffee.

"You do pretty well," I said to Chekotikhin.

"We have our own farms, our own dairies and our own livestock," he said. "These are some distance outside the city and the products are brought directly to our six restaurants. We have a rather good commissary too, where we buy our clothes. I think we are a little better taken care of than workers in your factories."

Chekotikhin was obviously a very fervent member of the Party. He was anxious to know about working conditions in America. When Steele and I painted perhaps an overbright picture, he looked courteously dubious.

"But you are always having strikes," he pondered. "Why? We never have strikes. But then we don't have one man at

191

the head of a business whose only interest is to make as much profit for himself and his stockholders as possible. So we have no need of strikes. I am in complete charge of this factory. I wonder," he smiled, "if there is anyone of my age in charge of a factory as large and as important as this in America."

I doubted if the head of du Pont or General Motors or Ford or General Electric was a thirty-one-year-old man who had earned his job by sheer ability and had worked from the bottom up. But as to that I couldn't enlighten him.

"Your unions are always squabbling among themselves." He shook his head in wonderment. "Why, I wonder. Our unions are in complete accord. But our unions are State unions, interested only in developing the best working conditions possible, in so far as they are compatible with our main object —which is to increase production. We don't have such things as seasonal employment as you do in your automobile industry. You have thousands of men thrown out of work for several months of every year. The State wouldn't allow that primitive sort of thing to happen. I get your American papers occasionally. I am horrified when I read of big companies hiring armed thugs to intimidate the workers and occasionally murder them. That has happened in Detroit, has it not, and in Pennsylvania and in Kentucky?"

I had to admit sadly that it happened frequently in America.

"I wonder why you people are so afraid of Communism," this strangely enlightened man in the interior of Russia said, thoughtfully. "It is a red flag in front of a bull to you. Yet there are only a handful of Communists in America. Who stirs up the people so that they think all Communists have long black beards and carry bombs under their coats?" He laughed. "I have seen your newspaper cartoons. Well, were

192

I the owner of a big factory in America and interested only in profits, I, too, would be afraid of Communism. I would be afraid that my factory would end up being run like this factory is run—by the workers and for the workers who, in the long run, are the State. Then, too, your factories make money out of war production, don't they? That is something we can't understand. Maybe it's because we love our country and your business men love only their bank accounts."

Steele took up the cudgels on behalf of his own union, the American Newspaper Guild. He explained about severance pay and how anyone discharged could not be tossed out into the street without a cent. He explained about the *Chicago Daily News* insurance scheme for its employees and about social security. The good-looking young Russian listened politely and skeptically. He didn't want to offend us, but he obviously didn't believe these things at all. It couldn't happen in America.

Steele and I left on our long drive home, rather thoughtful. Neither of us had ever seen a better-run factory nor had we seen more cheerful or harder-working employees. It was one more glimpse behind the veil, one more bit in the huge jigsaw puzzle which is Communism. It was an attractive bit, too. We drove on through the steppes and approached Kuibyshev. It was seven o'clock now and quite dark. We slowed down as we saw a long file of people marching ahead of us. They were the women we had seen working on the roads that morning. Now they were on the way home, if the huge wooden barracks surrounded by walls could be called home. They trudged on wearily, led and followed by soldiers carrying guns. That was another bit of the jigsaw puzzle—not such an attractive bit.

16

I Hate Censors

THAT LONG WALK around the factory grounds had opened both of my cuts again. Norman bandaged them and tossed me into bed for a few days. The trouble with staying in bed all the time is that you wake up so early, and in Kuibyshev there was nothing to wake up for. In normal circumstances, it would have been pleasant. The maternal instincts of Moats had come strongly to the fore, and she made an excellent nurse, occasionally scrounging pilaf of rice, cigarettes or a bottle of something drinkable from His Excellency, the Iran Ambassador. Affable Saed himself visited me and so did General Anders, and I had lots of fun trying to follow their quick German. Steinhardt dropped in, a bit disappointed because my carbuncles had not as yet run to seven. The Guinea Pigs were in and out, bringing bits of sausage or bottles of vodka. We were a closely knit group, the fourteen correspondents and the half dozen diplomats and military men whom we liked. I often thought that we correspondents had a pretty good conception of Communism ourselves. If one of us got a pound of cheese, a pack of cigarettes, a bottle, he invariably divided it with everyone else. If someone managed to snare some rubles at the diplomatic rate (much better than the official rate of exchange) he would share them with us. We even shared typewriters, and sacrifices for one's fellows

194

can go no further than to share a fragile portable in a city where there are no typewriter ribbons or repair shops available.

I usually awoke at about eight, a ghastly hour anywhere, but more ghastly in my cold room in the Grand Hotel. There were no bells to push in our luxury quarters, so we had to yell for one of the ancient but good-natured crones who served as maids and who brought us tea in the morning. The tea came in tall glasses and was a dreary affair. It was weak, made from pressed blocks of tea, and we couldn't get milk to hide its flat taste. The coffee was impossible. It was made from acorns. In fact, when we bought a box of it at our food shop, the box was emblazoned proudly and honestly with the picture of an acorn.

One morning, I had ordered tea and was waiting for it when there was a knock on my door. Amazed at such formality, quite unknown among us, I yelled, "Come in." It was Oumansky. He lived just across the hall with three unidentified bearded men who looked as though they had been invented by Walt Disney. Who they were no one knew. We had heard well-substantiated rumors that Oumansky would not return to Washington as Ambassador. We had heard that Litvinov was to get the job, but had not been allowed to release the story. Oumansky and I talked awhile, and I wondered what had brought him to my room at the unholy hour of 8:30 A.M.

"You know, Reynolds," he finally said, smiling, "I had heard that you were a sociable sort of chap. A good host, I've heard, generous to your guests. And yet," he added sadly, "I have been here ten minutes and you have not yet asked me to have a drink."

"Please have a drink. There's a bottle of vodka and there's half a bottle of Scotch on the table."

195

He poured himself a generous slice of Scotch and added some Narzan water to it. "Aren't you going to join me?" he asked.

I shuddered. The thought of a drink before breakfast was something that I couldn't face.

"I'm waiting for some tea," I said. "You go ahead. I'm not used to having a drink in the morning."

"I like whisky," Oumansky said gently. "And if you like whisky, you like it at eight in the morning as well as eight in the evening."

"Not me," I said, looking at him in fascination as he sipped the drink. Happily, my tea came and Oumansky sat down and we went on talking.

"I hear Litvinov is going to Washington in your place," I said bluntly.

He nodded. "Yes, and what a splendid appointment it is! He and I are very old friends and I can think of no one better equipped for the Washington post. By the way, the BBC announced the appointment this morning over the seven o'clock news."

"And you ask why we hate your censorship?" I said bitterly. "All of us heard the report of Litvinov's appointment. We were not allowed to send it even as a rumor. Now we hear a Kuibyshev story on the BBC. How will Fleet Street and New York like paying men to be here on the spot and then, when the first decent story out of Kuibyshev in weeks breaks here, we are beaten by a radio announcer 3,000 miles from Kuibyshev?"

"Well, you see, Tass announced it and the BBC and the American radio picked it up from Tass." Tass is the official Soviet radio.

"Our editors will, of course, be satisfied with that explanation," I said, sarcastically. "You people do everything you

196

can to make enemies of us. We only want a decent break on news stories and a chance to see something so we can write features. But we can't even get that."

"It will be different perhaps," Oumansky said, pouring another drink. "My new post is one I like very much. I am to be in charge of Tass."

"In charge of Tass!" I yelled. "That means it'll be worse than ever. You who know propaganda better than anyone in Russia, you who know what America and Britain want to hear will make Tass and the radio the real news source from Russia, and we'll be left out of things even worse than we are now."

"Come, now," Oumansky smiled. "It won't be that bad. You know I did my best to get you that interview with Stalin. If we hadn't been forced to leave Moscow, I know it would have been arranged. It didn't come off through no fault of ours. Perhaps when the pressure on Moscow is less we can all go back and then I am sure we can arrange something."

The breaking of the Litvinov story by BBC and the American radio was the last straw. All of us felt utterly defeated. Then came one more incident which made me realize sadly that I wasn't earning my keep in Russia. I wrote a feature story about the city of Kuibyshev. There was not a word in it harmful to Soviet home security, not a word that would give information to the enemy. There was not even a word of criticism in it. It was nothing but an innocuous story about this colorful city which had suddenly sprung from obscurity into world-wide prominence. I handed it to Pulgonov and muttered, "Here's one you won't be able to cut." To my horrified amazement I was wrong. My story had run twenty-five hundred words. Twenty-one hundred of them had been crossed out by Pulgonov's blue pencil. He had no reason, as far as I could see, for the deletion of one word of this harmless story. I went screaming to Lozovsky and showed him the copy.

"People are not interested in what you eat and drink," he said. "They are not interested in the Kuibyshev ballet or the marionette show you write about. You write of Molotov walking the streets unrecognized; of Vyshinsky and Oumansky living in your hotel. None of this is important."

"Of course it isn't important," I told him. "But the world is curious about this city. The people want to know what it is like. I tell them in this story. It's a human-interest story. In the absence of any important story it is all right."

"Save such stories for after the war," he smiled. "Important things are happening. Write of them. Write about the daily communiqué and comment on it."

"That's all dead by the time it gets to London or New York. Already Tass has given it out. We get the communiqué at noon here. Do you know we hear that same communiqué on the BBC at nine in the morning? We are obliged to write features like this story of mine. And how does it harm Russia? There is nothing but praise in it for the Red Army and the Red Air Force and for the way Moscow is fighting back."

Throwing words at Lozovsky was like throwing punches at a pillow. Nothing ruffled his urbane suaveness. I couldn't get anywhere with him.

"I give up," I told him. "I'm licked. You've beaten me. I'm leaving as soon as I can get out. I can't earn a living here. None of us can. We're taking money from our papers and magazines under false pretenses. Will you fix my exit visa as soon as you can?"

He was really distressed. "But how can you leave?" he wailed. "We want you all to stay. We know you are friends of Russia and we need friends."

"I'll leave admiring and respecting Russia a great deal

more than when I arrived. I love the Russian people and can't write enough about the heroic Red Air Force and Navy. But I hate your censorship. I just can't work under it. None of us can. To prove that my only hard feelings are against your censorship and not against your country I'll finish that Moscow picture if you'll find Eisenstein and get us together on it again."

We talked of little else but the censorship those days. Now that we are in the war we'll have censorship in America, and if the one taste of American censorship we had in Britain last summer is any criterion, it promises to be pretty bad. That was the time when American Marines went to Iceland to relieve the British troops. The story had been printed, but we wanted to get to Iceland to write the story of the Marines who replaced them. The Ministry of Information thought it a fine idea. We got great co-operation, too, from the Air Ministry. They would send us in a Catalina. The first batch (quite properly the three news association representatives) were to leave immediately, and the rest of us would follow when additional Catalinas were available. The three correspondents, Ned Russell of the UP, Red Mueller of INS and Tom Yarborough of AP, packed and hopped a train to Scotland. They expected to be in Iceland within twenty-four hours. However, before their train trip was finished, they had been hauled off it by messages from the Ministry of Information that the Iceland junket was off. They returned to London in a furious state. Why had they been recalled? The Ministry of Information would give no reason. Neither would the Air Ministry. Then we found that the American Embassy, acting on orders from Washington, had caused the trip to be canceled. To this day we don't know why it was canceled. Some weeks later a group of New York reporters were allowed to visit Iceland, but by then the story had faded. If that is an example of the bureaucracy we are to expect from American censorship, we should all feel right at home after our Russian experience.

During the first year of the war nothing was so absurd as the British censorship. It was stupid, infuriating and without any basis. Let me recount just a few of the cuts made by British censors in those days.

Craig Thompson, of the *New York Times'* London bureau, is an enterprising reporter. About a year ago he unearthed what he thought to be a good story. He found that the Army and RAF doctors were treating open wounds with sulfathiozole and that the overworked miracle drug had come through nicely once more. He saw several doctors and verified the fact that the treatment was amazingly successful. The doctors seemed surprised at Thompson's interest. Everyone knew about it, the doctors said. It was, nevertheless, a nice story and Craig used it.

In London, of course, all stories go through the censors attached to the Ministry of Information. The censor looked at the story Thompson handed in, glared angrily, and flatly refused to send it in. Craig wanted to know why.

"Don't try to fool me," the censor said. "I know perfectly well that sulfathiozole is a code word."

Thompson, who had never tried to "bootleg" a story through the censor, counted ten and then spent a half hour convincing the censor that there was actually a drug called sulfathiozole. The censor had never heard of it.

If the incident were an isolated one, it would not be worthy of comment. Unfortunately, things like that did happen in London every day and account to a great degree for the graying hair of the American correspondents who have been stationed in England's capital these past two years.

In London, when a censor cuts something out of a story

with a short "Home Security Reasons," we almost invariably agree with him. The services have issued several "bans," most of which are quite reasonable. Duff Cooper, former Minister of Information, once said in a press conference, "We cannot let you say anything which will endanger the lives of British citizens or the continuance of war production."

Correspondents enthusiastically endorsed Mr. Cooper's statement, and this harangue is not directed toward any reasonable rules which make for home security. It is directed toward the petty, absurd, tyrannical censorship that was for so long imposed upon American and Dominion correspondents by the three war services, all of which superseded the Ministry of Information as final arbiters of what might or might not be said. The three war services (Army, Navy and RAF) still labored under the happy delusion that they had been fighting the war and that therefore they should be allowed to run it.

They forget that this, for once, was truly a people's war. The battle of Britain was won by 250,000 civilian fire fighters, the thousands of civilian air wardens, ambulance drivers and canteen workers, and, if invasion comes, the home guard of nearly two million civilians is expected to play a big part in defense. London has twice been saved from complete destruction by the civilians—by the people's army. Yet, until recently, the three war services with typical pompous bureaucracy consistently refused to tell the people of England and the people of America just what was going on. We wanted to write only the truth, but the half-truths, the evasions, and the general refusal of the services to let us "See for ourselves," prevented first-class reporting. Things became so desperate in the spring of 1941 that the American correspondents seriously considered going on a one-day strike to show their indignation. In turn, Duff Cooper and Lord

Beaverbrook pleaded our cause, but the services still reigned supreme. Appeal to the Prime Minister was equally futile.

In wartime, censorship is regrettably but absolutely necessary for home security reasons. A study of the mistakes made by the censors and the services in England and Russia during the past year might show those to whom American censorship is now entrusted a few pitfalls that might intelligently be avoided. Lest anyone think that this is the sour bleat of a reporter who is excusing the ineffectiveness of his own poor stories by making the censor a scapegoat, let me list a few incidents of the kind of censorship we used to be up against in England.

Last winter Lord Haw Haw on the German radio told, with great glee, how it was that the Nazi bomber pilots found it so easy to locate London. He told us something that everyone in London and Berlin knew—that the Thames pointed the way to London. You cannot black-out the Thames any more than you could black-out the Hudson or the Mississippi. Raymond Daniell of the *New York Times* wrote an article in which he referred to this, and told how the "silver stream of the Thames pointed out the way to London." He sent his story off and went to bed. Later the censor phoned him and told him sternly that he could not mention the Thames. "It would give the enemy important information." The very capable Mr. Daniell, one of the most respected journalists on either side of the Atlantic, argued at great length, but the censor was obdurate. Exasperated, Daniell, with a final, "I suppose if I said the Amazon instead of the Thames it would be all right," hung up. An hour later the cable editor of the *New York Times,* sitting in the New York office, was shocked to receive a story from Daniell in which there was a line, "the silver stream of the Amazon River pointed the way to London."

George Lait, of the International News Service, wrote a

nice innocuous story on Christmas Eve, 1940. In the "cablese" used by foreign correspondents to save cable tolls, he wrote, "Despite un-Christmasy weather, London tonight, etc." In those days German airplanes were overhead twenty-four hours a day, knowing just as much about the weather in London as did the traffic cop at Piccadilly Circus, yet the censor withered Lait with a look and said, coldly, "You are not allowed to give weather information to the enemy."

Lait trailed along when Wendell Willkie visited Manchester on his trip to Britain. Thousands stood outside of Willkie's hotel in almost freezing weather, waiting for him to appear. Lait, impressed by their patience and their desire to see Private Citizen Number One, wrote: "The crowd stood there for hours in the wintry blasts, etc." This was cut out by the censor. Lait, fed up with the absurdity of such nonsense, rewrote his message to read, "The crowd stood in front of the hotel for hours, slapping their arms against their sides to keep warm." The censor passed this, with the remark that, "It was not weather information."

Perhaps the most ludicrous censorship story we all chuckle over in Fleet Street was one in which the aforementioned George Lait again took part. Brilliant teamwork on the part of Lait and Tommy Watson, another International News Service reporter, resulted in a ten-minute beat for INS on the story of Rudolf Hess' arrival in Scotland. They merely told the meager information that Hess had landed in Scotland and gave the few details available. Canny Watson was on his way to Scotland before the papers with the story were on the streets in New York. He got a magnificent story and on it put the date line "Somewhere in Scotland." His first story went through in full. Later that day correspondents were notified that they could not mention Scotland in connection with the Hess case. By now, of course, Watson's story was in 600 newspapers in America. But one must play out the farce. Earl Reeves, then head of the International News Service Bureau, solemnly sent a cable to his New York office which read: "In Watson's story please delete the word 'Scotland' as mention of this word has become dangerous to the security of the British Isles." The censor beamed with pleasure, and quickly approved the message.

The nasty series of Plymouth blitzes gave the censors additional scope for their smothering tactics. Mary Welsh of *Life* magazine obtained a magnificent and tragically sympathetic picture of a large billboard in Plymouth which was merely headed "Deaths." Under this heading, in finely printed type, was a list of names of several hundred dead. These names on the magazine picture could not have been read (literally) with a magnifying glass. The censor refused to pass the picture. They didn't want the Germans to know who and how many were killed at Plymouth. That same day an American photographer got another beauty in Plymouth—a picture of a long line of people waiting for buses to take them out into the country to sleep. The London papers published similar pictures and were filled with stories of those who left tortured Plymouth each night. But the picture was never sent. For some obscure reason, which the photographer still doesn't understand, this picture was killed. Yet London papers, with similar pictures and stories, with estimates of casualties, went by air mail to Lisbon each day and arrived in Berlin eight hours later.

I could give 200 similar examples. Let me give two or three more and rest my case: During the Battle of Britain we all spent a lot of time at Dover watching the air battles. One day we saw a beautiful dogfight over the Channel between a squadron of Spitfires and a squadron of Messerschmidts. We saw seven German airplanes shot down and we saw three

British aircraft destroyed. The combat was so close that we could not be mistaken in our identification. Ben Robertson of *PM* sent his story, telling of the seven-to-three ratio in losses. It was, we all thought, a grand story and a fine tribute to the RAF. The censor thought otherwise. Ben could say that seven German airplanes had been shot down, but he couldn't mention the three British losses. Robertson is a tenacious young man. He refused to accept the censor's edict. He went to the censor's boss, and then to that man's boss and to his boss, and finally he got to the top—Duff Cooper. The story was eventually sent, but it took Robertson thirteen hours to have it released.

Robertson was also the victim of the oddest bit of censorship any of us has been subject to. A line of his was cut from a story because of "bad manners." Two girls, Diana Brand (niece of Lady Astor) and Lady Mary Rose Fitzroy, were doing a magnificent job of serving tea, sandwiches and chocolate to balloon-barrage stations in the East End of London during the heavy blitzes of last winter. Robertson went around with them one day. He noticed the friendly way the troops greeted the two women. One would call to Lady Mary Rose, "Hi, Blondy, 'ow about a bit of a dance tonight?" Another would yell to Diana, "Hey, Sparky, got anything on for tonight?" It was the good-natured sort of joking common to troops of every nation and the two girls accepted it as such. Robertson wrote the story, but the censor took out his big, blue pencil. He cut all of the facetious remarks out of it with the stern admonition, "Such remarks cast reflections on the manners of His Majesty's armed forces." Robertson was kept from tossing himself into the Thames only when we reminded him that Berlin censorship was probably even worse.

I have had as many futile arguments with the censorship during the past two years as any of my colleagues. However,

205

I will mention only one example, although, if urged, I could very happily oblige with a hundred. The British Broadcasting Corporation was even more moribund and more stupid in its censorship than were the censors of written copy. The BBC proposed a Sunday-night broadcast. I submitted a script containing a few slighting remarks about Germany. The BBC told me that these must be deleted. My astonishment turned to dull numbness when they gave their reason. "Many of our Sunday-night listeners are churchgoers," I was told. "It is all right to hate the Germans on week days but not on Sundays."

The next day, which was Sunday, Winston Churchill made his now famous broadcast in which, to the glee of all Britain, he referred to Hitler as that "guttersnipe." His entire broadcast breathed hatred. When I heard that magnificent example of vituperation, I went screaming to Brendan Bracken, then Parliamentary Secretary to the Prime Minister, and to Duff Cooper. I put my case before them. If the Prime Minister could hate Germans on a Sunday night, why couldn't I hate them as well? Bracken and Duff Cooper rolled up their sleeves and went into battle. The BBC recanted. I was allowed to hate the Germans as I had in my original script.

When Brendan Bracken succeeded Duff Cooper we expected things to be better—and they were. Duff Cooper was always in our corner battling for us, but he didn't get very far. The service heads were too steeped in the old traditions of red tape; the Whitehall warriors ruled supreme. Bracken was known to be closer to Winston Churchill than any man in Britain. When Bracken stormed into the War Office or the Admiralty or the Air Ministry he did it with the force of a Churchill, and the bigwigs, anxious not to incur the displeasure of the Prime Minister, handled Bracken with kid gloves. Our main trouble was always with the censor himself, the little civil servant, badly paid, who had been given a set

206

of rules and who would never allow himself to digress from them. Once we got to Bracken, or Sir Walter Monckton, his director general, we could argue our case, knowing that a reasonable case would get a reasonable response.

During the past few months I have had no quarrel with the British censors, and my colleagues in London have found things much easier. In the main, British censorship is very reasonable. Bracken, like Duff Cooper, says that only home security reasons should be the basis of censorship. If we want to criticize the Prime Minister or go to work on Ernest Bevin or Lord Woolton, that's all right. That comes under the head of "Comment." I did what I thought to be a vitriolic blast on British censorship several months ago. I quoted some twenty examples of stupid censorship. I was amazed to find that every line of it went through. In fact the censor who read it laughed at a few of the quips and said to me, chuckling, "You didn't half give it to us." So I added a line to my story. I wrote, "Although there is strict censorship in Britain there is also freedom of speech. As proof of that, this article has gone through the censor without a word having been cut out of it."

But of course the Russian censorship was so smothering that it made me entirely forget the petty quarrels I'd had with the British Ministry of Information. As I say, we do have freedom of speech in Britain. Even after twenty-four years of life, the Soviet Union, so smart in most things, has not as yet discovered freedom of speech. But the youngster is young and will soon learn from the older democracies. Give her a chance. Russia will work things out all right.

17

Poker in French

PHILIP JORDAN and Moats were resolved to leave Kuibyshev. Moats had done six articles for *Collier's* and only three of them had been passed by Lozovsky. The others had been cut badly. She would go to Singapore or Chungking and find something there to write about. You could drop clever Miss Moats into a potato patch in the County Donegal and she would find something to write about. It might not be important, but it would be cleverly done. Jordan cabled Gerald Barry, his London editor, for permission to pull out. Obviously Russia had become what we called a "news-agency story." That meant that ordinary communiqués and an occasional brief news item would cover whatever was happening. The agencies were adequately equipped for this kind of service, especially since they had men like Cassidy and Magidoff of the UP, and Shapiro and Meyer of the AP on the job.

The question now was how to get out of Russia. Archangel was freezing up; occasionally, freighters went from there to Britain, but it was apt to be a month's trip by Volga, rail and road to Archangel. Then came the happy news that Sir Walter Monckton was en route to Kuibyshev. Monckton was the Number Two man in the Ministry of Information. He was a great friend of Jordan's and mine. We were all excited about his visit; a new face in Kuibyshev would be welcome.

Then, too, perhaps he could do something with Vyshinsky and Lozovsky in the matter of easing censorship. His mission, we heard, was to "insure better co-operation between British and Russian sources of information." Our constant groans to London about the difficulties under which we were working had evidently been heard. Jordan and I decided to have a cocktail party for Walter. Of course, cocktail party wasn't quite the word for it, because cocktails were unknown in Kuibyshev, but it sounded rather nice. He was to arrive on a Monday. Tuesday was Guy Fawkes Day; we would hold it on the British holiday. Jordan decided we would be really protocol and issue invitations. He typed out:

PHILIP JORDAN AND QUENTIN REYNOLDS
INVITE YOU TO A COCKTAIL PARTY
IN HONOR OF
SIR WALTER MONCKTON AND THE LATE GUY FAWKES
HOTEL GRAND, KUIBYSHEV
(*Everything free*)

There was a little man named Jack running the hotel now. We had a long conference with him. We explained that Sir Walter was as important in England as Molotov or Vyshinsky were in Russia. We wanted to have the best food and drinks that Kuibyshev could provide. Jack and the chef fell into the spirit of the party. There was a large room off the dining room which we could have. He would get cold pork pies, ham, cheese, chicken salad, and then he said he might be able to spring a real surprise as the *pièce de résistance*.

"Fried potatoes," he said, proudly.

We looked our admiration. If Jack could do that the party would be a success. We hadn't had any potatoes since we arrived in Kuibyshev. Potatoes, like children, are things you never miss until you don't see them around. Sophiana haunted the food store, getting beer and cheese, five bottles of champagne one day, six the next, getting vodka—pink vodka, white vodka, any kind of vodka. Charlie Dickerson of the Embassy gave me a bottle of Scotch; John Russell of the British Embassy contributed another; Jordan grabbed a couple more, and good old Henry Cassidy, one of the grandest fellows in the world as well as one of the best correspondents, gave us two bottles of Scotch which he had been hoarding. Moats fluttered her eyelashes at Saed and bobbed up with a bottle of brandy. It was going to be a bacchanalian feast.

Sophiana, Jack and the chef worked all afternoon fixing the table. They did a beautiful job. They had five kinds of cold meat. They had three different pastries. Jordan and I looked at the table in ecstasy. It was just five o'clock—and then the lights went out. We stood in the darkness of the cold room, sick at heart. Whoever heard of a cocktail party being held in the dark? But Sophiana and Jack were equal to the occasion. They scurried about and soon had a dozen candles glowing. The soft light hid the bare ugliness of the room and made our long, heavily laden table look even more attractive.

Our guests arrived on time—about forty of them. Everyone we had invited came, except Sir Stafford Cripps.

Monckton was a great friend of Cripps'. In fact, we had a shrewd suspicion that Walter had come to suggest to Cripps that his time was coming soon. People in England were getting fed up with defeats. Churchill's personal popularity had not waned, but people were sick of his dreary Cabinet. Sooner or later lightning might strike, and Monckton wanted Cripps to be where it might hit him. The friendship between the two men dated back to the time when they were two of Britain's greatest lawyers. The convivial, affable, friendly Monckton seemed to have little in common with the austere reserved Ambassador, but the two thought a lot of each other.

Cripps, for some obscure reason, hated Beaverbrook. In Moscow he had seen me constantly with Beaverbrook, and he transferred his dislike to me. I couldn't quite see the logic of it, but that didn't bother me. After all, Sir Stafford was not only a teetotaler but an ardent vegetarian. One must humor such people. Cripps, a fine man who in law practice was accustomed to giving half his time and income to the defense of those unable to hire legal talent, was a strange man. He had a great love for humanity as a whole but, like so many men of that type, he didn't care much for humanity individually. He was a lone figure even in his own Embassy—respected, but hardly liked. Cripps thinks that he will one day be Prime Minister of England. Cripps' fierce integrity and faithful adherence to the cause of labor are two factors in his favor. But I doubt if England will ever select a Prime Minister who neither drinks nor eats. Those are two defects in character that the people of Britain cannot tolerate. But I may well be wrong about Cripps.

A half dozen other ambassadors made up for the absence of Cripps. We had our magnificent General Anders and the Guinea Pigs and the rest of the British and American Embassy crowd as well as our own gang. Walter was obviously pleased, and the party was a huge success. Jordan and I fluttered about (I was fluttering on one leg) acting beautifully as hosts. Neither of us had ever done it before. Before the guests arrived I impressed upon Jordan the importance of getting rid of our vodka rather than the rare Scotch or champagne. It cost so much less. We both did our best. We kept stalking people whose glasses weren't full of vodka. We feared that if they found an empty glass in hand they'd switch to something more palatable and, of course, more expensive. Monckton was entranced with Chollerton, who would stand out in any gathering. Chollerton was here, there, everywhere, eating hugely, drinking magnificently, everybody's friend, loving everybody and knowing that everybody loved him.

"He's amazing," Monckton said admiringly to me. "Do you know what he just did? He poured a drink of Scotch while he was talking to me. He reached for a bottle of water that was on the table and filled his glass with it. He took a drink and said calmly, 'My, my, I made a mistake! That wasn't a bottle of water. Ah, well, we can't waste it. That wouldn't be fair to Philip or Quent.' It was vodka, and so help me, Quent, he calmly drank the whole thing—half whisky, half vodka. He's a wonderful man."

"He is indeed," I said solemnly. "We're trying to persuade him to get out of Russia for awhile. He's been here fifteen years. That's too long. And incidentally, Walter, I want to leave with you."

"I expected you would," he said dryly. "In fact, I was going to suggest it. I'm going directly to Cairo, and that's the place for you now."

"I want to get back to London," I said. "I don't care about Cairo."

"Take my word for it," he said, looking at me oddly. "You won't regret it. You'll be glad to be in Cairo."

I didn't know what he was talking about at the time but, knowing Monckton, the hint was enough. I told him that Moats and Jordan wanted to get out too and that he was our only hope.

"Litvinov is coming along," he said, "with his wife and secretary. Steinhardt is coming and bringing Professor Brown. Group Captain Hallowell from the Embassy is coming. I've only got Tony Greenwood with me so that leaves plenty of seats in the airplane. It's a big D C-3. You, Philip and Miss Moats are in. I'll make you and Miss Moats King's Messengers if I have to."

Everyone, including Philip and myself, voted the party the grandest ever held in Kuibyshev. Jordan and I were very pleased to have been such successful hosts. Then we got the bill. The party cost two hundred dollars. We didn't mind, but practical Sophiana filled the hotel with Russian invective. By clever argument and some brow-beating she managed to get twenty dollars knocked off. The same party, at the Savoy in London, with real cocktails instead of vodka, with really tasty food, would have cost us perhaps a hundred dollars. Russia is not an inexpensive place to live, even if you don't give cocktail parties. But Jordan and I wouldn't have minded if the bill had been twice what it was.

Monckton stayed for nearly three weeks. He had several conferences with Vyshinsky. Jordan and I would always ask him how he got along with the great man.

"He was very affable," Walter would say, "very pleasant."

He held conferences with Lozovsky. He went to them well primed by Jordan and myself about all our difficulties. When he emerged he would say, "Lozovsky was very affable, very pleasant. His French is excellent." Then we knew that Monckton was licked. He had run up against the same wall of polite evasiveness that we had met. We could not have had a better advocate than Walter, but the same old censorship remained unchanged. There would not be any additional or better "co-operation between British and Russian sources of information." It was such a pity, too. We were all anxious to go on operational trips as we had done in Britain, anxious to glorify the Red heroes at the front, anxious to get under the skin of those magnificent people, anxious to get behind the scenes so we could get the feel of the whole wonderful battle the Red

213

Army was putting up. But no. Not even Walter's persuasiveness could break down the distrust which Soviet officialdom felt for the American and British press.

Jordan received a shock in the form of a cable from Gerald Barry, editor of the *News Chronicle*. "Use your own judgment but am anxious for you to remain Kuibyshev." Unfortunately, Barry, in addition to being Philip's boss, was also his best friend. He could have ignored Editor Barry but not pal Barry. Reluctantly, he decided to remain. My office in New York was pleased enough when I cabled that Moats and I were leaving. They evidently realized that it was impossible to do my kind of work in Russia under existing conditions. Before I left, Oumansky came to see me.

"You feel pretty bitter towards my country, don't you," he said sadly, "being forced to leave like this?"

"Not at all," I told him emphatically. "I feel bitter towards your ridiculous censorship and refusal to trust us. Don't think I'm one of those half-wits who spends a couple of minutes here and then rushes out to write a book, *The Truth about Russia*. I like Russia a lot and I like the people a lot and I greatly admire the very little I've been allowed to see of the Russian war effort. But don't think I'm going to hurry to London to rap Russia. You know I haven't written anything but the truth about your country. I'll blast your censorship, but that isn't blasting Russia. I want to come back to this country. I want to learn something about it under less difficult conditions. Can I get a visa to return?"

"Of course you can," Oumansky smiled. "And when you come back perhaps you will be able to work as you like to work."

We shook hands on that. I can think of nothing more exciting than to spend enough time in Russia and really get to know the country and its people. You can't get to know Russia by daily visits to the Foreign Office, by having *Pravda* and *Izvestia* translated for you every day or by chatting with Oumansky or Molotov or Vyshinsky. But then you could never get to know America by living in Washington.

The boys had a dinner for us the night before we left, and Moats and I were properly sentimental. We meant it, too, because we had grown very fond of fellows like Cassidy and Steele and Magidoff and Chollerton and the others. The Embassy bunch was there, bringing their last offering of cigarettes. Norman was very depressed; his only decent customer was leaving. I hated to leave Kuibyshev, but there was nothing else to do.

It was impossible to learn much about the people of Russia during my brief visit. It wasn't, however, from lack of trying. All I had seen was a small section of a huge kaleidoscope, a vast picture which in its entirety was Communism. Too much was missing from my view for me to form any real idea of the whole picture. I had seen only small portions of the people's struggle and shared only a little of their hopes. I had seen enough hardship and poverty and sickness among the people. But I had also seen their love for and belief in their new world. When they walked, their feet were in the mud, and the cold winds numbed their bodies, but they looked upward, not downward. They knew that each five years would bring something that they now lacked. It had been like that since 1918. They knew that they had a long road to travel but were secure in their faith and were willing to keep on—not looking for easier walking every day or every year but always putting their faith in what another five years would do. And there is no doubt that at the end of each five years' plan the people of Russia do have something they lacked at the beginning of that half decade.

The world hasn't given Communism much of a chance to

work out its own destiny. I had gone to Russia with an open mind, hoping to penetrate the veil of prejudice and confusion that has hidden the essentials of practical Communism from the world. I left realizing that I had been permitted to peer behind that veil only occasionally; I left almost as ignorant of Communism as when I arrived. I comforted myself by the thought that no intelligent Russian could have gone to America for ten weeks and then left confident that he knew the answer to our type of democracy. You can't learn a whole new world, even a twenty-four-year-old world, in two and a half months.

We left Kuibyshev at 6 A.M. in the first real blizzard of the year. Our destination was Teheran, Iran, and a last-minute passenger was Saed, complete with luncheon baskets filled with food and drink for Moats. Sir Stafford Cripps came to see Walter off. He and his unhappy Airedale, Joe, shivered in the zero weather while we waited for weather reports. Charlie Dickerson and Charlie Thayer of our Embassy had come to see Litvinov and Steinhardt off.

"We should have hired a couple of stooges to see us off," I told Moats. "I'm afraid we're losing face rapidly."

"My God," Moats said, "it will be nice to fly back to the warm arms of Capitalism." Then she fell quietly asleep on a bench in the frigid waiting room. Finally the weather was all right and we walked the hundred yards to our airplane. The wind was cold and biting; the thermometer said zero. The snow flurries whirled all over the field, whining as they hit the big airplane, lifting it slightly, making it tug at its moorings anxiously. We had four additional passengers in black caps and black leather coats. The "Y.M.C.A." boys were with us to the last. Moats turned our baggage over to them, and she told them in Russian to take care of it. They smiled and bowed, happy to serve.

"At last we'll find a use for them," Moats said. She didn't like the "Y.M.C.A." boys.

And then we were off.

After we were out two hours I thought that it was time for Saed to give Moats something to eat and drink. I yelled to him in German, "Poor Moatsie didn't have any breakfast," and his honest, kindly face frowned in concern. He hurriedly opened his big box of food and took out hardboiled eggs, buttered rolls, cold chicken, a bottle of Madeira, and began to ply our Moats with these beautiful offerings.

"I get half, you rat," I told her. She deftly passed on eggs, chicken and the bottle of wine.

"You're a very fine character, Moats," I told her, happily munching on a leg of chicken. Madame Litvinov opened a huge box of caviar sandwiches, and I immediately turned my back on Moats and Saed. She passed them around. The airplane now began to look like a picnic ground in Central Park. If we only had ants to get into the mayonnaise we couldn't have told the difference.

This was Litvinov's first flight and, happily, it was a smooth one. There was something very likable about the newly appointed Ambassador to Washington. Most Russians seem Oriental. Litvinov was definitely European, and he looked as though he would be as much at home in London as Leningrad, Washington as Moscow.

Litvinov is an amazing man. Correspondents in London, Berlin, Paris and Geneva have always liked him. Big, jovial, affable, shrewd, he never told us anything that he didn't want to tell us, but he always did it nicely.

Back in 1939 when Litvinov was removed from his office as Commissar of Foreign Affairs we all thought that he was on his way to the salt mines. But he was still a member of the Congress. Everyone thought that his removal from office meant that he was in considerable personal disfavor. Subsequent events proved that political expediency had prompted Stalin to replace his old friend with Molotov. Soviet Russia knew that sooner or later she would have to fight Germany. But she wasn't ready. Litvinov was not the man to stall for time, not the man to placate fascist Germany. His record was too anti-fascist for that. Molotov could be the conciliator.

The Silent Man in the Kremlin said nothing. He never does. Molotov did the talking. Molotov greeted Von Ribbentrop when he visited Moscow. Litvinov was home playing chess and having the first vacation he has had in thirty years. Then the blow came. He was given the most difficult and most important diplomatic post in the world. He should do well in that post. There are people in America (I know there are in Britain) who still distrust and fear Soviet Russia. They still wonder if Stalin won't somehow negotiate a separate peace with Hitler. A short talk with Litvinov would overcome all their doubts. There isn't an ounce of appeasement in Litvinov's big, friendly body. He can be blunt and tough, if the occasion calls for it; he can be suave and diplomatic, if necessary.

I borrowed a detective story from Madame Litvinov and read it while eating her lovely caviar sandwiches all the way from Kuibyshev to Teheran. Every fifteen minutes she'd turn around and say, "Do you know who did it yet?"

I would yell over the sound of the motors, "No, and don't tell me."

I hurried through it, afraid that she couldn't resist letting me know that it had been the doctor after all. She sighed with relief when I finished. It is awfully hard for one detec-

218

tive-story fan to keep from telling another detective-story fan who did it.

We had flown out of the snow. The land below us was flat and uninteresting. We flew very low to duck the unwelcome attention of any German aircraft that might be in the vicinity. Late in the afternoon we landed at the Astrakhan airport to refuel. Even as we landed, the weather closed in on us and we knew that we were there for the night. The "Y.M.C.A." boys came in handy now. They found a phone; within half an hour six black automobiles showed up. We had twelve miles of driving before we reached the city, twelve miles of thick slush, with our cars weaving and bobbing all over the place. Once again they were the imitation 1936 Buicks and once more they didn't let us down. I made a mental note of thanks to Red Curtice, president of Buick, who was responsible for that 1936 wonder car.

Our party was received at the hotel as if we were royalty. One complete floor of the hotel had been hurriedly evacuated. Clean bedding had been put on the beds and we were surprised to find that there was steam heat in the hotel. We were even happier when waitresses came bearing tables and utensils. I, by dint of clever leg work in reaching this floor first, had a room to myself while the others doubled up. Moats too, had run up those stairs like a startled fawn and had grabbed a single room. There were only two of them. We had three Ambassadors and a British representative with the rank of Minister with us, but all had to double up except Moats and myself. We were very proud of ourselves. All of us had dinner in my room, except Litvinov, his wife and his secretary. Madame Litvinov wasn't well and all three of them were tired. We ate great quantities of cold meat and ham and drank many bottles of vodka. This being a diplomatic trip and Moats and I being extra baggage, so to speak, I suggested that the two Ambassadors, Steinhardt and Saed, share the expense of the dinner with Monckton. They protested feebly, but Moats and I were insistent upon being treated as guests. Besides, I had only a hundred rubles and Moats had less than fifty.

It was fun that night. Steinhardt began to talk of some of the cases he had watched Samuel Untermeyer try. Steinhardt had been a junior member of the Untermeyer firm. It was good to get away from politics and war and the Hotel Grand bathrooms and through Steinhardt's eloquence find ourselves in the Criminal Courts Building on Center Street, New York. Monckton, one of Britain's greatest lawyers, told of cases in which he had taken part. Saed, like a gentle Buddha, sat smiling at the head of the table, growing in stature almost before our eyes as we approached his country. Moats left for a few minutes and came back with some startling news.

"I turned down my bed," she gasped. "The sheets are new. The blankets are new. I turned the mattress over and what do you think I found?"

"The usual dozen or so," I said, with memories of Kuibyshev.

"I found not one bug," she said solemnly. "My goodness, it will be good to sleep alone for a change. Imagine not having to share your bed with a single bug."

I woke once during the night. The room was warm. I heard measured steps outside my door. The sound grew fainter and then returned. The "Y.M.C.A." boys were taking no chances. They were on guard all night. Litvinov, Saed, Monckton and Steinhardt were precious cargo which must be delivered unharmed. Their pacing through the halls of the National Hotel in Moscow had annoyed me in the beginning but now the sound was rather comforting.

We only got as far as Baku the next day. Once more when

220

we stopped to refuel we heard of bad weather ahead and our cautious pilots were taking no chances with their diplomatic live stock. Once more we waited for automobiles. Once more we had a long dreary trip into the city. It was about twenty-five miles, most of it past the ugly oil derricks. There were thousands of them. This was territory dearly coveted by Herr Hitler. The old-fashioned oil derricks pumped slowly and huge pipes ran from the fields toward the city. Baku is on the Caspian Sea and (if you like to travel, which I don't) an interesting place.

To us the most interesting feature was a modern hotel. The Intourist Hotel at Baku is probably the best in Russia. It is the kind of good commercial hotel one would find in Detroit or St. Louis. Moats and I ran ahead, as usual, to get the single rooms, but the floor which was reserved for us only had double rooms and there weren't enough to go around. So I doubled up with Professor Douglas Brown of Massachusetts Institute of Technology who had come to Moscow as an economic adviser to the Harriman mission and was returning with us. Doug Brown was not quite the bearded professorial type of the comic pages. He was young, keen and a hell of a poker player. How he applied the principles of Stuart Chase to the game as standardized by Hoyle I don't know; I do know he cheerfully drew to inside straights all the time and seldom missed.

There was a bathroom (a real bathroom) in each room, and it wasn't long before we were all steaming happily. By undressing quickly and keeping Brownie in conversation I hit the bathroom and the bathtub first. It was the first time I'd been in a bathtub since Moscow—about six weeks before. It was a gleaming white bathtub, and there was soap and I slipped down into the bath and didn't care whether school kept or not. There isn't anything in life better than a hot bath

221

when you're cold and filthy. In fact, there's nothing in life any better than a hot bath.

I got out to give Brownie a chance. Steinhardt burst into the room with a dazed expression on his face.

"Quent, suppose you were in New York tonight, where would you go to eat?" he asked excitedly.

"I'd go home, of course," I told him.

"What would you ask them to have for dinner?" he asked.

We had gone over this before. "I'd want a thick steak and fried onions and French fried potatoes for openers and from there on I wouldn't care," I told him.

"Well," he said, "don't drop dead, but I've been talking to the manager about dinner and I took the liberty of ordering for all of us. I ordered thick steaks and, so help me, they have them. I ordered French fried potatoes and onions and told him to take it away from there. How does that sound?"

"You're a very fine character," I told him.

"Of course, we're having caviar and vodka first," he added, "and they have a red burgundy we can have."

I dressed and hurried down the hall to tell Moats. I yelled through her door and told her to come out.

"I'm taking a bath," she yelled back.

"How will we know you when we see you again?" I said, and, thinking that wasn't a bad exit line, went down the hall to spread the gastronomic news to Monckton and Tony Greenwood, his assistant.

During dinner we were told that the visit of Litvinov to Baku was considered by the local population as only slightly less important than the visitation of the Holy Mother to Saint Bernadette was regarded by the good citizens of Lourdes. Litvinov had once been stationed here, and the local citizenry were going to fete him and his fellow travelers to the ears. Tonight a concert had been arranged by the local

222

wielders of larynx, fiddle and guitar. The cars would be ready at eight-thirty. At eight-thirty Moats and I were still knee-deep in the first real, thick steak we had seen in many months and we were in no mood to hurry. Besides, we weren't diplomats and didn't have to be polite. The others left and we finished at our leisure. That was a meal to remember. About nine o'clock we sauntered out into the lobby and there were four "Y.M.C.A." boys waiting for us. Two were our own and two were local products.

"The car is waiting," one of them smiled. It was easier to go along than try to explain that we didn't want to go. Besides, our refusal to go might be construed as an affront to Litvinov. We got into the back of the big black car. The "Y.M.C.A." lads covered us with robes. One of them climbed in front with our driver. A car shot ahead of us carrying four of the boys. Another car with four more followed. We seemed fairly well attended.

"Stick with me, kid, and see how well you get treated," I told Moats complacently.

"Nuts," she said. "Litvinov probably caught you eyeing my fur coat today. He thinks you're trying to steal it to give to some dame in London. The 'Y.M.C.A.' boys are assigned to me to protect me, my coat and my honor."

"I would like that coat," I admitted.

The first half of the concert was just finished when we entered. When the intermission came we were all ushered into a room off the auditorium and to our horror we saw that it was a table set for dinner. We sat down and it began. One course, one wine followed another. We had to make a show of eating but the steak made it difficult. Finally the bell sounded and we staggered back into the auditorium. Tony Greenwood and I slept during the second half. The others said the Caucasian music and dancing were very good.

223

We went out to find that a blinding snowstorm had sneaked into town while we weren't looking. At the hotel we were told that flying the next day was out of the question. In fact, it might be two or three days before we got away. Steinhardt and Monckton were a little anxious because they had cabled Teheran from Kuibyshev saying they'd be along in a day or two. Investigation disclosed the illuminating fact that there was no telephone connection between Baku and Teheran. A cable? A cable would have to be routed through Kuibyshev, Moscow and London. It would take seven or eight days to reach Teheran. In short, we were incommunicado.

"I haven't got a ruble," Moats said, "and you've only got fifty. You better get the boys into a poker game, but for God's sake don't get careless."

We played nearly every afternoon. When we didn't have to go to another Litvinov concert or opera we played at night. We had a good game, Steinhardt, Brown, Group Captain Hallowell, Saed and myself. Because Ambassador Saed spoke no English we played in French. French is well fitted for poker. A flush in French is quite logically *couleur* while a straight is even more logically *séquence*. I won enough to pay the hotel bill. I couldn't get Steinhardt, though. Saed was my pigeon. I couldn't lose when he and I were all alone.

We were at Baku four days and four nights, but we didn't mind it in the delight of rediscovering good food and hot baths and comfortable beds. That was by far the best hotel I saw in Russia, superior even to the Metropole and National in Moscow. Baku seemed a bright, cheerful place. The bitter cold in the north seldom hit Baku. In fact, this was the first time in twenty years it had snowed in November. When the weather cleared, we left on the fourth day for the last six-

224

hour hop to Teheran. We were very happy on our way to the airdrome. Monckton, Moats and I had a big car with fur robes over us and the weather was crisp without being too cold and the sun gleamed down brightly on the blue Caspian.

"And now, Moats," I said, in the doleful tone of that man who does travelogues, "we leave Baku, this little jewel of the Caspian. We will never forget the kindness of our welcome, nor will we forget the quaint tribal customs, the exotic food and the cry of the caviar in the stillness of the night. And so we take our leave of Baku . . ."

"Shut up, you heel," Moats said. "You'll jinx us, sure. We probably won't be able to take off."

We took off, all right. We took off beautifully and flew nicely south for three hours, and then ahead we could see dark gray skies and our plane began to bump gently and then we circled over what looked to be a very small and muddy airdrome. Something had jinxed us all right. As we landed the rain slanted down in the most unfriendly fashion and we wondered if we would have to stay on the airfield all night. But our four bright "Y.M.C.A." boys were equal to the occasion. It was beginning to be routine now. One of them scurried away to telephone for cars; the other three unloaded our baggage. This was a flat, desolate-looking place. We piled into cars and went to a hotel that looked as though it had hopped out of the script of *Rain*. It was a very tropical-looking place with huge rooms, each of which had an old-fashioned coal stove in the middle. But we were over the border. We were in Persia or Iran. The weather ahead was bad and we were doomed to stay here for the night. Kuibyshev seemed so far back that we hardly remembered it.

To contribute to the tropical touch, it rained all night. We sat around playing a game Moats had taught us called "Who Am I?" or "Twenty Questions." We played it until four in the morning and between us drank many bottles of Persian brandy, which isn't brandy at all but a pleasant almond-flavored drink with about the same harmful effect on the nervous or digestive system as limeade or Coca Cola.

The rain was still beating at our windows when we were called at seven o'clock. We were given the happy news that His Excellency, Ambassador Saed, had paid our bills because, after all, we were in his home country and that was swell. We got into our airplane with the "Y.M.C.A." boys being helpful with the baggage and then hung on nervously as we taxied down a field that was knee-deep in mud. The field was about three-quarters of a mile long. At the end of it there was a clump of rather tall trees. We gathered speed and the mud spattered our windows. We went faster and then slowly, agonizingly, the airplane lifted itself. Looking below I could see the tops of the trees just a few feet below, bending, almost flattened by the rush of our flight. I felt a little sick. I looked around, but Steinhardt was cleaning his nails, Moats was asleep, Monckton was wrapping a blanket around his legs, Saed was biting into a big red apple and Litvinov was reading a detective story which I had given him. They were all unaware of our close call. I turned directly around and met the eyes of Group Captain Hallowell. Large beads of perspiration stood out on his forehead. His hands trembled as he lit a cigarette.

"I've been flying all my life," he said to me, "and that's the closest I've been to it."

I told the others afterwards, but none of them believed me. It had been a nice ordinary take-off, they said, and I was being silly to dramatize it. I told them to ask Hallowell. He said it was nothing. "Nothing at all," he said cheerfully. "We missed those trees by at least four feet."

The trip from there on was uneventful, although it rained

for an hour, and flurries of snow played tag with our plane. There were mountains ahead of us, grim, brown mountains, snow-capped, and we seemed to aim straight for them. They looked very high and unfriendly, and then there was a gap. We went through the gap and suddenly we were in a different world. The dull brown earth had changed to patches of green and the sun gleamed down brightly, dancing on the ground beneath, and this, of course, was Shan-gri-la. It was like that in the picture, *Lost Horizons,* and I felt sure if we landed we'd find Ronald Colman trying to discover the secret of immortality and Frank Capra directing the whole show. I looked back at Saed. He was smiling gently. This was his country, whether it was called Persia or Iran. What a nice little man Saed was!

There were large patches of sheer brown desert, but there was nothing forbidding looking about this desert. Occasionally, a square white block would catch the sun and from 5,000 feet we could see cultivated gardens and cattle and people on mule-back. And then suddenly there was Teheran. We had been so long getting there. We circled once and we got a good view of one of the best airdromes in the world. It had two concrete runways, but hardly needed them. The hard-baked sand stretched for miles. Our airplane landed softly, and we stepped out into sun-drenched warmth and the warmth crept into us and drove the chill of Russia out of us and we all laughed and felt a bit giddy, as though with too much champagne. We were surprised to find quite a delegation on hand to greet us. The British Ambassador rushed up to Monckton and said fervently, "Thank God, you're safe, Sir Walter." Walter smiled uncertainly, wondering what he meant, and said, "We had a nice trip, a little long, that's all." The American Minister greeted Steinhardt, shook his head and said, "Oh, but you've had us worried." Steinhardt, not understanding, said, "We were a bit longer than we expected to be."

There was a United Press man there named Peters. I'd worked with him in London. He shook hands fervently too and said, "We never expected to see any of you alive."

"What the hell is this all about?" I asked him.

"My God, you've all been missing for five days," he said. "There have been no reports of your airplane since it left Kuibyshev. We got one report that you'd crashed in a snowstorm and had been picked up by a boat on the Caspian, but we couldn't verify it. The BBC announced that you were all missing and hope was gradually going."

Monckton, who had been hearing the same story from the British Ambassador, turned to me. "You're a fine reporter, you are. Here we've been missing for five days and none of us knew it. You, at least, should have known it."

"Nobody ever tells me anything," I said, very unhappy about it all.

18

Overlooking the Pyramids

MOATS AND I spent a few hours window shopping in Teheran. We couldn't do anything else because we didn't have
any money. In fact, we were all broke. Steinhardt had a few
American dollars; Monckton had about five English pounds
and I had a few rubles which of course meant nothing at all
in Iran. So we just looked at the windows and saw nothing
at all that we would be found dead owning. Moats and I had
both finished stories since leaving Kuibyshev, and we scurried to the Foreign Office to see if there was a censor. A nice-
looking gentleman was emerging from the building as we
entered, and Moats asked him in French where we could find
the censor. He fluttered his hands helplessly. Apparently he
didn't understand French. Moats tried in German and then
Spanish and finally in Russian. He still looked blank.

"What the hell language does he speak?" I said angrily
to Moats.

"English," the foreign-looking man said, unexpectedly. "I
am British, you see. I'm the local Reuter's correspondent."

"Never a dull moment," I said. "We're looking for the
censor. Is this the right building?"

"Yes," he said precisely. "You'll find the Iran censor in
an office to the left. Go to him first. Then bring your copy

to the British censor. He is one office beyond. And then, of course, there is a Russian censor who must approve your copy too. You may find the Iran censor a bit difficult. He is married to a German woman, and he is not quite what you would call a neutral."

"I'll file my story from Cairo," I said. One censor was bad enough, but to have to go through three would be just a little bit worse than going through a major operation without an anaesthetic.

We asked our new-found friend who happened to talk English how we could get to the British Legation. Being an obliging Englishman, he offered to drive us there. He looked in awe at this smart-looking girl in the lovely fur coat who seemed able to drag any known language out of her throat at a given moment and drove us to the Legation. It occupied a full square block, surrounded by high walls. Birds walked all over the place screaming their silly heads off. Heavy trees bent down over small houses and leaned companionably against the larger buildings.

"Good show, this," our guide said. "The whole British Legation is housed in here. Have their own swimming pool, tennis courts; do themselves right."

We found the Ambassador's house and sent word for Monckton or Tony Greenwood. The flunkey who admitted us didn't like the idea of disturbing Sir Walter or Mr. Greenwood right after dinner. Fortunately, he reconsidered before Moats lost her temper.

Tony came out beaming. "Thank God, you've come! They're having what you call a musical evening. Walter couldn't leave, so he tipped me the wink."

"When are we going to Cairo?" I asked him. By now, Cairo was looming as a sanctuary, a home of sorts, even though I had never been to Egypt before.

230

"We are leaving tomorrow," Tony said. "It is a special RAF plane, and I'm afraid Moatsie can't go along."

"Moatsie doesn't want to go along or else she damn well would," Moats said decisively. "I have things to do here. I have a lot of shopping for the boys in Kuibyshev. There is a plane for Cairo in the afternoon I can get, but I'm thinking of going to Singapore instead."

"Litvinov and his party aren't coming with us," Tony said. "He and Mrs. L. are pretty tired, and they don't want to get up at 5 A.M. tomorrow. To reach Cairo by daylight, we have to leave the airport at six. You can't land at Cairo by night; they don't use flare paths. Walter tried to persuade Litvinov to come with us, but he said he'd wait for a later airplane. He's just tired of flying."

A week later we heard of the "Litvinov incident." There was even a question asked in Parliament about the so-called discourtesy shown to the Russian Ambassador. Someone had sent a story from Teheran to the effect that Litvinov had been refused passage on an RAF airplane. All sorts of apologies were made to Litvinov. I'll bet Litvinov himself wondered what it was all about. He and Monckton were good friends, and Monckton admired him more than any other Russian official. In addition, Monckton is constitutionally incapable of being discourteous to any of his fellow men. Moats or I could be discourteous at the drop of a lip and enjoy it. Monckton is one of those pre-eminently "nice" men who would go a long way to avoid being discourteous.

"Tony, before you leave, talk to your Ambassador and tell him Moats has no money. She'll come around to see him tomorrow, and she'll want his okay at the local bank. It would take a week for money to be cabled from home. You fix."

"Sure, I fix." Tony was a charming young man, the son

231

of Arthur Greenwood, M.P., member of Britain's War Cabinet.

Moats and I walked back to our hotel. Teheran was an odd place. There was a ten-o'clock curfew and not a car, not a person walked the streets after that hour. The streets were blacked-out for some unknown reason. No one was going to bomb Teheran.

I had to rouse myself at five and get out with my baggage. No one else in the hotel was awake. I left my hotel bill for Moats, and felt a temptation to leave her a note suggesting that when it came to settling the bill, she should disclaim all knowledge of me and just pay her own. She probably would have gotten away with it, with her bright impudence. But 5 A.M., even after a good night's sleep, is far too early to write a note, so I reluctantly put the temptation aside.

Monckton picked me up at 5:15 in front of the hotel. I climbed sleepily into the back of his car and we were off to the airport. The dawn was just yawning over the horizon, and a big RAF airplane was warming up. It was nice to see those youngsters again in their blue RAF uniforms with their silver wings.

We aimed for Cairo, some ten hours' flying time away. For hours we flew over the most desolate-looking land I have ever seen. Finally, we hit Iraq and the desert became even more barren. And then, suddenly, there was Palestine. We landed at an RAF airport to refuel. It was about two in the afternoon, and we had lunch in the RAF mess. It was a good mess, and it was nice to have cocktails again and fresh vegetables and hear officers talk of London theatres and of Nat Gubbins' column and of the last *New Yorker,* six months old, which had arrived. It was nice until we were told that in landing we had done something to a wheel and it might take two days to repair it. An RAF station in the desert hardly seemed a desirable place to spend two full days. We felt pretty bad until we were told that Jerusalem was only thirty-five miles away. Steinhardt, Monckton, Tony Greenwood and I were delighted. We would go to the Holy Land and be tourists for a day or two. It would be fun actually to see some of these places I had read about for so many years. We would get a guide and see the Tomb and the Mount of Olives and the other shrines we had heard about since childhood.

It took some time for cars to arrive, and darkness overtook us before we reached Jerusalem. The Holy Land is blacked-out these days, so we didn't see a thing. We decided to get to bed at a reasonable hour and arranged to meet very early in the morning. There was a plain-clothes man who had been assigned to us, and I asked him to have a drink with me. We went into the bar at the King David Hotel, and a very lovely bar it was. The Inspector was homesick for news of London and he was thrilled by even my three-month-old gossip. I told him the new gags Flanagan and Allen were using in their radio program, the most popular program in England. I had no money to pay for our drinks, so I just signed "British Embassy."

The Inspector gave me some of the historical background on the fight between the Arabs and the Jews in Palestine. After listening to it for an hour, I was more confused than ever. Apparently, both were rushing to join the British Army.

"That ought to promote unity between them," I suggested. "They'll get to know each other and understand each other, and when the war is over they'll settle down and be good neighbors."

"No bloody fear," he said morosely. "I know them both well. The Jews are joining the Army to learn everything they can about modern warfare so they'll really be able to

233

go to work on the Arabs when the war is over. The Arabs are doing the same thing."

"There ought to be some good stories here after the war," I said. "Maybe I'd better reserve a room for the week after the armistice."

My cop friend had led an interesting life. He was always assigned to protect visiting celebrities. Young King Peter of Jugoslavia had been one of his charges. He was very fond of the young King.

"He loved to drive a car—but fast," my Inspector said. "We drove all over the desert together. He has a great sense of humor, too. Once we were on the shore of the Dead Sea and he got a bottle and filled it up with water from the sea. He laughed and told me he had a hell of a gag he wanted to pull. When we got back that night he called all his staff together. He told them that they were all leaving for Eng-land; everything had been arranged. They were tickled to death, of course. Then he told them that they ought to cele-brate by having a drink of native English wine. He got a waiter to bring in wine glasses and filled the glasses with the water from the Dead Sea. Then he solemnly lifted his glass and asked them to drink a toast to England. They knocked their drinks down and looked at each other a bit puzzled. But they were polite chaps and thought they might offend Eng-land by making a crack about the native British wine. So they just smacked their lips as though it were champagne. I bet when they got to England none of them ordered any British drinks. To this day, they don't know they were drinking water from the Dead Sea."

I went to bed early, expecting to be called about eight. I was really excited. I was called early all right—at 5 A.M. A voice said, "Your airplane has been fixed and a car is wait-ing for you at the door."

It was still pitch black in Jerusalem. We drove out of town quickly. After spending a night in the Holy Land, all I know about it is that Room 540 at the King David Hotel in Jerusalem is very comfortable and costs five dollars a night. I know just how the White Rabbit in *Alice in Wonderland* felt. This life of ours is a silly one—traveling so fast you never see anything.

We took off at daylight and headed once more for Cairo. I was grimly determined to take a vacation there. For the moment, I had forgotten Walter Monckton's soft, "Better come to Cairo with me. You'll be sorry if you don't." I was looking forward to seeing the Pyramids and the Sphinx, which I had only seen on postcards, and the camels, which I had only seen on cigarette packages. We crossed the Suez Canal. From the air it was a slender little ribbon of water in the sand. Then I fell asleep and didn't wake up until we bumped to a landing at Cairo.

"Wasn't that a great sight of the Pyramids?" Monckton said. "From the air they certainly are magnificent."

I told him that I had been asleep but that I was going to see them tomorrow. He looked at me and laughed. I didn't like that laugh. I stepped out of the plane and fell into the arms of Bob Low. Bob writes for *Liberty Magazine*. I introduced him to Monckton.

Low and I lived together in London during the bad times, and it was great to see him. He looked very tanned and handsome in his uniform. He had been in the East for nearly a year. Low has gone on more operational trips than any of us. He was the only one of the correspondents to go on a submarine trip—three weeks in the Mediterranean—during which his sub sank two Italian transports. He had gone dive-bombing over Italy and he had been out with the British Fleet. A trade that produces men like Bob Low, Ken Downs,

235

Bill Stoneman, Ed Beattie, Arch Steele and Bob Casey must be a pretty good racket.

"I'm going to take a week off, Bob," I told Low. "I'm fed up with working for awhile. I'm going to be a tourist here. I want to see the Pyramids and the Sphinx. I want to ride a camel and wallow in this sun."

"You'll wallow in the sun, all right, sweetheart," Bob said. "You're leaving for the desert at six in the morning. I've fixed your credentials; you're accredited to the British Army. In case you don't know it, the big British push started yesterday. It's going to be a hell of a story."

I looked coldly at Walter Monckton. "So that's what you meant?"

Walter nodded. "I knew it was coming, but it was so confidential I couldn't do more than hint."

"But the Pyramids," I protested weakly.

"Nuts to the Pyramids," Low said coldly. "Ken Downs is in the desert. What would you rather see, Ken or the lousy Pyramids?"

I brightened at that. We had been through France together and we had had a great time. Ken had been in charge of the Paris INS office. Now Low told me that Ken and INS had come to the parting of the ways and that Ken had gone over to United Press. The desert began to look attractive. Downs, Low and Reynolds—we were a good team.

"I've got a nice suite reserved for you at Shepherd's Hotel," Low said. "Best suite they got."

"What does it cost?" I asked suspiciously.

"What do you care?" Low said expansively. "You want the best, don't you? I told them that you were a big dealer and money was no object. Don't let me down now, chum."

I had read about the famed Shepherd's Hotel ever since I started to read. I started reading detective stories when I was

236

thirteen, and I've never gotten over it. How often I have read stories of "international love and intrigue," with Shepherd's Hotel as a setting! I was in for a disappointment. It was just another hotel, with the worst service I've ever suffered. The help was all native, and they seemed to talk no other language but Egyptian.

Bob did have a beautiful suite for me. It should have been beautiful—it cost fifteen dollars a day. There was money waiting for me from *Collier's,* however, so it didn't matter. I think if I cabled *Collier's* from the South Pole saying, "Send ten thousand. Want to buy an iceberg," *Collier's* would do it.

That afternoon Low took me to a military tailor's and ordered a uniform for me. I found out afterward that there were a half dozen tailors in town who would have made the uniform for practically half the price, but Low has a great disregard for money, whether it is his own or someone else's. He used to buy me wonderful presents in London: a flask from Simpson's, a lighter from Dunhill, a flashlight from some Regent Street shop, and when I'd thank him he'd say modestly, "I only want you to have the best, pal." I'd show my gifts proudly to everyone, although I worried a little about how Bob was tossing his money away, but I really shouldn't have worried—when the first of the month came I'd always get the bill. Bob just liked buying presents for people. What if he did charge them to the people to whom he sent the presents? As he insisted, his inclinations were right; it was the spirit of the thing that counted.

I knew several British correspondents in Cairo, and we sat around drinking with them at cocktail time. They all wanted news of Philip Jordan and our other colleagues in Russia, and they talked about their own experiences during the past year. Two of them had just returned from India. They had had an amazing adventure with a couple of dancing girls.

237

"I got this dame up to my room," one of them explained, "and she was a honey. A big dame who danced in the local night club. I got into bed, and she stripped and said, 'I dance for you.' So she danced. She moved everything but her feet. I kept saying, 'Stop that nonsense and climb into the hay, Sugarlips,' but she didn't understand English. I lay there in bed yawning; the drinks were wearing off. Every few minutes she'd stop dancing and say 'Backsheesh?' I kept saying, 'Afterwards.' She kept saying 'Backsheesh.' She wanted her dough before she got into the kip with me. I kept getting sleepier and sleepier, and the last thing I remember is her yelling, 'Backsheesh' and then when I woke up it was morning and I was alone."

"South Africa is the place for poon," another said. "Poon" is a wonderful word. It came from Texas originally, and was brought to Europe many years ago by my red-headed friend, H. R. Knickerbocker. Originally, it was "poon-taang," and who first coined the expression I don't know. Knick, Ed Angley of the *Herald Tribune* and other noted Texans who worked abroad, made it a household word in London. There is nothing derogatory in it. You would be walking down the street and pass a beautiful girl and someone would say, "What a hunk of poon!" It was merely a tribute to the girl's beauty and even to her virtue. You would never call one of those horrible tarts who still infest London "a hunk of poon." A good, serviceable word.

"I got off the train and looked for a taxicab," he went on. "I was amazed to see that the cab drivers were all girls. There was a line of them, so I just picked out the best-looking one and hired her cab. She was a hunk of poon, if ever I saw one. I figured she was some local society girl who was doing this as her bit in the war effort. My God, was I ever wrong! We got to the hotel and she helped with my luggage. She came

238

up to the room with me and I said, 'How about a drink?' She said, 'I'd love a drink, but I didn't turn my meter off.' I said, 'The hell with the meter, sweetheart, I've been in the desert for six months and I'm on an expense account.' So we had a drink and another drink and then a million drinks and she was pretty wonderful. She stayed all night and then after breakfast she turned practical. She said she'd have to see what the meter on her cab read. My God, it was six pounds ten shillings—that's about twenty-six dollars in American money."

"Was it worth it, pal?" I asked.

"My God, yes! Have you ever been on the desert for eight months?"

I told him I hadn't. One of the others told us about an experience he had had in Ankara, Turkey. It was a good story, I thought.

"Arthur and I were in Athens, Greece, when we got the B'Jesus knocked out of us," he said. "But I liked Greece. Those Greek dames somehow went for me. I don't want to brag, but, honest, I did all right in Greece. Then we wound up in Turkey in that lousy town of Ankara. If I was a married woman and wanted to be sure my husband would be faithful to me I'd send him to Ankara," he went on. "Arthur and I had an awful time there. There was one good restaurant, the Cosmopolitan, and we usually dined there. One night we saw two good-looking dolls sitting together. They looked awfully good, but they were strictly class, and I knew there was no use making a pitch at them. Well, damned if the bell-boy didn't come in the next morning and tell me he had a message from the telephone operator. Seems that these two gals had actually phoned her to find out who we were. They wanted to meet us. I talked to the telephone girl, and she told me they were two Greek dames. She told me where they lived and added that they'd like us to come to tea that afternoon.

"We felt pretty good, Arthur and I. Hell, we hadn't talked to a dame for six weeks. When we got to the house where they lived, it was just what I expected—a swell house in the best part of town. I figured they were two rich Greek society girls whose husbands had probably sent them to Ankara for safety. We went in, and they were even better than we remembered. Both young and good-looking, and it was fun to just sit and talk with them. Hell, I knew there was no use trying to get anywhere with them. They really had class. Now, I had the mother and father of a hangover, and the girls started to kid me about it. We had a few drinks, but my hangover only got worse. One of the dames finally said, 'You'd better go in and lie down. Come on, I'll make you comfortable.' I protested, but I really felt like death on wheels. So she led me into a bedroom and there was the biggest double bed I ever saw. I took off my shoes and lay on it. This dame got some cologne and stroked my forehead, and that was all right. I felt better each minute, and then she undid my tie and opened my shirt and I just lay there purring. Yeah, those Greek dolls always did go for me. Then damned if she didn't bend over and kiss me, so I pulled her into bed and there we were." He sighed. "That was a wonderful afternoon, especially because it was so unexpected. Arthur and I had a date for dinner at the British Embassy, so we had to leave about seven. Seemed that he had the same experience with the other dame that I had had. Going back in the taxi, we felt pretty satisfied with ourselves. I told Arthur, 'I don't want to brag, but if it hadn't been for me you wouldn't have gotten anywhere. It's just one of those things. I'm no good in London or Cairo, but in Athens I'm red hot. Yeah, those Greek dames go for me. And these were obviously a couple of high-class gals.' Arthur nodded. He was giving me full credit. When we got back the bell-boy asked us if we'd enjoyed ourselves. I didn't like the way he said it, but let it pass. Arthur and I wondered if we ought to send them flowers. We thought we would. I called the telephone operator and told her to send them at least five dollars' worth of the best flowers in Ankara.

"She said she would, and then she added, 'Those two girls just phoned to ask me if I'd remind you that you forgot to pay them.' I yelled, 'Forgot to pay them? Forgot to pay them for what?' The telephone girl seemed hurt. 'Well, didn't you enjoy yourselves? I never heard any of the men who spend afternoons with them who didn't enjoy themselves.'

"Then I realized that these two Greek society girls had been two hookers, two lousy tarts. Did Arthur go to work on me! 'Yeah, those Greek dames sure fall for you, chum,' he said. 'Now see how much you can get us out for. Maybe these society girls come high.' We let the telephone girl be our broker. The girls wanted twenty dollars from each of us. We made a counter offer of five dollars each. They came back with a quotation of fifteen or two for twenty-five. We settled for fifteen dollars, American money. We were glad to get out of Ankara the next day."

"You war correspondents lead a romantic life," I told him. "It must be very interesting. My, my, the people you meet, dancing girls in India, taxi-cab drivers in South Africa and tarts in Ankara."

Ken Downs walked into the bar at that moment, so I heard no more about the love life of the war correspondent. Downs had heard that I had arrived. He had been 200 miles north in the desert but he had hitch-hiked on an RAF plane that was headed for Cairo.

"Thought we might have a little poker game tonight, pal,"

241

he said casually. "Randolph Churchill would like to play and Douglas Williams and Philip Berry and maybe we could persuade Low to take a hand."

"You might," Low said smoothly.

"Where will we play?" I asked.

"I hear Bob got you that nice suite on the second floor," Downs said. "Best suite in the hotel. It would be a grand place for a game. In fact," he added modestly, "on my way in I told the clerk to fix up a table and to have plenty of drinks up there and some sandwiches. And, of course, cards and chips." ·

"You guys aren't just laying for the visiting fireman, are you?" I asked suspiciously.

"Really, pal!" Downs was hurt. "Do you think we'd gang up on you?"

"Fine talk, I must say." Low, too, was practically shedding crocodile tears. "It's a good chance for you to get to know Randolph well. He's very important out here; he's in charge of press relations. And you know Douglas Williams of the Ministry of Information? Then young Berry; he's the son of Lord Camrose who owns the *Daily Telegraph*."

"They're all solvent, I presume?"

"You presume correctly, Dr. Livingstone," Downs said.

"Just a friendly game," Low added.

Low was banker. I winced when he gave us each a hundred dollars' worth of chips. They were one-shilling chips, ten-shilling chips and one-pound chips.

"It'll save bookkeeping," Low explained, "to have a lot of chips. The game we play is just ordinary dealer's choice. You can open for one shilling."

That seemed reasonable. A nice two-bit game made me feel much more friendly toward my pals. Low dealt while I

242

told Randolph about his family. I'd seen his father and his mother and his lovely wife, Pamela, since he had.

"What can you raise?" I asked, casually looking at the three aces Low had dealt me.

"Our usual game," Low said blandly. "Table stakes. You can raise what you got in front of you."

"It's like that, hey?" I said.

"Yes, sweetheart," Downs answered. "No blows barred and look after yourself in the clinches."

I did. We played all night and when the smoke of battle had cleared, Low had won $100, Downs had won $140 and the visiting fireman had won just $2,000. It had been a very friendly game.

"Seems a strange coincidence," Low purred, counting out the money which Churchill, Williams and Berry passed over, "that we three Americans all won and you three Englishmen all lost. Could it be that we're just that much smarter than you?"

Churchill answered in language such as his father had never used, even in the heat of parliamentary debate.

"We've had a lot of drinks sent up tonight," I reminded them. "And dozens of sandwiches. Now suppose we deal a cold hand and the low hand pays for them."

"You win $2,000 in your own room and won't even pay for a few lousy drinks and some sandwiches," Low stormed.

"Not me, sweetheart," I told him. "I never believe in giving a sucker an even break."

Downs and Low incredibly had the same low hands, so they paid for the drinks and sandwiches, which came to $40. It had been a pleasant night and then Downs, Low and I changed into our uniforms, went to the Cairo airport, and headed for the front.

243

19

Eagles Over Africa

MADDALENA WAS ONLY a pinprick on a map. All of the desert locations were simply that and nothing more. When the surveyors went to work on the desert they picked certain points, named them, and put them on the war maps. Maddalena was important because it was "on the line." The "line" was the closely guarded telegraph wire that ran back to Cairo. Maddalena was also Advanced Battle Headquarters. Here General Sir Alan Cunningham had his tent and from here the New Zealander, Air Vice Marshal "Maori" Coningham ran the RAF.

The day we arrived at Maddalena things weren't very happy. Rommel had checked Cunningham's advance south of Tobruk. Sir Claude Auchinleck, Commander in Chief of the British Army in the desert, took prompt measures. He had succeeded Sir Archibald Wavell only two months before. Wavell, a popular hero in Britain, never quite did live up to his reputation. Wavell fought by the book. He was a pedestrian sort of leader, logical, sound. Rommel, a master of the unorthodox, would knock anyone's brains out who fought a conventional war. The "Auk" was the one to take chances and to make sacrifices of men, if need be. Some generals lose battles trying to save men. Not the "Auk." He didn't like the way Cunningham had hesitated. Cunningham was driv-

244

ing at Tobruk, and was well on his way to taking the battered old city. But then he slowed down. He kept worrying about his railhead some sixty miles away, and he diverted part of his attacking forces to the East to protect it. That is like stopping to tie your shoelace when you're fighting Joe Louis. Rommel moved in, divided Cunningham's forces, and for the moment disrupted the British advance. The "Auk" immediately fired Cunningham. It was a courageous thing to do. To begin with, the success of the whole Libyan campaign depended on the co-operation between the Army and the British Navy, commanded by Admiral Sir Andrew Cunningham, brother of Alan. By firing Alan, the "Auk" risked the personal antagonism of the Admiral. But Alan Cunningham had committed the major military blunder; he had looked over his shoulder. Jockeys don't win Derbies by looking over their shoulders. You don't win battles that way either, so General Cunningham had to take the rap. He was replaced by General Ritchie, whom the "Auk" called a "thrusting General."

Life at Maddalena was as pleasant as the Press Relations Department of the Army could make it for us. Major Randolph Churchill and Colonel Philip Astley were in charge of press relations and censorship and they did a magnificent job. Those of us who had known Randolph as merely a pleasant, convivial young man-about-London were amazed at the way he had taken over the thankless task. He awoke at dawn, as we all did, and often worked far into the night. Every time he cut a line from our copy he was willing to argue the reason for it with us. He only had one rule: "home security." Not one line was ever cut from a story of mine that shouldn't have been cut.

A Bob Low story suffered slightly when a line was cut from it, but that was done by an assistant of Churchill's. Bob

245

had been present when the German, Major-General von Ravenstein, was captured. Low, who was educated at Heidelberg, speaks perfect German, and he had a long talk with the General. In his story he described him as a very soft-spoken man with steady blue eyes. The young assistant censor didn't like that flattering description, so he blue-penciled the line. Low raised particular hell about it. "Are all German Generals supposed to have harsh guttural voices and shifty eyes?" he stormed.

Churchill agreed with Bob's protest and the censor got a call-down. Low stumbled across one of the most amusing incidents the desert had to produce. He and Downs were off on a sortie somewhere at the front. They passed a casualty station and asked if there were any wounded prisoners there. There was one, a German Staff Captain. The Captain was sitting on the running board of a truck with his head in his hands. He was suffering from concussion. He had been found lying along the side of a road, unconscious, but with no marks on him. So far, he had been too befuddled to talk, but Low's excellent German brought results.

"How did it happen, *Herr Kapitan?*" Low asked sympathetically.

"Well . . ." The Captain tried to reconstruct the events leading up to his being found unconscious beside a road. "I was riding in the back seat of a staff car. . . . Let me see . . . Yes, there were seven of us in the car. General Rommel was sitting in the front. . . . Suddenly, he turned around and said, 'This car is too crowded.' That's the last thing I remember."

With that, the good Captain collapsed, probably in horror at the thought that his General had jettisoned him. I wouldn't have believed the story, except that Downs was there too and swore that Low hadn't colored it a bit.

246

The desert front was a correspondents' paradise. We could go wherever we wished. We could go out on night patrols far in advance of the front. We could talk to prisoners freely. During two years in England I had never been allowed to see a German prisoner. When we wrote a story, all we had to do was toss it to Randolph Churchill or Philip Astley, and we knew that it was as good as in New York. After they censored it, the story went right to Cairo by airplane. If no aircraft was leaving Maddalena at the moment, Randolph would bully, cajole, and somehow a plane would take off within a few minutes. Churchill and Astley had the quaint and, to us, surprising attitude that they were working for us. Accustomed to the disinterest and patronizing attitude of the War Office, the Admiralty and the Air Ministry in London, to the rigid censorship and strict supervision of Russia, the desert, as far as working conditions went, was sheer heaven.

The desert seemed to breed a strange spirit of friendship which touched us all. We all felt that we were slightly batty to be out there and that gave us a kinship. We lived closely together, had the same problems and suffered the same discomforts. Men who might not nod to each other in Shepherd's Bar back in Cairo, were blood brothers here.

We had a truck at our disposal for our kits, and there was sleeping room in it for five. Downs, Low and I, having come up last, were out of luck. The five places were taken. We had sleeping bags with us and each night we'd roll them out, button our coats up tightly, crawl into the bags and sleep. We usually went to sleep around nine because there wasn't much point in staying up. We couldn't show a light anywhere and, anyhow, we were always awakened at dawn. If the sun didn't wake us the sound of the airplanes taking off on the dawn patrol did.

There were about 8,000 men at Maddalena and about 200

fighter and bomber aircraft. Sometimes we'd lie there at night and hear a single airplane motor overhead. We would wait nervously, wondering if it would drop a flare and go to work on us; we knew none of our aircraft was up there. Yet we never were bombed. For once the RAF had air superiority. The whole swift advance in November, 1941, was based on that air superiority. It was the first time since the war began that the RAF had enjoyed such an advantage. It was really thrilling to watch a squadron of Blenheims coming over our airport lazily. These were flown by the Free French, who called themselves the Lorraine Squadron. They'd fly high, circling the airport and then the Tomahawks (Curtis-Wright P-40) would go up to escort them on their errand. Usually two squadrons of Tommies would escort one squadron of Blenheims or Wellingtons. The boys invariably called the Wellington the Wimpies. This is the only aircraft in the world ever named after a comic-strip character. The Wimpies took their name from that estimable connoisseur of the hamburger and friend of Popeye, Mr. J. Wellington Wimpy.

Air Vice Marshal Coningham was in charge of all RAF operations. I wanted to meet him. Randolph fixed it in about two minutes. That Randolph got things done. Coningham looks the part of an RAF Commander. He is tall and hard, his face is tanned and lean, and he has bushy eyebrows which are never in repose.

"Met you before." He smiled when we shook hands. "It was at York about a year ago. Almost sent you over Germany on a Whitley that night."

I was amazed at his remarkable memory. He had been in charge of night bombing then, with headquarters in York. I had gone up to spend a night with the bombing squadron at Driffield. For months I had been trying to get an operational trip on a night bomber, preferably over Berlin. Such permission had always been refused. When I met Coningham at York I suggested that I'd like to go along that night.

"Why not?" he said unexpectedly. "Have you permission from the Air Ministry?"

I waved a casual hand. "It is entirely up to you, sir. The Air Ministry has told us that operational flights are under the jurisdiction of the officer commanding. They leave it to you."

"We could leave the observer off," he said thoughtfully. "It would be a good story, a fine story, and the fighter lads are getting all the credit these days. I'm for it. Sure, you can go along tonight. It's an interesting operation we have in mind. We are going to try and sink the *Bremen*."

By then I was sweating. I was on the verge of getting the best story of the war. No one, as yet, had been on a night operational flight and only Low had managed to wangle a day operational trip. That had been over Norway with the Coastal Command. But to go out on an aircraft that might sink the *Bremen*—that was a story! I was already thinking of my lead. . . .

"Just as a matter of form," Coningham said casually, "I suppose I ought to phone the Air Ministry and tell them."

"Oh, don't bother," I said desperately, my house of cards beginning to topple. "It's Sunday, anyhow. I doubt if you'll get anyone there."

"Oh, well, if we don't, you can go along. However, I'll call."

Our *bête noir* at the Air Ministry was in. Air Commodore Peake was in charge of press relations at the Ministry. A director of Rolls-Royce, the Air Commodore was smooth and suave, but he was a stickler for regulations. As soon as I heard Coningham say, "Peake? Hello, there. I have a man here . . ." I knew that I was finished. I never did get that story.

249

On the desert some 3,000 miles from York, Coningham recalled that afternoon. Coningham and I walked out of his tent and he talked of the aircraft he had under his charge. He talked of the desert campaign as a whole, and he talked of the German aircraft. No swivel-chair commander, Coningham. He had been a pilot himself. He was a great leader of men and a realist. We walked over to the airport, about a half mile from his headquarters. A squadron of Glenn Martin Maryland's was taking off. These were the two-motored aircraft used for reconnaissance, for ground strafing and light bombing. They circled once, as though waiting for their fighter escort, and then headed north.

"Where are they picking up the fighters?" I asked Coningham. In the United States Army and Navy the terms "pursuit" and "interceptor" are used. In the RAF all pursuit and interceptor planes are called "fighters."

"Those Maryland's don't need any protection," he laughed. "I'm sending them out alone. If they have to fight they can fight. If they have to run away, they can run away. They are great aircraft; all American aircraft are good. They're so well made, sturdy, they can take a beating."

"Things are going well, aren't they?"

Coningham shook his head. "For the moment—yes. But Rommel is getting a lot of supplies from Sicily. Every time the Jerries bomb Malta—and they're hitting the place every day—it means that our Beaufighters are kept on the ground. Meanwhile, ships are shooting over from Sicily. Up to now the Beaufighters were getting most of those supply ships, but now that they're grounded, I'm worried. I think Rommel is planning on a counter-attack, and, if he has the equipment, he can do plenty of damage."

Coningham made more sense than any commanding officer I had ever met. He wasn't blinded by the early success of the

250

Libyan campaign. He had air superiority for once, and he knew that anyone who has air superiority can advance. He knew, too, that it was only a matter of time when the Germans would catch up to him.

One day at Maddalena was pretty much like another. Breakfast was not elaborate—porridge and a piece of bully beef. We got a cup of water each morning for shaving, teeth brushing and washing.

Over at the airport one morning three squadrons of Tomahawks were just coming home to roost. They had been out on an early-morning sweep over the tank battle that was raging not far away. The air was filled with the high, happy singing of the Allison motors. One squadron landed, then another, and clouds of sand rose where their feet had skimmed the desert ground.

The third squadron circled, waited until the dust settled and then came down. All except one plane. One lone Tomahawk continued to circle unsteadily. Its left wing drooped forlornly. At least three feet of the wing hung untidily from the tip. I stood beside the Wing Commander, a tall, bronzed, curly-haired youngster, wearing khaki shorts. He was known as "Rosie" to everyone.

"Take your time," Rosie whispered, half talking to himself. "Come in fast . . . That's it. . . . Leave your flaps up . . ."

Two hundred pilots and the ground crew were watching this crippled bird. Each was mentally landing that airplane himself.

"Good! Good!" Only the sound of Rosie's voice and the hum of the motor disturbed the deep silence of the desert. The world had stopped breathing for the moment to encourage this helmeted lad and his wounded aircraft.

"He's landing by the book," Rosie said, and there was relief in his voice. "That's it, kid, come in fast—faster! Good! Oh, a good show!"

The Tommy landed at 120 miles an hour. It didn't even bump. The pilot jumped out and looked dejectedly at the crumpled wing. "I hit an Eyetie—fifty," he said ruefully. "I came at him sideways, got in a burst, and he almost stopped. I swiped his tail—knocked a hunk of it off."

"Didn't you go into a spin?" I asked.

"This airplane doesn't go into spins," he laughed, patting the nose of the Tommy affectionately, as though it were a pet dog. The kid was from Zululand. He should be able to handle a Tomahawk. The Tomahawks proved themselves the glamor boys of the Libyan show. There were several squadrons of them in the desert bearing the brunt of the attack.

The Tomahawks are great "infighters," as maneuverable as a Shetland pony. They stay low, ignoring the invitation of the Messerschmidt 109-F's, which hover in the substratosphere. Sooner or later the M.E.-109's will dive. That's what the Tommies are waiting for. It is true that the M.E.-109-F can outrun any fighter airplane in the desert today, but the Tommies don't run away. They get "inside" the Messerschmidts. They outmaneuver them, they outshoot them and, to date, in this Western battle, they have brought down four times as many Nazis as they themselves have lost. The pilots swear by them.

Drama was never absent from the stage of our desert airdrome. Three more squadrons of Hurricanes and Tomahawks took off to escort a squadron of bombers en route to a Nazi airport. The bombers circled solemnly as the little fighters buzzed around them, weaving and bobbing, crisscrossing and diving, having some fun before the serious business of escort began. The bombers were Blenheims and Wellingtons. They disappeared into the blue of the sky, merged with it, and, for the moment, all was quiet. A lone Douglas DB-7, known as

252

the Boston here, swept to a lazy landing. The pilot reported plenty of activity on the roads behind the German lines. Tanks and motor transport were being brought up in a desperate effort to stem the British tank advance. He gave his map to his Wing Commander, who rushed it to Coningham, waiting in a small tent just off the airport. Within fifteen minutes a dozen bombers and dive-bombers, Blenheims and Glenn Martin Marylands, were off to see that those Nazi tanks were shattered.

One by one, the pilots brought in their reports.

"We had a wizard show," the young leader of an Australian squadron said, trying to keep the excitement out of his voice. "Wizard" in the RAF means wonderful. He went on, "Twenty of them jumped us. The sky was full of the swine. But we gave them plenty. Rawley put on a wizard show, all right. Hey, Rawley, I saw you drop one. Tell us about it."

"I got on the tail of a Hun and gave him a long burst and he came apart." Rawley was a small, slim youngster with curly golden hair. He looked twelve. But he was nineteen. "Then, as I watched the Hun go down, I felt something popping around me, and damned if a Hun wasn't on my tail. I slipped away and almost ran head-on into another one. I gave it to him good, and he went down. Then I saw you were in trouble, sir, and I hustled over, but you'd gotten the Hun you were after before I reached you."

The sun was high now, and it was time for lunch. I thought I'd try the Army mess this time; they might have some water. I went to the public-relations tent. I stayed there until, in resigned discouragement, Churchill and Astley asked me to lunch. The lunch was cold bully beef with Worcestershire sauce, but there was tea. The tea tasted as though it had been used to wash down a truck.

253

"That's the chlorine in the water," Churchill said. "Tastes awful, but it keeps you from getting typhoid."

There was news of the tank battle. It was going well because of the amazing efficiency of the American tanks. They had completely routed a Nazi tank force superior in numbers by using tanks superior in armament. The American tanks weighed about thirteen tons and carried a thirty-seven-millimeter cannon that plowed through the seventeen-ton Nazi cruisers.

During the afternoon the desert lived up to advance notices. The sun poured down and baked the sand to a fiery whiteness. Some German airplanes had been over the night before, dropping flares, and there was some reason to believe that they had located our airdrome. If so, they would be over in force to bomb it, so it was suggested that we dig some slip trenches alongside the truck that we called home. Downs, Low and I went to work with pickax and shovel. The work went slowly and finally we abandoned it. It wasn't more than two feet deep.

"Deep enough for a grave," I told my two pals. "I'll be happy to bury either or both of you in it."

Low said, "Thanks, sweetheart."

Out on the airdrome there was great activity. Four huge Bombays dropped very slowly from the sky; they looked slow and leisurely alongside the quick, deft fighters. Bombays are really troop-carrying airplanes. They were flying ammunition up to the tanks. They are of the troop-carrying type used by the Nazi parachute troops. I talked to the squadron leader who had flown one of them. A feature of this desert battle is the amazing co-operation and split-second co-ordination between the Army and the Air Force. Airplanes took off, airplanes landed. At no time during the day was the sky free of them. One Tomahawk came back with its undercarriage smashed by

254

a Nazi cannon. Quite calmly, the young Australian landed the Tommy on its belly. It raised a mountainous cloud of dust as it hit the ground, completely hiding the aircraft. Gradually the dust settled and then we saw the slight figure of the pilot emerge. The airplane was sitting quite unharmed on the sand, and the pilot was cursing softly because it might be another twenty-four hours before he could get another one.

I was with the Australian squadron commanded by Rosie when it was ordered up. A road had been observed filled with armored cars rushing up to support the Nazi tanks. The boys hopped into their Tomahawks and away they went—twenty-one of them. They were due back in an hour and a half. The sun began to climb down toward the horizon and then suddenly, as happens in the desert, it plunged below it. Five Tomahawks came out of the semi-darkness to land. They had been jumped by a whole wing of Messerschmidts. It had been a dogfight all over the sky. They had knocked down plenty of the M.E.'s, all right, but the fight had lasted too long. These five had petrol enough to make our home port. The others? By now their gasoline would be exhausted. Somewhere or other, sixteen Tomahawks and sixteen pilots were down in the desert.

At dinner, which was bully beef and, incredibly, a sardine, we didn't talk much about the sixteen who were missing. Cold comes with the night. We had dinner in a tent, but the desert night air seeps through the strongest tent and you long for the comparative warmth of your sleeping bag. We sat there smoking, and then we heard the sound of airplane motors. The thoughts we had kept to ourselves tumbled out now. This must be Rosie and his crew. The vibration of the motors grew louder. Sound plays queer tricks in the desert. This may have been one airplane; it may have been fifty. The still, cold air was throbbing with the sound of airplane motors. Then, two miles away, something flashed through the darkness and for

255

a moment banished the night. It was a flare, and we knew that this was a Hun looking for our airport. The sound died away. It was hard to sleep that night, knowing that sixteen pilots were out beyond the horizon somewhere. Even if they landed safely, they'd be suffering from this same cold. The roar of planes woke us early the next morning. I looked up, and, against the deep blue, saw a dozen flashing shapes—unmistakably Tomahawks. They had come back. It was news good enough to banish any resentment at such an early awakening. The pilots, looking a bit blue with cold, hopped out. All of them had run out of petrol and had made for emergency fields where they knew petrol would be stored. In all, there were ten pilots. Six were missing; six pilots who were alive and vital and smiling only yesterday. Perhaps some bailed out on this side of the line. Rosie, who worried so much about the pilot with the broken wing, didn't come back.

20

Attack and Pursue

FOR DAYS Downs and Low had been talking about Colonel Desmond Young. Colonel Young was in charge of press relations for the Indian Army. A veteran of the last war, Young spent most of his time at the front escorting correspondents. He pulled into camp one afternoon, and I quite understood the enthusiasm of Low and Downs. The Colonel had a small pointed mustache, slightly graying hair, and his eyes twinkled when he smiled. Low and Downs said that he was the bravest man they had ever met. He was on his way to visit the Indian division which was storming a place called Sidi Omar. He wanted Downs and Low to join him. They, however, had just wangled a trip to a tank outfit that was in combat, and they suggested that I go along with Young.

"There's only room for Ken and me," Low explained apologetically, "on this trip to the tanks. You go along with Young. Nothing will happen probably, but you'll see the country."

"Thanks," I said sarcastically.

"It might be interesting," Young said thoughtfully. "I don't want you to go on a wild-goose chase, but I think we'll run into something."

I looked at the quiet Colonel, and somehow got the idea that wherever you went with him would be interesting. I was right. We stocked up with as much food as we could get from the commissary. I kidded Randolph into giving me a bottle of whisky and a half dozen packs of Chesterfields. Then we set off in the Colonel's staff car. You drive by the compass in the desert. There are very few roads, and even a mild breeze will raise the sand and obliterate the road.

Colonel Young was an interesting fellow. After the last war he had gone to work on a newspaper in India. He had become the editor, but now he was through with all that.

"After this war is over," he said, "there is only one job I want. I want to go to America and be a butler."

He wasn't fooling, either. To him a butler's life was the ideal existence. He would make a wonderful butler, too. But meanwhile, there was the war to be won. We drove on through the terrific heat of midday and then we saw lazy bursts of black smoke hanging on the horizon.

"They're doing some shelling," Colonel Young said casually. "Maybe Low and Downs missed something by not coming along. I hated to persuade them, but my mob is in the thick of it now, and I can promise you some action."

We drove on, and now we could hear the shells bursting. An hour later we were halted by barbed wire. This was a mine field. Mine fields have gaps in them about thirty feet wide. A mine is usually about a hundred yards across. We found the gap, and the Colonel began to drive gingerly through it. I found that I was holding my breath. The shells were landing fairly close now.

"That's from Sidi Barrani," Young said. "From here on we'll be under enemy observation. The Italians are doing that shelling. Not too accurate, is it?"

"Well," I said doubtfully, "these shells aren't landing in Cairo."

258

"It would be very silly," he said thoughtfully, "to be killed by the Italians."

"It would be very silly to be killed at all," I told him.

"But especially silly to be killed by Eyeties," he persisted.

Personally, I think it doesn't matter whether you are killed by an Eyetie, an Eskimo or a Japanese beetle. Once you are killed you are apt to be very dead indeed, and the manner in which you are killed and other extraneous details seem to me to be incompetent, irrelevant and immaterial. But the British feel differently. They dislike very much being killed by Italians. They hate the Germans with a healthy, honest hatred —but they despise the Italians. The Germans fight until their ammunition is exhausted, then quite sensibly run away to join another detachment. The Eyeties fight until their ammunition is low; then they calmly raise their hands and surrender. They are more treacherous than the Germans. Often they will raise their hands and wait until the British come up to nab them. Then they will hurl hand grenades, and stick their hands up again.

"They are aiming at us now," the Colonel said, "and that is good, because they seldom hit anything they aim at."

That was comforting, except that a shell landing on either side of us would probably explode a mine or two and that, of course, would have had the same effect as a direct hit. But we got through the mine field without incident, and hurried on.

Sidi Omar was a one-mile-square, slightly raised plateau. It was nothing but sand. The Indian division had captured it the day before. Of course, an Indian division is not composed entirely of Indians. The main force of the attack had been borne by a British regiment, the First Royal Sussex, an ordinary line regiment. Dusk was coming on as we crawled into Sidi Omar.

We heard the story of the attack from the General commanding. This line regiment, unable to find the gap in the mine field which surrounded Sidi Omar, had plunged straight through. You hear a lot about the New Zealanders, the Australians, the Canadians, and the South Africans, but you seldom hear the story of the ordinary British regiment. The British War Office policy has always been to shroud the deeds of British regiments in anonymity. In the report which London was reading of this successful attack there would be a line: "The attack was carried out by an Indian detachment." There would be no mention of the First Royal Sussex. Seventy per cent of these lads had been born in Sussex County. A great percentage of them had been farmers and the sons of farmers. Many others had come from Brighton. They had everything in the way of color, yet they remained anonymous.

Their losses had been heavy. Mines are buried about six inches below the surface of the sand. The tread of a man's foot will explode one—yet these British lads had rushed through the mines, ignoring the terrific machine-gun fire from the Eyeties who held Sidi Omar and the mines which were bursting all around them, sending so many of their mates to eternity. They had only one thought—they wanted to get in close with that steel. They did.

The victory was hard-earned. Twenty-eight tanks had been blown up as they stormed through the mine fields, but the plateau was now completely in British hands. The dead were being buried, and prisoners were being hustled back to the rear as the Colonel and I drove in at dusk. The dusk only lingers a few moments in the desert and then it is night and very cold. The General in command scratched his five-day growth of beard and explained the situation to us. The Italians were on two sides of us, the Germans on a third side and only the rear was free of enemy troops. "They shelled us most of the day," the General said encouragingly, cheerfully, "and I imagine tomorrow will be noisy, too."

In the desert your two masters are night and day. You can only build fires during the daytime and so you seldom have hot dinners at night. When darkness comes, you grab some cold bully beef and then go to sleep, even though it is only seven o'clock. You get up at dawn, which in December is six o'clock. That first night the Colonel and I prowled about, talking to the men and hearing amazing tales of their courage from the officers. One of the officers told us not to prowl around too much because there were German patrols out.

"Keep your guns handy, too," he said. "You haven't got one? Hop into any trench or dugout and pick one up."

The trenches were filled with equipment left by the Italians who had surrendered. I picked up a gun in a nice holster and tried to appear as if I were used to wearing it. Actually, I was scared the thing might go off. I had never shot a gun in my life and, with any luck, never will shoot one.

Sleeping at the front is a fairly simple affair. You put your coat on, throw your sleeping bag on the ground and crawl into it. The dawn woke us very gently, and we had tea with a shot of whisky in it and two biscuits. The Colonel and I parked our car alongside a shallow, three-foot trench about ten feet long. In the distance we heard a dull boom and then the swish of a shell feathering its way toward us. We dived into the shallow trench, lying flat. The shell whistled directly over us and landed with a sharp explosion three hundred yards beyond us.

We didn't know it then, but this was the beginning of a three-day nightmare. More shells came and all of them went directly over us. Sometimes the scream of them as they approached was uncertain and warbling, and that was bad, because we knew that they were about ready to drop. Some dropped quite close. They were sixty-pound shells. One exploded near a truck some forty yards from us and the blast, in some inexplicable manner, took the air out of three of its tires. Otherwise, the tires weren't touched, although the truck was riddled with shrapnel and shell fragments. We hugged the bottom of the trench and the shells kept coming for two hours. Then the British artillery, which was about a mile to our rear, opened up, and we heard its shells whistling over us. Ridiculous as it seems, they passed one another as they went over our trench, and soon the firing was so heavy that the whining of the shells almost obliterated the actual sound of the guns.

You hear the whine of the shell practically the whole way, and every shell sounds as though it were coming right at you. We had three solid hours of it and that exhausted us.

The sun was very high now and the air quite still. The Colonel and I went to investigate some of the unoccupied trenches. Some of the things we found were very unpleasant, because there had been no time to bury all of the dead. We also found a great many hand grenades and I found a bottle of something called *cognac alla uvova*. We had very little water and anything wet looked good. We opened the bottle and it was fine. It was a sort of brandy eggnog, and with a couple of biscuits it made a good luncheon.

Just after that we heard the hum of airplane motors and we looked up, waiting for them. They were RAF airplanes, Blenheim bombers escorted by Tomahawks. They looked very beautiful. They flew over us, heading for the place where that battery of Eytie guns was located. Within a few minutes we heard far-off crumphs and we knew that the Blenheims had found the guns. The airplanes came back looking very pleased with themselves.

That night, patrols of Sikhs and members of the Southern County regiment went on patrol looking for trouble. The

262

Sikhs faded into the night, their black beards and white turbans seeming to merge into the desert.

In the morning the Sikhs and British patrols brought in more than a thousand prisoners. The Italians were a sorry, pathetic-looking lot, absolutely weary and disgusted, and obviously glad to be out of it all.

The German prisoners were very young, and they looked half-starved. They were not the surly, arrogant prisoners one finds in Britain. They were utterly defeated, not caring much what happened to them. They also looked bewildered and, strangely enough, scared. It is rare to see a Hun who looks scared. In action he is a good fighter as long as things go according to plan and he has the benefit of his mechanical toys —tanks, armored cars and the like. But these Huns were definitely scared and bewildered. I talked to them and found that their bewilderment was easily explained. Their officers had misled them. They had been taught to believe that their tanks were invincible, and yet they had seen the lighter American-made tanks put their massive dreadnaughts out of action. They had been told that they had air superiority, and then they had seen swarms of Tomahawks and Bostons and Marylands clear the sky of their own M.E.-109-F's and their Heinkels. They had been told that the British soldiers would run. Instead, they had found a force which had been given and had carried out just one order: "Attack and pursue." They had found fighting devils who rushed through their mine fields regardless of casualties, and whose only burning desire was to close in with a bayonet.

We stood talking to the prisoners and then a fresh bunch came in—about a hundred Eyeties. A captain was in charge of them. He had ten men with him and this group of eleven had captured the whole hundred. But there was no jubilation on

263

the face of the tall, darkly handsome Indian Captain. He came directly to us. He recognized the Colonel and he saluted.

"I want permission to execute one of these prisoners," he said coldly. "These Eyeties had surrendered. Their hands were up and we stopped shooting. We started to march them along when one of them who had a hand grenade in his pocket got it out and threw it at us. It killed two men. I should like permission to execute the prisoner."

The Colonel hesitated. Technically, he had no right to give orders to this officer, but for the moment he was the ranking officer in the vicinity, even though his job was press relations.

"One of the men killed was my brother," the Captain said tonelessly.

"That's too bad," Young said softly, "but the man must be tried, Captain. Send him back with the others. Better search these to see if they have any more grenades."

The Captain spoke Italian. He barked an order to the prisoners and they threw their knapsacks on the sand. The Captain and his men went through them. Italian prisoners were always very well equipped. The blankets were fine, heavy, woolen affairs, and usually they had a bottle of wine in their kit. Their overcoats were of good material. They looked very miserable and forlorn standing there, and it was difficult not to feel sorry for them. The poor devils had no right being there in the first place. This certainly wasn't their war.

We weren't quite so sorry for them when the search disclosed six small, red, hand grenades, each about the size of an apple, but each capable of killing or maiming a half dozen men. War in the desert is a nasty affair. It is murder, and the side which is most successful at the business of murder wins.

The prisoners could not be sent to the rear because now there was no rear. We had been surrounded on three sides; now word had come from reconnaissance planes that fifty Hun

264

tanks were coming from the fourth side to attack us. Finally, in the distance, we heard the unmistakable quick, sharp bark of tank guns. They had opened fire with their seventy-fives at three thousand yards. Soon the artillery supporting this division began to answer. Reports came to the General commanding every few minutes. He stood there with a six-day beard on his face, his uniform in tatters, and there was something magnificent about his calmness. The reports were bad at first. Six British guns had been put out of action. The tanks were approaching closer to our plateau. They wanted it badly because it was a vantage point commanding this part of the desert. For the moment, this one-mile square of worthless desert land was the key position in the whole desert campaign. The General smiled when a grimy dispatch rider hopped off his motorcycle and blurted out: "We got seven of them." Then he repeated the message in more military terms. Seven of the big tanks lay burning in the desert less than three miles away. But the others came on, and then, suddenly, the General said casually, "There they are."

To be sure, there they were. They were in single file, a departure from their usual attacking methods. Now they were only a mile away, and I counted twenty-three of them. They were for the most part the big Mark Four type, General Rommel's pets. Shells burst around them, sending up quick bursts of sand and smoke that hung in the still air. Sharp red flashes broke from the tanks and lazy puffs of white smoke followed. We on the plateau were quiet and tense now. The guns from the other three sides began to throw shells at us, but we were too engrossed in this amazing desert drama to hide in our trenches. Then one of the tanks received a direct hit. Its nose rose slightly in the air; it leaned drunkenly on its side, and then a column of black smoke spiraled up from it. The soldiers with me let out a derisive yell. This might have been a football match, with ourselves as interested spectators.

Another tank was hit and still another and now a pall of smoke hung over the battleground. The tanks were close to the borders of the mine fields surrounding our plateau. They tried to keep their single file, flanked by armored cars. There were five of them burning now, and the rest looked like bewildered beetles being attacked by some small, vicious, but unseen insect. More messages came to the General, but he needed none, for the whole battle was laid in front of us now, less than a mile away, and brought much closer by the amazingly clear air of the desert.

It lasted for one hour. I saw ten tanks go up in smoke and then the Hun had enough. The surviving tanks crawled away painfully, slowly, uncertainly. Some limped badly and you knew that these were hurt. Their blunt noses swerved away from our plateau toward the west, toward the protection of their guns, which were still shelling us viciously. Slowly the tanks merged with the horizon and then they disappeared. The shelling stopped, and a heavy, exhausted quiet descended upon the desert. We realized that we were limp with tiredness and the burning heat of the sun. Official reports came in. The artillery had destroyed fifteen tanks within four hours—a nice morning's bag. We felt as though we had seen something historic. We had seen British mobile artillery, supported by nothing more substantial than our enthusiastic cheers, destroy a section of the best German tanks. The fight had been all in the open, for there is no cover in this desert. On paper, the heavily armored trucks had every advantage over the vulnerable guns which had nothing but a single plate of steel protecting the crews.

We lunched well, the Colonel and I, on a can of fresh peaches (canned in California) and two cans of beer (born on Bushwick Avenue, Brooklyn), which the Colonel had snared from the General's mess. We hoped that darkness would hurry. It took a long time to arrive. The patrols went out again to put any wounded tanks they might find out of their misery lest the Huns come back during the night and apply first aid. It was easy to sleep that night, despite the bitter cold. We slept well, but our awakening was rude. In my sleep I heard a persistent buzzing and it grew louder and automatically I brushed a mosquito that wasn't there, and then suddenly I was wide awake. The airplane was quite low. My watch said 4:45. The half moon gave little light to our battered plateau. The sky was a black curtain of velvet, splashed with a million golden stars. I got out of my blanket, wondering idly whether this plane was one of "ours" or one of "theirs." We were not left long in doubt. There was a soft swish of something flying through the air, and then high above a burst of light blossomed to hang against the blackness. He dropped two more flares, one directly over us. He was like a surgeon preparing for a major operation. The flares were arranged methodically and now our plateau was bathed in penetrating white light. Flares sink very slowly and burn for five minutes. Now we knew that we were in for it.

21

The Earth Trembles

THE WHOLE OF the flat one-mile-square desert plateau was bathed in brilliant, hard, white light from the flares the plane had dropped. For a minute or so the plane merely circled casually while we huddled down in our very shallow trenches, waiting for it to come at us. We knew that we were in for a taste of the most horrible attack that modern warfare has yet devised—dive-bombing. I looked up and saw the plane, ghostly white in the light of the flares, standing out distinctly against the black, star-specked dome of the sky. It was just 5 A.M. And then I ducked quickly into the trench, for the noise of the motor had changed from a steady drone to a high, singing whine as the pilot leaned against his stick and pointed his airplane earthward.

The whine changed to a scream as the plane, loaded with death, hurled itself through the air. He was coming directly for our small patch of four short trenches. He dove to what seemed a hundred feet, and then came the bombs. They landed and the world shook unsteadily and the earth trembled and the sides of my pitifully small trench dislodged sand and rock and covered me with it and the concussion threw me heavily against the side of the narrow trench and the blast sent sharp flashes of agony through my head. And then he was gone. There was quiet, except for the drone of his motors

268

above. There was the smell of smoke, and then a new sound, a crackling noise. I stood up and saw that a large supply truck forty yards from my trench had received a direct hit. It was burning brightly. This was disheartening, for it is the custom of German bombers to use fires as targets. They did it in France and over London and Plymouth and Coventry. Henceforth this burning truck would be his objective.

I looked at our car and saw that all the glass had been shattered and it had jagged holes torn in its sides. I heard the plane returning, and it was time to fall face downward in the loose sand at the bottom of the trench.

He was not alone this time. Word had gone out that there was good hunting to be had here on our plateau. They dropped more flares and circled casually. The drone of the motors insinuated itself into your brain, so that you wondered if the uneven hum would ever leave your consciousness. They waited, studying our plateau as a surgeon studies the operative field before he makes his cut. There were five of them. By now the Nazis knew that we had no anti-aircraft guns close enough to bother them, so they took their time. There was a sharp minor explosion close by, and I stuck my head above the trench. I did that by merely sitting up. The fire had reached the gas tank of the supply truck and the tank had exploded, a gentle explosion compared to the noise of the bombs.

Then, fantastically, the truck came to life. Roman candles shot from it in graceful curves. I could only think of the fireworks at the New York World's Fair, two years ago, and thinking of that sent a pang of homesickness through me. The truck, unluckily, had been full of flares and Very lights, and they cascaded beautifully from the wreck, blue and green and white. I could imagine the German pilots up there laughing and talking to one another through their radios and saying, "Good joke, eh, Franz? The English shooting fireworks at us." I was swept with a blind and quite illogical hatred of them. Hatred is a good, honest emotion and it is useful too, because when hatred grips you—fear leaves. Of the two, hatred is stronger, leaving room for no other feeling. They had decided to paste us again, and I flung myself into the trench and swore at them and hated them and hated all Germans, and that was good, because now I wasn't nearly as afraid as I had been when they first came. Our trenches, shallow as they were, threw black shadows in the amazingly white light of the flares, and we knew that from the air those shadows would stand out like broad charcoal marks on white paper.

All five of them dove at once. The bombs dropped all around my small trench and time stood still and nothing was real except the horrible cacophony of warfare at its worst. Soon we were beyond sensation when blasts swept around us and bullets and hunks of steel tore into the sides of our trench six inches above us. Only the noise and death were real. Of the two death, which we expected any moment, was the more welcome, even though death had sent his most hideous messenger, the dive-bomber, to summon us.

There were occasional three- or four-minute intervals, when the Nazi planes became bored with their sport. Then we breathed again and talked, although we talked disjointedly, because none of us on that plateau was quite normal now. Once, after a stick of bombs had landed only a few yards away, the Colonel, who was lying in the farther end of my trench, called, "Are you still with us?"

"I'm not at Sun Valley," I yelled back, with what I hoped was fine sarcasm.

"I mean, how are you doing? Still alive?"

He was yelling, too, and then I realized that we were both

yelling because our ears weren't functioning normally and each of us heard his own voice as a whisper.

"It isn't good, Colonel, is it?" I asked.

"This is it, I'm afraid," he called back cheerfully.

"I wouldn't mind it if Jim and Don were here," I said, really talking to myself.

The Colonel asked me who Jim and Don were. I told him that they were my brothers.

"You must be very fond of them to wish them here in this spot of hell," the Colonel said sarcastically.

"If they were here, you and Don and I would be having a drink, and Jim would be getting us out of this mess somehow. We would be laughing at the Hun because we'd know that Jim had some way of fixing the louse so he couldn't hurt us."

"Jim must be quite a man," the Colonel said.

"Jim is quite a man," I told the Colonel coldly. I felt a deep nostalgia then, and strange indifference to what the dive-bombers would do next. I knew quite well that there was little chance of any of us surviving the next half-hour because we were like fish in a barrel. It bothered me that I would have to die with this regiment of British infantry. They were magnificent, and I admired them tremendously, but they were British. I have never made any secret of my love for them and my admiration for the way the British have fought and suffered in this war. But if you are born in the Bronx and brought up in Brooklyn and have worked in New York most of your life, you have but one loyalty, one allegiance, and that is to the much-maligned sidewalks of New York and to our whole country.

When you are under sentence of death, as I thought all of us were there in the chill, tortured desert, you think of things like that. And I felt a little sick because these magnificent

271

men of Britain who were around me and who shouted rude, derisive remarks to the Huns above, who emptied their machine guns and rifles and revolvers so futilely every time the Huns dove at us, were not men of New York's Sixty-ninth. They would, I felt, have been just as good and as truculent and as disdainful of both death and the Hun as these farmers and sons of farmers of the First Royal Sussex. Life would be so much happier if we could only pick those with whom we wanted to die. As it is, we are only granted the lesser boon of being allowed to pick those with whom we want to live.

If one must die one could only feel honored in dying with this regiment. They are entitled to stand with the fabled British regiments of the past. They earned immortality those few bad days in the desert. But I felt annoyed that I was not to die with my own mob; with men from West Fifty-second Street and from Flatbush and from Harlem; with men I'd grown up with; with men I'd worked on papers with in New York; with taxicab drivers and lawyers and bartenders and writers and mobsters who have been my friends. And because I could not, I felt a great resentment, and a great hatred, too, for those lads above who were our potential executioners. Only blundering on their part would allow any of us to be alive when morning came.

By now there was a slight haze over our plateau, but the stars could still be seen through it. The stars looked incredibly calm; they don't twinkle in the desert, because the air is so dry. I looked up at them and was annoyed at their calm acceptance of this nightmare. Hatred hung in the air; we on the ground were sending up waves of hate toward those Germans above and they were hating us and expressing it most emphatically. Only the stars are neutral in a fight like this.

"Dig in, pal, here they come," the Colonel yelled. I suddenly realized that for three minutes my thoughts had been just about 6,000 miles away. They were jerked back quickly enough to Sidi Omar—a black speck on a war map, but now the center of both this world and the next to us who lay half hidden by the sand, but only half hidden. Stark, real terror is an anesthetic. I have been frightened in France and Britain a hundred times, and that was bad. This was something different. The feeling we had here transcended ordinary fear.

Every one of us, I am sure, on that plateau was convinced that death would come within a few minutes, and yet, I think, none of us felt the ordinary pain of fright. This death was inevitable; we couldn't duck it; and therefore, being ordained and ordered for us, it was merely something to accept. And this acceptance of our fate somehow so dulled our capacity to feel physical pain that stones and bomb fragments sprayed us all over and only touched the superficial layer of our skin. It drew blood, of course, but it didn't hurt. I knew that I'd be dead within a few minutes, but I was annoyed with myself because I felt that I wasn't reacting properly. I should pray, but I felt no inclination to pray. My whole past life should be flashing through my mind during these few moments. I tried to examine my state of mind objectively, and I realized with disgust that because all my life I had been a spectator I now found it impossible to be a participant. These things happened to other people; they didn't happen to me. A reporter isn't much good if he feels; he has to think. I had been so accustomed to writing about situations like these with other people as the actors that my mind refused to accept the fact that now I myself was part of this drama.

Then all conscious thought was banished by the hellish noise as the planes dove again. The bombs fell all around us and the world rocked and I found that I was talking to myself—out loud. I kept on talking while that part of my mind not affected so badly as the rest of it listened. I was saying,

273

"Mom, I'll be with you in a minute. Wait for me, Mom."
Then everything was all right because I had something to
hang onto. I kept talking to my mother, and when the planes
came again I didn't mind them because I wasn't alone now.
I found that as long as I kept talking to her I wasn't afraid.
I remember laughing and saying, "Mom, remember one
Sunday after church we were all sitting on the porch and you
made cocktails? You had learned a new kind of cocktail for
us, Dubonnet and gin. Jim Dwyer and Ellen were there and
Marj and Con and Jim and Don. We were all there. Bill and
Ralph were there, and Pop and you made the cocktails. Pop
tasted one and he said, "This is awfully strong," and you
took the shaker back into the kitchen and added more gin to
it. You thought it was the Dubonnet that made it too strong.
Mom, it was the gin that made it too strong, but we never
told you. . . . Here they come again. . . . Take care of me,
Mom. . . . Listen to them screaming, Mom. . . ."

I was probably yelling, but the air was so full of noise now
that it seemed a wonder it could hold that much. I lay there
snug enough now and not minding it so much but wishing
rather that the inevitable would hurry up and happen. This
kept up for forty-five minutes.

Then in the East a turquoise strip appeared on the horizon.
It broadened and lightened to aquamarine, and then the blue
faded into golden light, a merciful herald of the dawn. But
one more attack remained before the dawn banished these
malignant creatures of the night. This was perhaps the worst.
When a plane dive-bombs, it cannot drop the very heavy
bombs because it might itself be caught in the upward blast.
These Nazi planes had been dropping comparatively small
hundred-pounders—small, perhaps, but each one quite capable of killing a hundred men. Now the planes flew high above

274

us and, huddling there with our faces in the sand, we wondered what new deviltry they were hatching.

The big bombs they had been saving for last came screaming down at us. These were the bombs I had heard in London a hundred times, and in Moscow, too. They sounded as though some celestial giant was tearing a piece of heavy silk; they sounded like the screaming of a thousand, shrill-voiced, tortured demons—and then they landed. Again the world trembled and the blast swept through the trench, and we embraced the earth with our bodies. I kept talking to Mom, and I know darn well she was hearing me even over that noise. The world shook, and suddenly the dawn came to blast the darkness from the desert. All was quiet, except for the crackling of the flames from the burning trucks and the faint hum of the retreating Jerry planes.

I lay there for awhile, too dazed and exhausted to know or care whether I had been hit. Then, unsteadily, I climbed out of the trench and fell twice before I could stand. Others around me were doing the same thing. None of us said anything for awhile. We stared dumbly at the ground around our trench. It looked as though it had been chewed by giant teeth. The smell of destruction hung heavily in the air; it is an odor of burning that always follows bombing. I found that one of my hands was bleeding and then noticed blood soaking through my uniform at the knee. They were small cuts from flying bits of rock or bomb fragments, but they seemed very unimportant. Everything seemed unimportant compared to the unaccountable miracle of our being alive.

We had no right to be alive. The ground, pockmarked with ugly, gaping holes, the bomb splinters that could have been raked up like autumn leaves, told us that. I picked up a half dozen bits of bomb fragments in the trench where I had been huddling. No, we had no right to be alive. Our faces were

275

black with a four-days' growth of beard, with dirt and sand. Our uniforms were torn and filthy. But we were alive, and that was very nice. Oh, that was so nice.

Ambulance drivers appeared in the half-light, asking anxiously, "Anybody hit?" They went from trench to trench. In his official report of the dive-bombing an hour later, the General merely wrote, "The casualties were few."

Colonel Young had come through without a scratch. He had a first-aid kit in the car and he got it out. He took a look at my cuts, and, because he had no iodine, he poured whisky on them.

"A waste of good whisky," he grumbled, and then he put a bandage and some plaster on my knee. I had a cut about an inch long. It bled, but it didn't hurt, and that was probably because we were all so exhausted we were incapable of feeling pain any more. The day passed slowly with intermittent bursts of shelling, and then we went to see the General. I had a story, but no story is any good on a one-mile island of sand in the sea of the desert four hundred miles from the nearest cable office. I wanted to get to that cable office.

"You might be able to run the gantlet tonight," the General said thoughtfully. "I want to send some dispatches to Army Headquarters. If you'd take them along, why, I'd let you leave. At your own risk," he added hastily.

We decided to chance it. There was a gap in the mine field to the southeast of the plateau. We would go through it and from there on depend on compass bearings. Fighting or traveling in the desert is exactly like traveling on the sea. There are no landmarks and one section of the desert looks like every other section. Years ago, surveyors mapped the desert and built stone cairns about six feet high and gave them names. We, for instance, would head for Conference Cairn, some forty miles away. Once there, our compass would take us to Army Headquarters.

We ate a tin of bully beef and took another tin and a bottle of whisky with us. Whisky at the front is not a beverage. It is literally a medicine and is guarded as such. It is used sparingly when the chill has robbed you of all resistance and only whisky or hot tea can make you live again. Actually, I have found strong hot tea to be more of a stimulant than alcohol, but water is so scarce in the desert and the lighting of a fire so difficult (no trees grow in the desert) and revealing that you don't often get tea when you are in action.

The General plotted our course and then stood with us in the darkness looking for German flares. We knew that the Germans were on three sides of us, but we weren't sure about the southeast side, in which direction we were to make our effort. The German always moves according to plan, and he always acts according to the rule book. We knew his book of rules. We knew that tonight the German tanks and armored cars and trucks with equipment would not be grouped together. We knew that he would do as he always does in the desert. He would disperse his forces in small units or "leaguers," for the night. As we watched, a flare went up a good mile away. It was a greenish-white German flare and it shot up about a hundred yards. The flare would light up the surrounding territory for perhaps a radius of a quarter of a mile. Thus the Hun guards against surprise attack by patrols. We knew that he would keep this up all night, for he had always done so. The Hun is not a man to change his tactics in the middle of a campaign. Other flares went up, all in the direction that we intended to go.

"Just steer clear of the flares and you ought to be all right," the General said. "And if you get into trouble hurry back and we'll give you a ration of rum."

We got into our car, a nice American Ford station wagon, and set off. Going through a gap in a mine field at any time is very unpleasant. It is especially trying at night. A few fugitive clouds had come to hide the moon, and we had to feel our way, almost to pray our way, through the narrow gap between two fields sown with dynamite. We breathed a lot easier when we knew we were out on the other side and that the mine fields lay behind us. But now, of course, we were in No Man's Land, and why any man would want this land I could not see.

We were traveling at eight miles an hour. We found that our motor seemed to make less noise at this speed and then, too, if we went into an unexpected bomb crater or shell hole the wear and tear on the car wouldn't be so bad. For a while we had the desert to ourselves. The night seemed filled with an ominous quiet. Blood had been spilled on this land, and tanks had roared across it and guns had spoken loudly here today. And they had left this black, brooding silence that hung like a pall over the desert. We crawled along, whispering, and now and then shining a well-shaded flashlight on our compass. We hoped the compass was a truthful one.

Then to our left a flare cut the opaque wall of the night. It hung there, greenish-white against the black. We kept on going. Another flare went up, this time about a half mile to our right. We had Germans on either side of us but none, we hoped, in front of us.

The Colonel drove on. The canvas top of our car was rolled back so that we could get a good view of the sky and possible enemy aircraft. I stood up, acting as lookout. It was hard to see anything in the darkness and twice we went into bomb craters, but each time our gallant Ford pulled out easily enough. Fords, Chevrolets and Dodges act as the legs of the British Army in the desert. Once two flares burst directly ahead but perhaps a half mile apart. We drove between them very gingerly. The night was cold, but I found myself sweating. When we had gone a mile beyond them we breathed again.

Sight is deceptive in the desert at night. Often I would see what I thought to be a group of tanks silhouetted against the horizon, only to find when we reached them that it was only a high sand dune. We did pass three tanks, all lying on their sides, broken remnants of the afternoon's warfare. Suddenly, three tanks loomed out of the darkness to the right, less than a hundred yards away, and the moon had to pick that unfortunate moment to creep from behind the sheltering clouds. I gripped the Colonel's shoulder, but he, too, had seen. There was nothing to do except to appear nonchalant, a rather difficult thing to do at midnight in the desert in the shadow of three German tanks. We didn't increase our pace. We continued to crawl, veering slightly to the left. We could see no men near the tanks. They were probably huddled inside to escape the cold and a bitter wind which had sprung up. We were opposite them and I hoped the Colonel would step on the gas and run for it. But he was too wise. Sudden acceleration would be a signal that we were not friends; if they hadn't heard us or seen us it would be a dead giveaway. We crept on and the outline of the tanks blurred and finally disappeared completely into the night.

It was a long drive and a nerve-racking one. For three hours we went through German-held territory. We had driven past twenty-three flares, none more than a mile away. It was 5 A.M. now, and we were both exhausted.

"Shall we chance it?" the Colonel asked.

"Yes," I said, knowing quite well what he meant.

He nodded and handed me a cigarette. I crouched low in the car and lit it and then lit one for him. He stopped the

279

car and we sat there happily. Until now we had been afraid to show even a cigarette light. I have never enjoyed a smoke as I did that. What matter if the cigarettes were filthy German issue cigarettes we had found at the bottom of a trench? We had a drink, too, and that tasted only a little less heavenly than the nectar of the gods. Another hour of driving brought us to Conference Cairn. Our compass had not lied to us. We threw our sleeping bags on the ground and crawled into them. The sun woke us too soon and we headed for Army Headquarters.

Three hours later we drove into the camp. We were a horrible-looking pair. My sun poisoning had turned septic, and my face looked like something the rats had been nibbling at. By one of those miracles granted only to knaves and fools a big aircraft was leaving for Cairo within an hour. There was room for us.

There were four things I wanted to do very quickly as soon as I got into my room at Shepherd's Hotel. I wanted a doctor, a bath, a sleep between cool sheets, and then there was the most important thing of all. A doctor was there and he did things with lotions and salves and the fire began to leave my face and hands; the hot water was steaming in the tub and the bed was turned down. But these were unimportant. Some carry a rabbit's foot, some carry lucky coins and pilots often carry babies' shoes. I have two lucky talismans which are quite different, and I never go anywhere without them. I took them out of my duffel bag, dusted the sand from them and put them on the mantelpiece. They were two autographed pictures in leather frames. I was convinced that they had brought me luck at the front just as they'd brought me through a hundred London bombings without getting my hair mussed. I poured a drink and raised my glass to them.

"Here's to you both and thanks again," I said reverently,

and Franklin Roosevelt and Winston Churchill looked back at me from the mantelpiece, smiling with quiet confidence. Looking at those two fine faces and at the lines of determination which showed even through their smiles, you felt that everything would be all right. I felt very proud that they were there in the room with me. Then I crawled between the cool sheets and so wonderful did they feel that I decided to remain in bed for the next eight or nine years.

22

This Is It

THERE IS ONE nice thing about Cairo: the city is filled with book stores. The truth is that Cairo is such a dull place that there isn't much to do after dark but read books. And all of the book stores were loaded with mystery novels. I order them by the pound. I asked Bob Low to get me a hundred pounds of books, and hoped my sun poisoning would last forever. Sun poisoning is merely an extreme case of sunburn. The doctors in Cairo were expert in treating it. Anyone not accustomed to sun is an easy mark for it. Being strictly an indoor athlete I was very susceptible.

For a week I hugged my bed in the luxury suite which Low insisted that I keep, and, with an occasional poker game, time passed pleasantly enough. Then one night when both Low and Downs were back from the front we decided that I might investigate the bright lights of Shepherd's restaurant. We three dined and dined well. There was still champagne at Shepherd's, and we had a couple of bottles. About ten o'clock Douglas Williams of the Ministry of Information walked into the room. We called him over and asked him to have a drink. We always ask censors or men who arrange facilities for us to have drinks. In fact, if we happen to have wives and daughters around and if they become interested in them, we would gladly relinquish all claims. It is like that with censors. We do our best to keep on good terms with them.

"Any news tonight?" I asked Douglas.

"Only that Japanese thing," Williams said casually.

"Oh, those Japs," I said airily. "They talk and talk and never do anything about it."

Williams looked at me in amazement.

"Haven't you heard?" he said. "They did something about it tonight. They bombed the hell out of Pearl Harbor, and whether you three great reporters know it or not your country is now at war."

We made a dash for the lobby to read the ticker. It was true, all right. The whole story in sharp short takes was there.

"What date is this, anyhow?" I asked Downs.

"December 7th," he said.

"I guess that's a date to remember," I said.

"I guess it is," Downs nodded solemnly.

We went up to my rooms and held a council of war. All three of us wanted to get right home. I don't know exactly why. It just didn't seem right to be in Cairo with America at war. We talked big that night and made plans in which we'd be commandos, or intelligence officers or even Ministry of Information officials. We were pretty excited, especially in view of the fact that all three of us had been yelling, "We'll be next" for two years. But none of us had expected that it would be the Japs who'd go to work on us.

The next day all three of us went our separate ways in an effort to get early transportation out of Cairo. Downs went to General Brett, who was rumored to be on his way back to America. Low went to Randolph Churchill to arrange it through him, and I went to Sir Walter Monckton. I had always found Walter more than willing to help. This time was no exception.

"There's a plane going within three or four days," he said. "It goes via the Mediterranean, landing at Malta, Gibraltar and possibly Lisbon. Then it goes to Foynes and England. I might get you on it."

"If you get me on the thing, I might make home by Christmas," I said. "But get me on something that doesn't hit Lisbon. I doubt if I could get a visa to Portugal."

A year before I had written a rather disparaging story about Lisbon which the Portuguese didn't like. There were some blistering editorials in the papers there which threatened dire things to me if I ever returned. I've always thought it a great mistake to enter either barrooms or countries where you're not wanted.

"If you stop in Lisbon it will only be for a few hours," Monckton said. "And perhaps I can help with the visa. I may have to make you a King's Messenger and get you some kind of official visa."

That night I had dinner with Sir Miles Lampson, the British Ambassador to Egypt. It was a pleasant dinner, until Sir Miles started asking me questions about Russia. Time after time in answer to his penetrating questions I'd have to say, "I don't know."

Sir Miles looked a bit puzzled, and said with a gleam of mischief in his eye, "One of your chaps was through here not long ago. He'd just come out of Russia. He'd only been there three weeks, but he seemed to know a lot more about it than you do."

"Sure," I said. "After I'd been in Russia three weeks I knew everything about the place. I could have written a book about it. But I made the mistake of staying there three months. After three months I realized I didn't know a damn thing about the country."

Downs and Low were progressing well with their arrange-
284

ments, but I got away first. We took off from the Nile, as dirty-looking a river as ever a poet sang about. In Egypt, if you should happen to fall into the Nile, they rush you to a hospital and fill you with injections. There is some bug swimming around the Nile that is a very bad boy. We took off in a beautiful flying boat, one of the old Imperial Airways boats. There were seven of us; the other six were generals. We took off at ten o'clock at night. We would reach Malta at daylight, remain there all day, and when night came make our second hop. There were plenty of German and Italian fighter planes in the skies over the Mediterranean, and we were too vulnerable an aircraft to risk any encounter with them. I fell asleep. Some hours later, as the boat bumped on the surface of the water, I awoke. This indeed was a pleasant way to travel. You fall asleep in Cairo and wake up in Malta. Pretty good, if true. I was brought to a rude awakening. We were back in Cairo. One of our motors had quit four hours out, and the cautious pilots, detecting a cough in one of the other motors, had turned back. So we had to drive back to Shepherd's Hotel again. It was just 4 A.M.

I went with Low the next afternoon when he brought his baggage to the office of the Overseas Airways. He was going on a boat like mine, twenty-four hours later. We were allowed only forty pounds of baggage. Low, in addition to his three uniforms, four suitcases, duffel bag and typewriter, had a radio which must have weighed at least sixty pounds. He gave the officials two of his suitcases which weighed just forty pounds. These were checked in.

"But what is all that?" the puzzled official said, pointing to the mass of suitcases, duffel bag, typewriter and radio, which Low had placed in a separate pile.

"Oh, that?" Low said innocently. "That's just my hand baggage." And of course he got away with it.

285

That night we really did get away. The flight to Malta was serene. We flew over the island once, and I was amazed at its smallness. I knew that Malta was loaded with airports and airplanes, but couldn't detect one from the air. I learned afterward that the planes were kept in caves and that the airports were so beautifully camouflaged that it was virtually impossible to see them from above 2,000 feet. As we landed, the air was filled with the shrill scream of a siren.

"Reception for us I guess, hey, General?" I said to one of my fellow passengers. "Nice of them."

"Reception, hell!" he growled. "That's an air-raid siren."

And so it was. It was the 1,231st time that an alert had been sounded in or on Malta. As we stepped ashore a group of fighter aircraft shot up, and it was lovely to see them climb. We went into the RAF mess and had bacon and eggs and wonderful coffee. Most of Malta's air raids were as unimportant as this one. The German and Italian bombers constantly tried to take the island by surprise. However, when they saw the RAF fighter planes up there, they usually gave up and scurried back to their home ports. Malta is nothing but a big hunk of limestone, anyhow. Bombs either bounced off it or splintered the rock a bit, but didn't do much damage. I couldn't understand the reason for this constant attack on the rock by bombers.

"They're smart, giving it to us all the time," the Group Captain said. "You see, for months our Beaufighters have been sinking a lot of Eyetie shipping coming from Sicily to Tripoli. Those ships were filled with equipment for General Rommel. But now we can't send our Beaufighters up; they'd get their ears knocked off by the enemy fighters. So we know that lots of shipping is getting across to Rommel. It's only an overnight trip for a boat."

It was hard to find much bomb damage on Malta. The

impressive thing about Malta was the way the aircraft were dispersed. Unfortunately, there is no military censor within 3,000 miles of where I'm writing this, so how much of what I saw on Malta is "hush hush" I don't know. I have nothing but contempt for those who are given the run of a military stronghold and who then sneak out of the jurisdiction of the military authorities to write a complete story of what they saw without regard to bans which might exist for reason of home security. So I'll leave Malta alone, except to say that I'd hate to do a long stretch there.

The weather was so good the next night that instead of stopping at Gibraltar we went on to Lisbon. We landed there at 4 A.M., an hour ahead of schedule, and there was no one to meet us. The generals all changed into civilian clothes in the plane. It would have severely embarrassed neutral Portugal to have seven British generals in uniform parading about the streets. We waited an hour for sleepy but pleasant custom officials to appear. I was a bit nervous. My passport had a stamp—"Official Business"—on it, but, after all, mine was an American passport, and if any custom official had asked me what I was doing on a British mission, I might have had to give some double talk for an answer. I felt like practically any E. Phillips Oppenheim character, but no one asked me anything. They took us to the Grand Hotel, a small place near the excellent Palacio Hotel in Estirol. They didn't take us to the Palacio, we learned later, because it was headquarters for German agents who swarmed all over Lisbon. I had just gotten to sleep when there was a banging at my door. I froze and slid my hand under the pillow for the little gun that was always there in any Oppenheim novel. However, never having owned a gun in my life, I wasn't much disappointed to find nothing under my pillow but my other hand, which was still asleep. The banging kept up. It must be the

Portuguese authorities, I thought, coming to nab me. Or maybe Gestapo agents. If they were, I would smile and say, *"Wilkommen, meine Freunde,"* which, if my brief memory was right, meant, "Welcome, pals." But it was nobody but Bob Low. He had just landed.

"You've been asleep exactly twenty minutes, so don't give me that nonsense about waking you in the middle of the night," he said, before I could begin. "I ordered breakfast for us downstairs. Come on, I'm hungry."

"That was very charming of you," I told him. "You're everything I care for, everything I've dreamed about. Listen, you heel, I need breakfast like I need a hole in my head."

"Well, I ordered it, anyhow. Bacon and eggs and coffee."

"After two years you ought to know I drink tea for breakfast."

"I found out that they have American coffee here," he said. "Real American coffee, the kind they advertise in *Liberty* . . ."

"In *Collier's,* if you please."

I was awake and should have known better than to argue with Low. If he was in a talking mood there was no use trying to sleep. Besides, night had been turned into day, and for all I knew 7 A.M. was, in reality, 11 A.M., my usual breakfast time. I got dressed and we went down and had ham and eggs, and it was really American coffee. We sat on the terrace and talked of this and that, and it was all right. Low and I can talk to each other by the hour and enjoy ourselves. The reason is that both of us are non-listeners, so neither ever gets bored with the other's conversation. We talked of pals we'd be with in London in a couple of days. We talked of New York, and I described Radio City minutely to him. He hadn't been to New York in five years. I went on with my very colorful description of Radio City, and when I was through he re-

288

minded me that Radio City was already three years old when he left New York.

"You know what we have nothing of?" he said suddenly.

"What have we nothing of?"

"Money."

"I have about ten pounds," I reminded him.

"Ten pounds," he said in disgust. "There's a casino here. There's roulette. This is the casino Jimmy Sheean took for five grand last year. Are we going to pass that up? But we need capital. I find I have no money at all."

"I want to meet you some day when you have," I told him, but I admitted the justice of his argument. Money invested in roulette is strictly a sound investment, and anyone who says it is a speculation is a cad.

"Where are we going to get any money?"

"I know a man," Low said calmly, "a very nice man. His name is Frederick Hibbard, and he is the Consul here at our Embassy. He will give us money."

"He sounds like a very fine character," I suggested.

Low nodded, and went to phone him. You could drop Low anywhere in the world and he'd bob up with someone who'd cash a check or lend him money or just pay for food and drinks. Low came back from the phone looking thoughtful.

"Fred was fine. He'll cash checks for us either on New York or London banks. But he's worried about you. He says he'll be glad when you get the hell out of here. You wrote a nasty story about these people and you are definitely no dream prince in this town. He thinks you'd better stay under cover. Anyhow let's go and see him."

We got into a big Packard limousine and went to see Hibbard. As we drove past the Palacio Hotel the driver pointed with pride.

"One of beegest Gestapo spies, he leevs there." He grinned. "I drive heem often."

"He must be a very great spy for you to know him," Low said scornfully.

"Oh, yes, he very beeg spy," the driver said proudly.

Hibbard was just as good as Low had prophesied. He cashed checks for us and then shook his head dolefully at me.

"You were very mean to these people in your article on Lisbon," he said. "Frankly, I think they are right in resenting your article. You went off half-cocked."

"Should I go and apologize to them?" I asked sarcastically.

"It might be a good idea to go and straighten things out with their Minister of Propaganda," he said. "No? Well, don't send any more turkeys through Lisbon."

"Turkeys?" A light began to dawn. Amon Carter of Fort Worth had promised to send me a smoked turkey on my birthday the previous April. Knowing that Carter never made a promise that he didn't keep, I had counted on the turkey, but it had never arrived.

"Amon sent the turkey, all right," Hibbard said. "He sent it air mail, which must have cost a small fortune. However, then came the problem of transporting it from Lisbon to London. Ordinarily, they just put it on a British plane, and let it go at that. They're not obligated to you, you know. But they saw that it was addressed to you. That was enough. The turkey reposed in a warehouse here for some weeks, and then it was sent back to Texas. I imagine that it was a very old and tired turkey when it arrived."

We asked Hibbard to dinner with us at the Palacio and went back into our big Packard. It was still only eleven in the morning, but neither Bob nor I felt sleepy.

"You know, I never got to see the Pyramids in Cairo," I

told Low. "Let's be tourists for today. Columbus is buried here in Lisbon. Let's go and see his tomb."

Low was agreeable. Our genial driver shook his head enthusiastically when we told him where we wanted to go. He drove us about fifteen miles to a very old church, and then, with great ceremony, ushered us in. A guide began to show us around. One saint was buried here; another saint was buried in this vault; here was an exquisitely carved wooden altar; here was the tomb of Vasco da Gama.

"It's Columbus we want to see," I said, after an hour of weary tramping.

"Another church?" our guide smiled.

We went to four churches. We saw the tombs of a hundred saints and a thousand sinners, but late that afternoon we still hadn't found the resting place of Columbus.

"More Columbus?" our still unwearied guide asked.

"I have a hunch this dope doesn't understand English. He's just being obliging. Try him in French."

Low tried him in French, but with no luck. So we gave up and headed for the Palacio, a really lovely hotel. We wanted to see what Germans looked like in civilian clothes. But there were no Germans in the bar. There was no one in the bar, except two bartenders. We ordered drinks and they looked at us coldly while serving us.

"Let's give them a little double talk," Low whispered, and then he began to talk German.

"What a pity about poor Rommel," Bob said, practically shedding tears. "He was our best General, but when he lost those 5,000 tanks at Tobruk, there was nothing for him to do but to commit suicide. They've kept it out of the papers nicely."

The two bartenders looked pop-eyed. Bob kept it up, with me contributing only an occasional *"Schrecklich."* My German wouldn't fool a police dog. Bob told of the 50,000 Germans lost in the desert. He took on the role of a Gestapo agent, and his flawless German made him sound very authentic.

"And our poor Berlin," he sighed. "It is in ruins. Nothing left of the Adlon, the Bristol gone and Unter den Linden a shambles. Oh, it is sad . . ."

At this point we noticed one of the bartenders feverishly writing a note. He went to a dumbwaiter, put the note on it and sent it whirling down below. Maybe he was merely asking them to send up a bottle of vermouth. We preferred to think that he was a spy reporting to his boss.

"Will you have a drink on the house?" the other bartender said.

"A double martini," Low said promptly.

"Two," I added.

This kept up for some time, but when Low started to tell about how the *Scharnhorst* and *Gneisenau* had been sunk by a single bomb, I thought it was time to leave. We left for the casino, feeling very pleased with ourselves. We headed for the bar, and then I had an idea.

"We have one hundred dollars between us," I reminded Low. "If we have a drink now, we'll just have a Scotch or a Martini. If we play and win we can have champagne."

He agreed. We bought a hundred dollars' worth of chips, and went to the roulette table. I put some chips on my pet number, 23. I always star 23, putting chips on all corners of it. The ball whirled and it dropped into 23. I pulled my chips in nonchalantly. Low looked at me in disgust. He had a system. His system was to throw a handful of chips all over the board, and wherever they landed they stayed. Next time 19 came up. I got eight to one on that because 19 bordered on 23. Then on the third throw 23 came up again. By now people at the table were looking at me as though I were a Greek syndicate. I threw all of my chips to the croupier.

"I'll cash them in," I told him, yawning. "So fatiguing, this! One can play just so long, and then it gets boring."

Low was furious. He hadn't cashed a bet. I made him go to the bar with me, and we bought a bottle of champagne. I felt good. It was the first time I'd ever quit a roulette game a winner.

"We are fighting a very fine war, Bob," I told him, watching the bubbles dance in the glass.

"You shouldn't have quit," he grumbled. "You might have won as much as Jimmy Sheean if you'd kept on. I want you to be a big dealer."

Hibbard came up, a little startled to see two men who had been broke that afternoon buying wine. He asked us what we'd done with ourselves all afternoon. Low told him about looking for the tomb of Columbus.

"If you had found his tomb in Lisbon, it would have been the neatest trick of the week," he said, looking at us strangely. "It so happens that Columbus is buried in Seville, which is in Spain. Before that, he was buried several other places, but never in Lisbon."

"Twenty dollars that driver charged us," Low wailed. "Our feet are bleeding from walking. All because you never studied history!"

"We had a very good history teacher at Manual. I guess I got Seville mixed up with Lisbon."

We had a lot of fun that night. I admit that this sounds like an account of the Rover Boys in Europe, but it has been like that with Downs, Low and myself these past two years. Bad spots like that morning in Sidi Omar give you a hangover. You stay scared for awhile, and you find yourself waking up at night tense and wild-eyed, not knowing what is the matter with you. As an antidote you need laughter. Downs, Low, the rest of us have kept sane because we've looked for laughs.

During dinner there was a phone call for me. Our flying boat was ready to leave. I hurried back to the Grand, got my things and, within an hour, we were winging toward Foynes. I sent two cables before I left, one to Lord Beaverbrook and one to Brendan Bracken. I asked them to get me on the first ferry plane leaving for Canada. I could still make New York by Christmas, with any luck.

Foynes is on the River Shannon in Limerick. I hate dry states and neutral countries, but the greenness of the banks and the smiling friendliness of the officials who met us were heartwarming. We were taken to a pub and given sandwiches and tea. The Irish can make tea better than the British. To me, tea is the best drink in the world. If I were ever President, I'd forbid anyone in America to serve tea in those horrible little linen or paper sacks. Tea has to be brewed, and the Irish know how to brew it.

Meanwhile they were refueling our ship. We climbed aboard and started smoothly down the river. Suddenly a motor gave an unhappy scream, a moaning whine, and stopped. Then the enormous flying boat veered sharply to the right, and a moment later we crashed into the bank of the river. A pontoon was smashed, and a slice was taken off our port wing. We were a sick, unhappy lot. We had flown over the Mediterranean, through skies infested with enemy aircraft without mishap, and now we had to spoil everything because a motor had conked out at a critical time. Once more we were ferried ashore. The flying boat would be out of commission for weeks. We would have to take a bus and drive

294

right across Ireland to Dublin, where we would get a land plane the next morning. It was just getting dark when we got into the big bus. We traveled five hours through one of the most beautiful parts of Ireland, but there was no moon and we couldn't see a thing. They tell me that Ireland is a lovely country. I wouldn't know.

Early the next morning we took off for London, and that night it was business as usual at the Savoy. All of the boys were still alive. A couple of the waiters had been called up, but otherwise things were as I had left them in September. But there was some bad news. Lord Beaverbrook was in Washington with Winston Churchill, and Bracken was severely ill with the flu.

I ran like a homing pigeon to Ambassador John Winant. Winant is a very wonderful man. I remember the first press conference he held when he arrived in London. His gentleness, his sincerity and honesty completely won us all. As we left, I remember Bill Stoneman saying in a daze, "I don't know what it is about that guy, but all I know is that I feel like going to church right now."

Winant was the friend of every correspondent in London. He and his charming wife never went in for any social life in London. "Can't afford it," Winant said briefly once to an English reporter. It was no wonder that the British loved him as much as we did. We were very proud of John Winant in London. Now and then he and his wife would dine with Red Mueller and me at the Savoy. Winant had more fun with a reporter like Red than he would have had dining with the whole British Cabinet. His best friend was Ernest Bevin, and two or three nights a week they'd have dinner together at the Strand Palace, where Bevin lived.

Winant wasted no time in fixing me up. He called Sir Archibald Sinclair, Secretary for Air, and told him it was imperative that I get away on the first ferry plane leaving. But Sir Archibald had bad news. There was only one airplane now ferrying pilots. The others had been called to either the Far East or to Cairo. And the weather was very bad. That one plane was being held up in Canada and wasn't due for several days. Then it would have to be overhauled in Scotland. However, there was a fast boat leaving Christmas night. How about that? I felt sick at not being able to make New York by Christmas because, unless you're at home, Christmas is only another December 25th. It's like that in my family. But there was nothing to be done about it.

Meanwhile Low arrived. We both looked toward Christmas Day with horror. Then Ambassador Anthony Biddle phoned.

"Of course, you and Bob are having Christmas dinner with Margaret and me," he said. "And that room at our place is still reserved for you. You haven't used it for months."

Tony Biddle was like that. He and Mrs. Biddle were the patron saints of the correspondents in London. They had a guest house on their estate near Windsor which was reserved for us. We usually went there week ends, and if we happened to miss two consecutive week ends, the Biddles worried about us. For Christmas dinner, which they held at noon because Low and I had to be in Cardiff to catch the boat that night, they invited every American waif in London. Helen Kirkpatrick of the *Chicago Daily News,* Kathleen Harriman of INS, Bob Low, Ed Beattie and Ned Russell of UP, Joe Evans of the *Herald Tribune,* John Winant and I were the lonely ones they took in. It was quite impossible to feel homesick. The Biddles had a Christmas tree for us. They had presents for us.

"Tony wouldn't let me pick out the ties," Margaret Biddle said sadly.

"Thank God," I said fervently. There should be a law against even intelligent women selecting ties. The ties and scarves which Tony had for us were wonderful, but then for years Tony has had the reputation of being the best-dressed diplomat in Europe. Margaret Biddle gave us the kind of dinner we would have had at home. She must have been saving rationing cards for weeks. Everything we had was American. We even had old-fashioned cocktails with Kentucky Bourbon. We had turkey and cranberry sauce and plum pudding, and we had snappers and paper hats, and we had a hell of a time. We even got John Winant to take a drink of champagne—no mean feat! It was the next best thing to being home. Kathie Harriman even got over missing Averell and Marie. Then Low and I had to leave.

My efficient Betty had everything packed and our train tickets bought. Before we knew it we were on a train headed for Cardiff. People don't travel much on Christmas Day in England. We had the train to ourselves. It was a dreary four-hour trip. There were no porters at Cardiff. In Wales people go around singing on Christmas night; they have no time to cart trunks. Low and I just left our bags and trunks and typewriters on the platform and walked to our hotel. Walking eight blocks through a strange blacked-out city is not much fun. We arrived at the hotel to be greeted with a message that the boat would not be leaving for another twenty-four hours. There was a dance going on in the hotel. Bob and I sat in the empty bar listening to the singing and laughter, and sipping champagne which tasted like dish water. It was good champagne, but nothing would have tasted good that night.

"I'll bet you a thousand dollars to five dollars that I will never again spend Christmas night in a strange hotel with you," I told Low.

"Vice versa," he said gloomily.

297

So we went to bed.

The next day there was more bad news at the shipping office. The "fast" boat would take at least fourteen days. Low balked at that. He phoned our friend Commander Kenderdein at the Admiralty to see if there was any warship going toward New York on which we could hitch hike. There was a destroyer leaving within ten days. Low and I could go along if we wished. Low wished. I hated the thought of going back to London, unpacking and then hanging around for that long. Besides, if I took the freighter, I'd have a good rest and maybe I could write a book. Low went back to London. I got on the little *Lochkatrine*.

The next morning we went from Cardiff to another port in Wales to pick up part of our convoy; then we went to Belfast Harbor to gather the rest of it. I looked forward to the trip. I was tired of fast traveling; tired of picking myself up off the floor; tired of looking for news and arguing with censors and I was homesick, too. Even foreign correspondents get homesick. Yes, it would be a quiet, restful trip, and maybe I would write a book. I'd crossed the Atlantic before in convoy. It had been a nice voyage. The trip promised to be a pleasant escape from the war.

But I had forgotten one thing. I had entirely forgotten the fury of the North Atlantic and I'd forgotten that the ocean now was a battlefront, too. For twenty-three long days our small freighter had to fight the North Atlantic at its worst. Our convoy of fifty ships was blown all over the ocean by a hurricane. We were on our own most of the voyage, now and then getting heartbreaking S.O.S.'s from ships which had started out with us and which we were powerless to help. The horrible weather didn't bother the German submarines. It was easy enough for them to get close unobserved, discharge their gyroscopic-controlled torpedoes and then scurry

298

far below out of the range of depth charges. Ships were sunk within a hundred miles of us; but worse than the submarine hazard was the weather which so horribly battered our little ship.

There was no escape from the war on the North Atlantic. Everyone had to fight every knot of the way, every ship, every man. Everyone, even the weather had to be in it. I thought of that when I was on deck last night clinging desperately to an iron stanchion. The old *Lochkatrine* was groaning and sobbing as the waves lashed her and the wind pierced her. Most of our lifeboats had long since been smashed. This time the weather was certainly on the side of the Germans. Then there was a break in the clouds and looking up I saw the stars. They shone down with calm indifference. They were remote and cold, indifferent to the brutal struggle going on down here in the North Atlantic; indifferent to the fact that no one on this planet is neutral any more. No one can be neutral—except the stars. Only the stars are neutral.

Yes, it has been a long dreary trip, but it ends tomorrow in Halifax Harbor. I didn't have the rest I had planned, but I did write a book. This is it.

Cardiff Docks, December 26, 1941
Off Halifax, January 18, 1942